PRAISE FOR *LAST DAYS IN BABYLON*

"In March 2004, London journa into Baghdad, braving the hazards of ᴉsely personal goal—to examine the fac ʀge a connection with her family's past ients the astonishing swiftness with which the Iraqi Jewish community was shattered in the years after WWI, culminating in a mass exodus. . . . Benjamin's evocation of the routines and rituals of Iraqi Jewish life . . . makes her account of post-WWI turmoil all the more convulsing."

—*The Boston Globe*

"This is a book written from the inside; Benjamin brings to her subject not just the impressive research, elegant prose, and incisive intelligence she brought to her previous two books, but also a passion that imbues every line with urgency and zest. . . . Benjamin is writing as an Iraqi as much as she is writing as a Jew, and her book doesn't just tell the story of a community but is also a sidelong history of a country made up of minorities. . . . It is a world she has had to journey towards, from a sense of disconnection and loss to a point where she can try to understand it and make it her own. Her depiction of that journey is so brave and honest that the book can be enjoyed for that alone; her weaving together of her own story with that of a community and a country makes *Last Days in Babylon* essential reading for anyone interested in why Iraq went wrong."

—*The Jewish Quarterly*

"Benjamin honors her family by vivifying a once-thriving community that has dispersed worldwide, leaving only twelve souls struggling for survival in present-day war-torn Baghdad."

—*Publisher's Weekly*

"It is a potent mix of nostalgic recollection and incisive observation set on the shifting political and social landscape in Iraq."

—*Jewish News* (Arizona)

"This memoir, unlike many other current ones, resonates with the compelling urgency of today's headlines. . . . [An] insightful narrative."

—*Jewish Book World*

"An impassioned account of a multi-ethnic society. . . . An incisive exposé of the 20th-century political vicissitudes which transformed the Middle East from a Pandora's box kept somewhat shut by the Ottomans to the present amphitheatre of unrelenting religious, nationalistic and xenophobic conflicts. . . . This is a history unknown even to most Jews. Benjamin narrates it fluently and passionately."

—*The Independent* (London)

"*Last Days in Babylon* is a rich and moving family memoir, but it's much more, too: a fascinating and impassioned look at an unknown world."

—*The Evening Standard* (London)

ALSO BY MARINA BENJAMIN

Rocket Dreams
Living at the End of the World

Last Days in Babylon

The Exile of Iraq's Jews, the Story of My Family

ॐ~∞

MARINA BENJAMIN

FREE PRESS

NEW YORK LONDON TORONTO SYDNEY

*f*P
FREE PRESS
A Division of Simon & Schuster, Inc.
1230 Avenue of the Americas
New York, NY 10020

First Free Press trade paperback edition June 2008

FREE PRESS and colophon are trademarks
of Simon & Schuster, Inc.

For information about special discounts for bulk purchases,
please contact Simon & Schuster Special Sales at 1-800-456-6798
or business@simonandschuster.com

Designed by Davina Mock

Manufactured in the United States of America

10 9 8 7 6 5 4 3 2 1

Library of Congress Cataloging-in-Publication
Data Control No. 2006045657

ISBN-13: 978-0-7432-5843-2

ISBN-13: 978-1-4165-7204-6 (pbk)

For Marcelle, Bertha, and Soren
and in tribute to Regina Sehayek Levy (1905–1992)

CONTENTS

"I am Iraq, my tongue is her heart,
my blood her Euphrates,
my being from her branches formed."

Muhammad Mahdi Al-Jawahiri,
Fi dhikra al Maliki, 1957

PROLOGUE

At home in London during the cold Spring of 2006 I try to summon up images of Baghdad. I want to remember people's faces and voices, the traditional tilework I admired in their homes, the particular yellow of sunlight bouncing off sandy brick, the delicious skewered meat I ate in restaurants. It's an exercise I go through regularly, as an antidote to the litany of bad news that streams from my television screen.

The news, by now, has a numbing sameness to it. There has been another bombing, and more innocent people are dead. There's footage of cars burning at the roadside. Men in bloodstained clothing help other blood-smeared men to safety. Angry crowds remonstrate with shaven-scalped American soldiers. Women in chadors wail over lost husbands and sons. The city, I reflect for the umpteenth time, is lawless, unrelenting, and I feel a surge of relief that I live where I do, far away from all the violence and turmoil.

Two years earlier I witnessed similar scenes in Baghdad for myself—from the safety of a hired car, in the company of a hired guide, and, more often than not, by peering through darkened glass. After the bombing of the Mount Lebanon hotel, an early civilian target of the post-war violence, I was among the crowds of Western journalists who had talked their way past the police cordons to commiserate with the locals and trade theories as to why that particular hotel had been targeted. Too many Westerners stayed there, said one journalist. Too many American Jews said another. No, said a third, the car bomb was intended for the Al Jazeera offices next door.

At the time I had been sickened by all the purient onlookers' interest (of which I was part, straining as was everyone else for answers that put a rational gloss on the senseless) and by the metallic smell of death, and I'd wanted to leave. But now, with my access to such information confined to second-hand relay, I think about how the television cameras do not lie.

Firsthand, as on screen, much of Baghdad appears forsaken. It sprawls across a grid of lookalike suburbs built out of dust-colored concrete with tatty high streets that are permanently snarled with traffic and sporadically patrolled by U.S. tanks. Bomb damage is evident everywhere. Refuse and rubble litter the ground. Police checkpoints, flagged up by double rows of painted oil drums, block off numerous roads, and street fighting is rife after dark. Anywhere, at any time, something might explode.

And yet there exists another Baghdad where, even now, it remains possible to capture something of the fabled magic of the ancient city. You won't see Ali Baba thieves spring from earthenware jars brandishing giant scimitars, or stumble across walled gardens concealing tiled fountains. But you can lose yourself in a confusion of twisting streets and fill your lungs with the loamy, musty air of what feels like centuries past. In a small corner of northeastern Baghdad, known locally as the Old City, all the odds have been defied, and something wondrous of the mythic past has come through the wars intact.

I feel as if I've known this other Baghdad all my life. A Baghdad of history and cultural romance, consonant with my family's recollections of verdant palm and scented orange groves, of picnics by the Tigris, and sun-baked afternoons spent cooling one's heels indoors, sipping homemade lemonade. Its local characters are colourful, voluble, and opinionated. Its politics are as labyrinthine as its streets. Its crumbling buildings creak under the weight of stories untold. It is a Baghdad I believed no longer existed, until I had seen it for myself. And it is the Baghdad that I want to remember beyond the firewall of current carnage, and of seemingly endless and irrevocable change.

The Old City is one of the few places in Baghdad where you won't see American soldiers, since most of the streets are too narrow to support armoured convoys. Western civilians are thin on the ground, deterred by the palpable lack of policing. Yet Westerners who do venture into this vibrant mercantile hub come to experience something of the "real" Baghdad. They come for the antique charms of its twisting streets and dusty alleyways, many of them so narrow you can practically span them with outstretched arms; for the smells of *masgoof,* the local fish speciality, smoking in open doorways; the sweaty clangour of artisans at work beating metal and scraping leather; and to rub shoulders with upright Bedouin chiefs dressed in impeccably starched *dishdashas* going about their everyday business.

Often they are hunting for hidden treasures. They know that there are medieval churches in the Old City, built by Armenian and Nestorian Christians, and elaborately carved twelfth-century gates tucked away in neglected corners, between the noisy souks and bustling coffeehouses. There are also imposing stone buildings dating, mainly, from Ottoman times. Occasionally, a dark street opens up onto the banks of the River Tigris, where an unexpected burst of sunlight flashes up off the water. But mostly the narrow streets fold in on themselves, hugging their secrets.

At midday, when the sun is blisteringly hot, these streets are thronged with people, dodging the wooden carts of goods pushed by small, barefoot boys and the donkeys laden with burlap bags, and lifting their robes to avoid being splattered by the filthy water that trickles down the middle of the street. The Western visitors mingle in, revelling in the place's very survival, for while the rest of Baghdad seems to have been have been sucked into the prevailing chaos, in the Old City the rhythm of life carries on just as it has always done, undisturbed either by the occupation or the fierce resistance to it.

I, too, had come to the Old City in search of the past, my family's past, coloured by fond memories I'd been spoon-fed down the years. And the enduring mystery was this: why were my relatives still so eager to relive it all?

The date was March 2004, ten months after President George W. Bush announced the end of "major combat operations" in Iraq. Despite the presidential assurances, war was still raging across the country, as the Americans continued to root out Baathist sympathizers, largely comprised of the most hardened core of Saddam Hussein's supporters who'd lost their influence with his removal. For their part, the Baathists, along with other less readily identifiable resistance forces, continued to fight back, and with brutal consequences. Baghdad was extremely dangerous, especially for Westerners whose value as collateral or PR was just beginning to be recognised. Nick Berg, the Jewish-American contractor whose videotaped beheading shocked the world, was executed only weeks after I left. His death, in retrospect, marked the end of one kind of war and the beginning of another, more intractable kind.

In spite of planning my trip meticulously I was frankly terrified of going into the country. Determined to be as inconspicuous as possible, I'd arranged to be driven through the night from Amman along the notoriously dangerous desert highway, which passes directly through the towns of Ramadi and Fallujah. Already the towns were hotbeds of insurgent fury, and home to bandits who stalked the desert road in speeding Toyotas. For hours I kept a sleepless vigil. Then, as daylight broke, I spied the chilling evidence of the bandits' handiwork, as we zipped past the blackened carcasses of one burnt out vehicle after another.

In the main, I saw Baghdad only by blazing sunlight when everything looked yellow and the hot dusty air clogged my throat. By night, I observed a self-imposed curfew, resigning myself to listening to the sporadic gunfire that crackled and snapped across the city skies from the relative safety of my concrete-reinforced and security-patrolled hotel complex. There was even the occasional thudding mortar, sometimes rather too close for comfort and a sure indication that one of the hotels where Westerners stayed, or one of the restaurants they frequented, had been targeted, if not always reliably hit.

Even by day my movements were restricted, except when I was accompanied by my guide Mahmoud, an irrepressibly tender hearted and cheery Shiite who had worked as a schoolteacher for many years, but who, after the war, had taken up the more lucrative job of chaperoning foreigners around Baghdad. "Mahmoud Shaker, driver and interpreter," it said on his business card in neat English script, above his address and phone number.

Mahmoud was short and plump, with smooth skin the colour of milky coffee, a trim black moustache, large doe eyes, and an unfailing sense of sartorial pride. Whatever the time of day and however scorching the heat, he would arrive at my hotel turned out in carefully pressed shirts and trousers and polished black loafers teamed with pale silky socks. Even when I roasted in far lighter (and much scruffier) clothing, Mahmoud wore a light tweed jacket and always remained the picture of composure. He was the father of three teenage girls, all of whom covered their hair with black cloth hijabs. His wife, who insisted every morning on preparing me a breakfast of sweet tea, oven-hot bread and clotted cream, was a Sunni Muslim from the town of Hit, in the Anbar region the West was now calling, as code for trouble spot, "The Sunni Triangle". Mahmoud liked to boast of his connections in Baghdad and he promised that although our tour of the Old City would be full of surprises, come what may, he would make sure I was safe. He even hired an armed bodyguard to discretely tail us.

Mahmoud had taken a particular interest in planning our tour ever since I'd informed him that my grandmother was born and raised within the folds of the ancient city centre. She was an Iraqi Christian, I told him, knowing that a splendid Armenian church lay within the Old City, where it once served a small but vibrant local community. I confess that even as I fed this not-so-small lie to my guide, who would later become my friend, I could feel a prick of guilt beginning to bore itself into the back of my head. Later it grew into a persistent hammering. My grandmother, a Christian! This was no small travesty, more along the line of a dancing-on-the-grave order of transgression. Surely, somewhere, she was protesting against my faithlessness with an outstretched finger—the one poking against the walls of my skull.

I felt bad about lying to Mahmoud as well. In those perilous days there existed an implicit trust between journalists and their guides working in Baghdad. You were a team. You looked out for one another and decided between you how much danger you were willing to court. I had been lucky to hook up with Mahmoud as soon as I arrived in Baghdad. From the first he had been an excellent navigator and tactful interpreter, and he fast proved to be knowledgeable, reliable, punctual and discreet. He was curious about what I was up to so far from home, but he didn't press me for information. His gut told him that I was a "good person", and after I showed him pictures of my young daughter, he began addressing me familiarly as Umm Soren (the mother of Soren), Arabic-style.

Even so, I still couldn't bring myself to tell him that I was an Iraqi Jew. That my mother and grandmother were Iraqi Jews, and that one of the chief reasons I had come to Baghdad, putting myself in the way of danger when I would much rather have been back home in London with my daughter, was that I believed that this strange post-war hiatus in Iraq might be the only opportunity in years, perhaps even decades, for me to bridge the distance enforced by exile and get close to my past.

Instead, I told Mahmoud that I was working on a newspaper feature about the Jews of Baghdad, a minority group that had ancient roots in the land, dating from the Assyrian and Babylonian exiles of the eighth and sixth centuries BC, when much of the Jewish population of Judaea was deported. Jews had been here for more than a thousand years when the Islamic armies conquered Mesopotamia. They had flourished for centuries. From Ottoman times until the middle of the last century, Jews dominated trade and finance in Baghdad. They enjoyed religious and communal autonomy, hobnobbed with tribal dignitaries and government officials, and, in almost every sphere of life, they were conspicuous, prosperous and influential.

Mahmoud seemed interested to learn that the Iraqi Jews were so thoroughly Arabized that they spoke Arabic between themselves and were steeped in an Iraqi culture that they themselves had helped to shape, through literature, poetry, music and cuisine. They thought of themselves as Iraqis before Jews, I told him, and they cherished their religion as something that gave them communal rather than national distinction.

Of course, the Jews were now gone, I added, though this could hardly have surprised Mahmoud. Having once constituted more than a third of Baghdad's resident population—which, in proportional terms, is roughly equal to the number of Jews currently living in New York City—the Jews had been uprooted en masse, mostly in 1950 and 1951, after irreconcilable tensions between Iraq and the newly-founded Israeli state made it intolerable for them to remain.

Mahmoud was well aware of the Baghdadi Jews' legacy, as most educated Iraqis were. More to the point, he knew that the ancient Jewish Quarter had more or less overlapped large sections of the Old City. But when he realized that I was hoping to find traces of Jewish life in old Baghdad, he had shrugged his shoulders and frowned. "But there is nothing left," he said. "The place where the great synagogue used to stand is now a shopping centre. All the old houses that used to belong to Jews have been converted into tenements." Intending encouragement, he added that if we happened to strike up a conversation with some of the neighbourhood's older residents, they would be bound to remember the Jews. But if I was looking for evidence—for artefacts, vestiges, even resonances—I would be disappointed.

Unlike other ex-pats attempting to reconnect with a foreign homeland, at leisure to wander freely, talk to people, soak up the experience of being in a place at once familiar and unknown, I began to understand that I would have to make do with scraps. Given that this was Iraq, and that a war was on, I would be grateful even for that much. Nonetheless, I had heard it said that there were things that a keen observer might yet chance to discover; small cigarette-shaped indentations in the doorposts of houses to which Mezuzahs, long-ago pilfered for their silver, had once been nailed, and stars of David ingeniously incorporated into a building's brickwork.

And so we pushed on, my hope being that as Mahmoud guided my steps I could drift into a parallel universe, picking up echoes meant specifically for my eagerly attuned ear, while my eye alighted on hidden signs and symbols, invisible to all but an Iraqi Jew.

Our tour began on the eastern banks of the Tigris at the foot of the Maude Bridge, from where rolls of looping razor wire stretched away into the distance along the top of the pale stone embankment and vast piles of litter, heaped into neat mounds, awaited collection. The bridge had undergone a succession of name changes over the years, but it was still known colloquially as the Maude—after the British General who had liberated the city from the deadweight of Turkish rule back in 1917 and then promptly died.

Through the shimmering haze of the morning's heat, I could just make out the old British Residency directly opposite us on the river's western bank. It was a large villa-style building with tall windows and thin decorative pilasters. Its faded grandeur alluded to the influence that the British had enjoyed here between the two world wars. This was where the indefatigable Gertrude Bell, a gifted Arabist and contemporary of my grandmother's, had worked as oriental secretary. Bell was one of a handful of Britons who had fought for Iraqi self-rule. Famously, she is reputed to have drawn Iraq's borders in the sand for the young Winston Churchill's edification. She had also urged King Faisal—first king of this new-born nation, kludged together from provincial leftovers of the Ottoman Empire—to appoint an Istanbul-educated Jew to his very first cabinet as minister of finance. The Jews were then approaching the pinnacle of their power in Baghdad. They were well-connected, urbane and bent on self-advancement. It was a soaring peak to attain after centuries of being merely tolerated—but also, a dizzying height from which to fall.

Mahmoud parked beside the bridge, thinking that we would proceed on foot. He had already mapped out a zigzagg route that would take us along River Street, before doubling back to the water's edge to see the white stone seminary, or Mustansiriyah, now a museum and the best preserved example of Abbasid-era architecture remaining in Baghdad. After that, we would work our way back along Rashid Street to arrive at the Souk al-Serai, where book dealers, stationers, printers and sellers of political posters plied their wares under the invigilating shadow of the old Ottoman government buildings, as upright and dishevelled as a brace of calcified functionaries.

The Souk al-Serai occupies a set of interconnected and vaulted passageways, crammed with stalls displaying every kind of paper product: notebooks, cards, letter paper and, of course, books. It was crowded and dirty and smelled strongly like the public urinal it apparently doubled as. Most of the literature that I saw there was Arabic—some religious, some not—and there was a surprising availability of tattered John Grisham and Tom Clancy paperbacks. I stopped to buy colourful posters of Adb al-Karim Qasim and Grand Ayatollah Ali al-Sistani, champions past and present of Iraqi nationalism, before we moved swiftly on to a rendezvous with an aged barber who had been hairdresser to the young King Faisal II, Faisal I's only grandson and Iraq's last king, murdered in cold blood during the popular revolution of 1958.

The barber was one of Mahmoud's "surprises"—a living, breathing testament to the Baghdad of another era: the real thing, if you will. His grimy salon on Rashid Street consisted of a tiny, whitewashed space containing two battered red leather chairs with rollered headrests and a couple of tarnished mirrors, and the walls were covered with sticky-looking photographs of Iraq's former Hashemite kings. The barber himself cut a figure of crisp cleanliness. He wore a stiff white shirt and clip-on bow tie and his trousers were held up over his round belly by old fashioned, striped suspenders. He had large goggling eyes, giving his face an expression of perpetual amazement, and his voice was a hoarse croak that came from the deep wells of his body. It had the discomfiting effect of turning everything he said into a gurgling confidence.

When Mahmoud introduced me as British, the barber shook my hand and bowed theatrically. Then he rolled his large eyes and said, "There are some people in Baghdad who hate the British. Why? Because they don't realize that it was the British who built Baghdad". His praise of the British was so sincere, so fulsome, that I wondered if he was aware of the irony of his comment: that the former builders of Iraq had, along with their American allies, recently reduced large swathes of Baghdad to rubble.

Rashid Street is the Old City at its most dignified. Running parallel to the river, the street is grand on a pre-automobile scale. Its stately pale stone-and-plaster houses are built over colonnaded walkways paved with big square flagstones, and its architectural confections include Corinthian columns, curling cast-iron balconies and tall windows. It is grey and shabby now, with many buildings on the verge of crumbling. But its old-fashioned shops and tumbledown coffeehouses, where pots of tea sit simmering by the doorway on open-flame burners, are as busy as ever. Peering into one of these smoke-filled caverns, I spied a roomful of men, some in lightweight linen suits, others in *dishdashas*, reading the papers and playing backgammon, passing the time of day clicking and swishing strings of amber worry beads.

At last, on Rashid Street, we were somewhere that ought to have prickled my skin with its familiarity. In my family's recollections of life in Baghdad, the street was a destination, an upmarket hub, a place of finery and indulgence. My grandmother shopped here on a regular basis, hiring a horse-drawn carriage, or *arabana*, and loading it up with bags as she visited one outlet after another. Orozdibak, Baghdad's original and much-feted department store, built over three stories tall, was located here. My mother remembers buying her first grown-up dresses from its stylish fashion department. When she was younger, my grandmother took her to Bata shoes for sandals and to Abu Maurice's for an occasional ice-cream treat. When she fell sick, the medications she swallowed came from the local pharmacy.

Back then, much of Rashid Street would have been Jewish. The shop owners were Jewish. The customers were Jewish. Even the street vendors and beggars were Jewish. My grandmother would have felt entirely at ease here, among her kind. My grandfather's own barber, not to mention his cobbler and tailor, would have been based here. And yet, years later, as I stood in the street trying to conjure up their ghosts, I had to face up to the fact that this Jewish history was gone. It had been written over, rubbed out, vanquished. It remained alive in living memory, of course, but even that was now fading. My grandparents are gone, and my mother and her sister are both in their seventies. When they talk about Baghdad now, details slip, names get left out. They still remember Rashid Street. Only it no longer remembers them.

A particular frustration was that I knew that my grandparents had lived only blocks from where I now stood, in the house in which my mother and aunt were born. But I dared not give the game away by asking Mahmoud to take me there. Besides, I had no idea of the house number, or even if it was still standing. All I knew was that their street, Taht al-Takia, was now a shoe market, and I couldn't think of a suitable pretext for stopping off there.

Instead we visited the Shorja, once the Jewish Quarter's largest open-air souk. In a city where the names of streets, markets, bridges and squares are routinely changed to keep up with new regimes and ideologies, and where, as a consequence, history has a strange way of disappearing, the Shorja has endured for more than a hundred years. That alone seemed promising, suggestive of other continuities.

The Shorja is literally a tunnel of commerce. You enter at one end and emerge at the other, and while you are in it you have no awareness of anything besides the constant clamour of people haggling over goods at the innumerable stands. I had to grab hold of Mahmoud's arm as we pushed our way forward with the rest of the crowd over shifting sheets of cardboard that covered the muddy ground underfoot. Glancing from side to side as we were thrust unhappily along, I glimpsed all too briefly the spice stands and soap-sellers, sweet stalls and nut vendors that lined the narrow street and also formed a pinched ridge along its middle. There were stalls piled high with plastic gew-gaws, children's toys and cheap clothing, gaudy stationery and coloured yarns. The sheer quantity of products was overwhelming, and together with the aggression of the shoppers and the sense of being pressed in on from all sides, I felt as if I were suffocating. When Mahmoud finally yanked me into daylight, I was panting for air.

As he dusted off his tweed jacket, Mahmoud looked at me expectantly, searching for confirmation that we'd just experienced a slice of authentic Baghdad. I babbled enthusiastically to say that we had. But, in truth, the Shorja has been a steaming, heaving, maddening disappointment. Unlike Rashid Street, which was at least a relic of its former self, the Shorja refused to speak to me. It offered up none of its secrets and none of its history and it left me feeling that I had come all this way on the basis of an illusion: namely, the faint but firm conviction that I somehow belonged here, and that this sense of belonging would be sharpened by the varied sensations of being here.

I expected the Old City to serve as my own personal medium, allowing me to commune directly with the past. I hoped it would be a conduit through which my grandmother would walk towards me as I'd never seen her, flushed with the ardour of youth, to tell me all about her life. In my innermost imaginings, I believed that our eyes would meet and our hands would touch; that some invisible knowledge would pass between us and fill me with a sense of who she was—and therefore who I was. But it was not to be. There was no "footsteps" moment in my journey. Only clamour and heat and dust. The worst of it is that had my grandmother still been alive she would have been as much a stranger to the Shorja as I was.

In the heat of my disappointment, felt most keenly as we sought refuge from the mayhem of the souk in the dark emptiness of the Armenian Church, it seemed that I had not only lied to Mahmoud about my identity, I had lied to myself. How could I be an Iraqi Jew and yet feel so disconnected from my ancestry?

The Armenian Church is a wonderful building, fashioned out of reddish brick. From the inside it appears to be shaped a like a monarch's crown—tall, multi-chambered, and with rounded, almost pillowy ceilings. It had been looted repeatedly after the war, stripped of every painting and statue, every altar cloth, candle and vestment, until it stood utterly bare, bereft of all ornament and cover, lacking, somehow, in dignity.

The church, in its present miserable condition, looked very much like I felt: disarmed, exposed and uncertain of its provenance. It was then that I knew that any claim I had on the country would need to be staked indirectly. That if I wished to revisit my grandmother's life I would have to re-imagine it rather than simply unearth it. That if I wanted to understand in what way I belonged to Iraq—and it to me— I would have to journey across the landscape of my family's collective memory.

If my history had been erased, I would re-write it, rejoining the tributary of my family's personal story to the fast-flowing and better-known narrative of public history.

Family Chronology

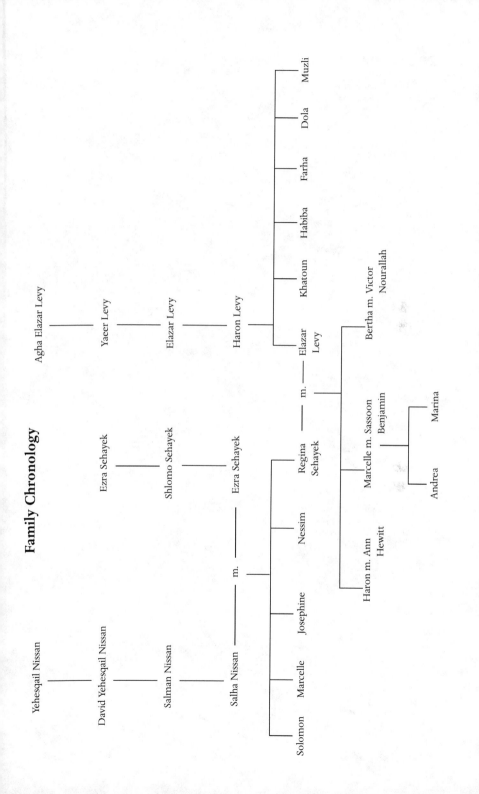

Part One
THE LOST WORLD

One

BLOODLINES

I take after my Baghdadi grandmother Regina in good ways and bad. I've inherited her appetite for life, her love of independence, her quick tongue, and her inability to suffer fools gladly. I also have her impatience. My hasty hands are routinely covered with burns from the kitchen, just as hers always were, and I have her dreadful habit of not listening to what people are saying if I think I've caught their drift early on. Now that Regina is gone, I find it's little things like these that conjure up her presence. And if I let myself sink into the softness of tender recollection, I can hear her gently scolding my childhood self, more amused than angry, *"Wi ash milouna*—you little devil. What have you done now?"

Most of my early memories of Regina are purely visceral. I remember the conspiratorial looks we'd exchange when she visited our home and unclasped her old-fashioned leather handbag in order to fish around for a packet of Maltesers to put into my eight-year-old hands. I remember her itchy embrace, when I would fold myself into the woolly cardigans she knitted herself in bold colors like cherry red or turquoise, and inhale the faint smell of mothballs mixed with sharp notes of coriander and cumin. And I remember how laughter used to break over her in uncontrollable waves, setting her whole body ashudder, helpless to stop the stream of tears springing from the corners of her eyes.

Regina and I were always close, our relationship defined against the more fractious one that existed between me and my mother. She indulged my child's clowning and asked me detailed questions about school. She played checkers with me and let me win. Tucked me in to her spare bed and poured out stories about high-minded sultans and veiled princesses. Fed my chocolate habit and hemmed my too-long skirts. She also cooked for me when I was sick—a soupy stew of rice and chicken laced with powdered dried lemon that I'd lap up like the cat who'd got the proverbial cream—and let me run amok in her well-tended garden. When my mother complained that her English-born daughter had turned out to be a rebel, reluctant to learn Arabic or eat Iraqi food, Regina would wave a forgiving hand. "She's young, Marcelle," she'd say. "She'll change." The change was a long time coming, but my grandmother was right.

Physically Regina was unremarkable. She was small in stature and somewhat heavyset, with broad, even features that were pleasing rather than pretty. Her complexion, like mine, was a light shade of olive, and her hair was dark and wavy. As a young woman she used to coax her waves into a distinctive face-framing style of the kind made popular by the silent screen star Mary Pickford. But by the time I knew her, her hair had thinned, and to make the most of what was still left she used to cover it with a fine hairnet. Age had exacted its toll in other ways. Where she had once stood firm and upright, she now stooped, unchecked osteoporosis causing her spine to slope gently outward beneath her shoulder blades, giving her the beginnings of an unsightly hump. Her voice had acquired the shakiness of the elderly. Her body had softened and spread.

Picturing her as I knew her in her twilight days, it is difficult to convey the larger-than-life character that Regina represented to my child's mind. She was a cunning heroine and guiding light, a marvel, a phenomenon. For as long as I can remember, Regina was at the center of my family's very own creation myth. She was the figure who single-handedly whisked her children out of an Iraq that had become deadly for Jews, rising to the challenges of secrecy and guile and successfully dodging the police, spies, port-authority officials, and the power-tripping whims of petty bureaucrats, all of whom were on her trail like tracker dogs.

She was also the person who made it possible for her children to re-make themselves in the face of incalculable loss, shepherding them from one safe haven to the next until they arrived in England in 1958. Whether in different circumstances Regina would have stepped forward from the silent masses and declared herself in this way, acting with defiance where others shrank into the shadows, is difficult to say because, in retrospect, it looks as if her entire preceding life had some-how prepared her for this one moment of greatness.

I have always understood that had it not been for my grand-mother's bravery, I would not own my Western freedoms. But, as with so many individual acts of everyday heroism, Regina's coura-geous tale has been lost amid the larger movements of history and the humdrum obligations of a life lived on a small scale and in an ordinary fashion.

I wish now that I had asked Regina more about her Baghdadi past when she was alive and I was old enough to be curious about it. But, back then, I badly needed her to be a champion of the present: my present, an English present. Caught between two cultures, I was under tremendous pressure to conform to the mores of a world that no longer existed, to forgo my university ambitions, marry young, take over my father's retail clothing business. It seems almost unreal to me now, but my parents began considering marriage matches for me almost as soon as I'd turned sixteen. Sometimes I'd come upon them, heads together across the kitchen table, whispering about this or that boy, picking over who was rich, who was clever, and who came from a good Baghdadi family, trying to spin their idle speculation into something that had substance. At family weddings and bar mitzvahs, they'd invariably want to know what boy I was sitting next to and what we talked about, and if my mother felt sufficiently emboldened, she'd saunter over, eyes beaming like headlights, and check out the possibilities herself. My instinct, always, was to run a mile.

Years later I'm still not sure what my parents actually meant when they so forcefully enjoined me to "be Iraqi." Most of the time being Iraqi felt like some abstract birthright that had no legitimate outlet of expression in England. The only place it held any purchase at all was within Iraqi homes. And when I was growing up these blurred into a contiguous space where exiles banded together to marshall their own rearguard action against the forces of assimilation.

All Iraqi homes looked the same to me. They were full of Persian carpets, gilt-framed mirrors, colorful ornaments made of glass and china, and plump, velour-covered sofas. In place of the soft glow given off by lampshades, they were lit by crystal chandeliers that made everything gleam. My parents went to a lot of parties in those days, thrown by fellow Iraqi Jews living in London. Usually I went along too and had my cheeks pinched by relatives from the older generation. *"Mashallah,"* someone might croon, drawing out the last syllable of this singsong exclamation in an extended *aaahhh.* "How she's grown," they'd say. Then they'd follow it up with a toast to my mother: *"Befra-ha!"*—To her wedding!—and my mother's face would dissolve into ripples of gratified smiles.

Regina went to a lot of parties herself back then. But she tended to sit quietly to one side of things with her ankles neatly crossed, observing rather than participating, lost in her own thoughts. What was she thinking about? I wonder now. Her faded youth? Her life with her late husband? A cherished past in Baghdad when she'd thrown such parties herself? Or was she simply acknowledging that her time had been and gone and that her pleasure now lay in handing over to the next generation the cares and responsibilities of cooking, entertaining, and matchmaking.

Regina lived through most of the twentieth century. She was born in 1905 as the Ottoman Empire was drawing its final rasping breaths. As a young girl she watched the British march into Baghdad to claim the spoils that once belonged to Turkey, while as a woman she saw her country rocked by the rise of Arab nationalism, followed in fairly swift succession by regicide, revolution, and the repeated backfirings of Baathism. From her exile in Calcutta, and then London, she would intermittently take the temperature of the situation back home, wondering if she'd ever return. She didn't.

Though she did not live long enough to witness Saddam Hussein's fall, Regina got to watch Desert Storm on television in 1991. Conflicting emotions of pain and nostalgia, recognition and alienation, churned inside her, unresolved, especially when Baghdad appeared on-screen and a roving camera hovered with apparent concern over whole suburbs that were about to be bombed. At that point, more than forty years had passed since she last set eyes on its river, gardens, streets, and squares.

My grandmother died in 1992, of natural causes. Having led a life marked by an act of genuine heroism, she left it succumbing to ancient terrors. In the obscure nursing home in northern England where she spent her last years battling Parkinson's disease, she suffered repeated nightmares in which the doctors and nurses who attended her were transformed into syringe-wielding Nazis with deadly intent. I never found out whether these phantom Nazis were the goose-stepping kind that she'd probably seen depicted in a hundred movies, or Arab nationalists drawn from memory and then cut in the German mold. Either way, she seems to have spent her last days combating her own inner demons.

W hen I first came into Regina's life in 1964, things were much different. Those inner demons were well hidden, and my grandmother radiated her usual aura of capability. She was living in Hounslow, a rough-hewn suburb on the western edge of London that is now predominantly Asian and given over in large part to curry restaurants and secondhand-car dealerships. Back then it was white, working class, and distinctly lacking in the sort of resident my mother regarded as "proper." Regina owned a two-story red-brick house on the Great West Road, which is the main artery that connects Heathrow Airport to central London. It is a route of arrival and departures, crisscrossed by constant traffic, but she was there to stay. Built in the 1920s, the house was a period classic, with bay windows and a stucco exterior, and it had a long thin garden with a vegetable patch at the back where Regina tended bumper harvests of raspberries and rhubarb.

Regina had worked hard to turn that house into a home. She had supervised works as her daughters Bertha and Marcelle rolled up their sleeves and painted the woodwork a blinding shade of white. Then she'd sat up nights, her nimble foot working her beetle black Singer, to sew curtains for all the windows. On the advice of her late husband's nephew Albert, she scored her *coup de grâce* and furnished the entire place with a job lot of heavy oak castoffs bought at Phillips, the auctioneers. In the matter of arranging her domestic affairs, as in all other things, Regina was a dynamo, her vim and sparkle disguising the fact that apart from a huge, battered baking pan in which she made syrupy *baklava* perfumed with rose water, a nest of curvaceous pots for brewing Turkish coffee, and a couple of fine carpets, very few things from her Baghdad life were arrayed around her.

To bring in a bit of extra money, my grandmother took a part-time job at Crowns, a wallpaper shop on the local main street. There she worked alongside Englishwomen who had somehow slipped past retirement age without anyone noticing and who smelled of cats and face powder. I don't remember the shop ever being very busy, but I do remember the tinkling bell perched high above the door frame that rang whenever the door opened, and I can still picture the long wooden counter with its smooth-grained surface and scored metal yardstick, behind which my grandmother stood ready to roll out the best that Crowns had to offer: regency stripes, ebullient florals, colored flocks, and anaglypta.

On the rare occasions my mother took me to visit Regina at Crowns, my grandmother made a memorable fuss. She lifted me onto the counter and let me finger the rolls of wallpaper. She plied me with chocolate and showed me off to the other shop assistants as though I were something she'd won at the fair. I remember eyeing those women suspiciously, thinking that they offered clues to another, perhaps better life that Regina lived outside the family circle. But I need not have worried, for while my grandmother indulged them in their banter, laughing as if she understood all the jokes, these women with dyed nested hair and musty twin sets remained as foreign to her as they were to me. Nor did they ever become her friends. That closed loop, was, like my mother's, peopled entirely by Iraqi expats.

Regina's friends were principally widows like herself, and most of them lived within a narrow orbit of London's West End. There was

Toba in Kensington, Fahima in Hammersmith, and Naima, who'd ventured out as far as Cheam. More or less the same age as Regina, these were women who maintained themselves in a state of coiffed perfection. Their hair had that airy, buoyant spring that defies weather. Their nails had the shapeliness and polished luster that only a manicurist can provide. They were always heavily made up, and wreathes of smoke from their menthol cigarettes mingled with their expensive perfume. They also had a taste for chunky and sometimes garish gold jewelry.

Though Regina was never so flashy, with these women she could be herself, speaking Arabic and reminiscing about the old life in Baghdad. Together they would while away whole afternoons munching sweet almond pastries and discussing the latest fashions, and their ears would burn with gossip as they raked over the latest Iraqi Jewish scandal to set the community alight—divorce, bankruptcy, adultery— adding up the mounting cost of exile on each count. Only when the gossip was exhausted did they lament and discuss the seemingly unstoppable rise of the Baath Party, which purported to stand for socialism and Arab unity but whose notoriously anti-Jewish leadership made the likelihood of their returning to Baghdad more remote than ever.

At the end of these sessions Regina, tanked up on nostalgia and bonhomie, was brought home to herself in a way that no amount of engagement in English life could affect. Popping one last pastry into her mouth she would whip up a froth of effusive praise for its maker's delicate fingerwork, zip up her fleece-lined boots, button her red wool coat, and complain about having to take the Tube home to Hounslow. In all her years in England, she never did get used to the cold.

If you had chanced to see my grandmother on the street in those days, a tiny figure, trudging to and from work with the rest of Hounslow's willing and able, blending in, making the best of it, you would never have guessed at the torments in her past. Like countless other ordinary people, she carried her burdens invisibly. What's more, she had learned that in London few people were interested in the life she'd led before she arrived in England on Boxing Day morning 1958, trailing half a dozen suitcases containing her worldly possessions and bringing with her two daughters and one son, whom she'd bundled up in woolly scarves and hats in anticipation of England's legendary biting winds.

My mother tends to underplay the material hardships she encountered when the family first arrived: the cold, the darkness, the constant moving from one unsavory accommodation to another, the lack of home comforts, the hunt for work. These realities she could somehow deal with. It is the indifference and casual disregard that my family met with almost everywhere that still rankles. The landlady at their very first lodgings made an indelible impression, begrudging them the use of a few matches to light the gas heater and rolling her eyes at their innocent questions about how things worked in England. She even groused that their comings and goings were wearing out her carpets.

When she first laid eyes on the small, upright woman who had come to see her room, this landlady had looked my grandmother up and down, taken in her sallow skin, dark eyes, and dark hair and said, "So you're from Baghdad, are you?" When Regina started to reply, tentatively elaborating the various reasons for her flight, the landlady began examining her chipped nails and poking at her hair to give it a bit more puff. By the time the bank manager, milkman, grocer, and almost all the neighbors had asked the same question, Regina understood that it was not the opening gambit to conversation she'd first thought, and privately hoped for—only a prelude to a swift dismissal, such as "Very interesting, I'm sure." No further questions asked. From then on she kept her personal history for those who loved her.

As a child I was completely taken in by my grandmother's surface self. I was convinced that she was the start of the line, a kind of bulwark between the palpable now and a distinctly hazy then. I knew that after her came my mother and then me; but in those rare moments when I tried to wind history back beyond my grandmother, I saw nothing but a blank. Every now and then Regina would pull out a photograph of her own mother, Salha, to show me, by way of indicating that she too came from a long line of grandmothers and mothers and daughters, that we were all of us links in a single chain. But I never felt that this bony old woman, swathed in a headscarf and bent almost double, had anything to do with me. She belonged to the foreign world of Baghdad: the rest of us were Londoners. It took me years to appreciate the extent of the journey my grandmother had had to make to get to the decisive point where she might count as a beginning, and not an end.

Nowadays, of course, I cannot get enough of the family photographs, every one of them a concrete testimonial to a past I can see all too clearly even if I cannot reach it. Pictures of Regina and her children, pictures of Regina and her husband, pictures of her brothers, her mother, her father, her friends. The family album is teeming with quiet evidence of Jewish life in Baghdad, lived happily and well, as if in an Eden before The Fall.

Though it's hard to say exactly when I began to feel the pull of my Baghdadi heritage and, as a result, to think of myself more as Iraqi, I can point to a number of trigger moments. Regina's death was the most important, for with it came the fear that her stories would die with her. The politics of multiculturalism and the self-acceptance it preached were another trigger, the shift on the geopolitical horizon after 9/11 yet another. That said, there are still moments when I think I'd simply swung out so wide, rejecting every cultural heirloom that my mother wished to hand me, that I was bound at one time or another to come boomeranging back into the fold.

Though I've never embraced the life my mother might have wanted for me, in recent years I've no longer felt an impulse to bolt whenever I run across a fellow Iraqi Jew. I'm attuned now to the unspoken kinship that exists between us as second-generation exiles, and I want to linger awhile, as if warming my hands in front of a fire. I've begun to learn Arabic, to collect recipes for Iraqi food, to listen for echoes from the past. I've learned that exile isn't something one gets over. It is something one endures.

And so I return over and again to Regina. To my memories of her. To the stories she told me, and to the family album.

One photograph in particular haunts me. It is a picture of my grandparents as newlyweds. They are standing on a jetty, beside my grandfather's sister and her husband, and with the wide, murky Tigris flowing silently behind them. The picture is black and white, but I imagine the scene in the colors of dust: the yellow of stone, the dusky shades of skin and clothing, the muddy gray-green river. My grandfather Elazar wears a European suit and a fez. Regina, diminutive, upright, and somewhat imperious looking, wears a black *abaya*—that traditional garment of Muslim modesty, which in those days was worn by Jews as well. The picture dates from good times when my grandfather was doing well for himself as a merchant, trading in tea and coffee, which he shipped from India and Africa to Iraq, and in leathers and carpets, which he bought in the East and sold in London.

Whenever I look at this photograph I catch myself scanning my grandmother's face for clues as to how she would deal with what life would soon throw at her, as if her fate were somehow written in her young features. But my grandmother stares back at the camera unsmiling. Not a wisp of dark hair is visible beneath her headband. Her face is closed. If I'd only asked Regina about her experiences when I had the chance, I might have had the retrospective wisdom I now seek. But the photograph remains a silent rebuke, reminding me that for too long I was never much interested in my grandmother's life.

Two

BAGHDAD

Y ou couldn't really call the Baghdad of my grandmother's day a beautiful city. By then nothing was left of Caliph Mansur's original round city, a genuine wonder of the eighth-century world, with a towering encircling wall, wrought-iron gates, sumptuous palaces, gilded mosques, and fairy-tale gardens. The only remnant was its old Sassanid name, Baghdad, which meant "Gift of God."

The famed seminaries and observatories built by the Abbasid caliphs who followed Mansur had long ago turned to dust. The once-magnificent palaces were in ruins. And while Baghdad's residents continued to speak of the glorious reign of Haroun al-Rashid, whose military victories across the Arab world earned him comparison to Charlemagne, they had to suffer the indifferent rule of a succession of Turkish governors. These *walis* cared nothing for the city's proud past, and after four hundred years of running Baghdad as a neglected frontier province of the Ottoman Empire, they presided over a largely lawless city. By the start of the twentieth century, Baghdad was rife with corruption and crime, its streets teemed with beggars, and its crumbling infrastructure stood in desperate need of attention.

Travelers lured by the myth of Baghdad were invariably disappointed by what they saw. Only from a distance, when its shining domes and verdant date and orange groves beckoned, could the city still work its spell. Or else at the witching hour of dusk, when the city's oil lamps appeared as a shimmering crescent on the banks of the Tigris and all was quiet save for the gentle lapping of water. At such times Baghdad was like a veiled courtesan, offering hints of promise to those who wooed her, without revealing any of her flaws. The rest of the time her wrinkles and battle scars were unforgivingly exposed.

A handful of sights stood out by day. Of these, the most magnificent was the domed shrine of the mystic and scholar Abd al-Qadir al-Gaylani. Housed within a vast rectangular walled compound, the shrine was visited by thousands of pilgrims of every nationality, who washed under the fountains, strolled under the arcades, and shared news about the state of Islam in the world. The medieval Talisman and al-Wastani gates, each with their splendid octagonal towers and domed inner chambers, were equally esteemed by visitors to Baghdad, in that they offered a glimpse into the city's dignified past. But other relics from Abbasid times could be counted on the fingers of a single hand. Among them a beautiful minaret, dating from 1236, stood next to the souk el-Ghazl, looking like a tall church candle, and the magnificent tomb of Zumarad Khatoun boasted an unusual carved stone dome, prickly and pointy as a pinecone.

Stripped of these baubles, Baghdad looked tired and run-down. Here and there, you might stumble across an ancient wooden doorway studded with squat iron nails, or glimpse in passing the glinting blue tilework of Persian craftsmen, but the city's principal buildings, its barracks, baths, mosques, even its palaces, had all seen better days. Viewed as a whole Baghdad was an eye-numbing blur of earth-colored buildings, one or two stories high. Many of the buildings were windowless and cavelike, and almost all were made of sunbaked bricks that were formed from alluvial mud and apt to dissolve back into the earth at the first heavy rainfall.

To compound this impression of neglect, the city's ancient walls lay around it in ruins after Midhat Pasha, the most dynamic of Baghdad's nineteenth-century *walis*, knocked them down, intending to replace them with wide leafy boulevards. But the boulevards were never constructed, and no one could be bothered to clear up the rubble. The streets were overcrowded and dirty, making the city a haven for a comprehensive range of serious and fatal diseases: malaria, sandfly fever, bilharzia, hookworm, dysentery, typhoid, smallpox, and cholera topped this deadly list. Baghdad's public services—its water supply, sewage system, electricity, and street cleaning—were either deficient or nonexistent, earning Baghdad an unpleasant twist on a legendary nickname: "the city of a thousand and one smells." And Bedouin tribes regularly stormed in from the desert on horseback to loot the city's souks, causing terrorized shopkeepers and their hapless customers to dive for the nearest cover. To the outsider Baghdad appeared to exist in a constant state of tension, with the forces of chaos forever threatening to ambush the city's reluctant march toward civilization.

Whenever the Turkish authorities made some attempt at maintaining law and order, conditions would improve a little. But the Baghdad *vilayet,* or administrative region, was situated too far from the base of imperial power at Istanbul for either its welfare or its intrigues to matter very much, with the result that no one was held to account if standards of policing slipped. Likewise no one noticed if monyes set aside for urban improvement ended up lining the silken purses of the *walis* and their political allies.

And yet beyond the dirt and the disease, the beggars and brigands, the lack of civic amenities and the unchecked crime, Baghdad's streets were thronged with people of every race and religious stripe engaged in purposeful activity, as they moved from market to vaulted bazaar to warehouse, or *khan,* and back again: hawkers, peddlers, merchants, gentlemen *effendi*s, tricksters, entrepreneurial street vendors, meat sellers, ironmongers, candlemakers, coppersmiths, basket weavers, moneylenders, fishermen, tanners, spice sellers, and landowners. Everywhere you looked trade was underway, deals were being brokered, and money bought and sold. The air was thick with speculation. Like no other city in the Fertile Crescent, Baghdad reveled in the beauty of business. And in business the Jews excelled.

In a dispatch dating from 1904, the year before Regina was born, the French vice-consul at Baghdad put the city's Jewish population at forty thousand, almost one-third of the total number of people resid-ing in Baghdad. He went on to claim that the Jews were not only the most numerous ethnic minority in the city but also the richest and most industrious. Six years later, in a report prepared for the British consulate, H. D. Shohet, himself a Jew, estimated that Baghdad was home to fifty thousand Jews. Offering an insiders' vision of a commu-nity on the rise, he wrote: "[Jews] have literally monopolized the local trade, and neither Muhammadans nor Christians can compete with them. Even the few leading Muhammadan merchants owe their pros-perity to the capable and industrious Jews whom they have for years employed as clerks. The Jewish clerks are practically the managers of their firms."

According to Shohet, the chief item of Jewish trade was Manchester piece goods. Local merchants had amassed riches by importing these goods from Manchester and exporting them to Persia, making use of subsidiary offices they'd set up in Manchester, London, Kermanshah (now Bakhtaran), and Hamadan that allowed them to circumvent the use of intermediaries. In fact, Baghdadi Jews had been busy establish-ing trading posts outside Mesopotamia since the middle of the nine-teenth century. Beyond England and Persia, there were pockets of Baghdadi Jews trading in Bombay and Calcutta; in Rangoon, the for-mer capital of Burma; and in Hong Kong, Shanghai, and Japan. It was from these satellite communities that the famous Sassoon and Kadoorie dynasties sprang, the former responsible for a vast textile empire strung across India's major urban centers, and the latter for founding the largest finance house in Shanghai.

Various external factors aided the ascendancy of the Jewish mer-chants of Baghdad: the end of the monopoly of the British East India Company, the expansion of the port of Basra, and the opening of the Suez Canal in 1869. With this enormous boost to commerce, by the end of the nineteenth century long-distance trade from the Tigris-Euphrates Valley to India, Europe, and the Far East was booming, fi-nanced by Jewish bankers willing to extend credit to family members and trusted coreligionists based abroad, and pioneered by Jewish mer-chants ever alert to the potential of new markets.

By 1910, when H. D. Shohet prepared his report, the Jews were comfortably handling the vast bulk of Baghdad's commercial and financial business. The next development they awaited, apparently with "breathless impatience," was for Baghdad to emerge as a trading megalopolis, a development they hoped would be hastened by the implementation of Sir William Willcocks's new irrigation schemes and the building of a projected railway line across the Syrian desert. (Willcocks was the British civil engineer behind the Aswan Dam, completed in 1902.) "They think that Baghdad will soon be a very important center of commerce and residence," wrote Shohet, "and that they will then be able to throw themselves into a stream of speculations." Poised on the brink of modernity, Baghdad's Jews looked forward to a future more glorious than anything previously hinted at over the course of their long history in Mesopotamia.

"Jews, Sunnis, Shias, Kurds, Turkomans, Assyrians, Armenians, Yazidis: all have equal standing in this city." This is what Regina's father, Ezra Sehayek, used to tell his Muslim friends before winking and adding, "But the Jews were here before all the others." Jews were indigenous to ancient Mesopotamia. Abraham, Judaism's founding patriarch, originally hailed from Ur of the Chaldees. Ezekiel, Ezra, and Daniel had all lived in Babylon. The Talmud was penned by Babylonian scholars and scribes. Even the royal line of David survived in Mesopotamia down to the Middle Ages. Though Ezra's friends already knew this much, they'd tease him back, saying "Yes, yes, we know how you Jews are plotting to claim Mesopotamia for yourselves. You want it for your fabled Jewish homeland."

After almost a century of Arab-Zionist conflict, it is difficult for those with no direct experience of the Middle East to imagine Jews like my great-grandfather as a vital presence in Muslim societies and cultures, or indeed to appreciate the extent to which Arab Jews lived in peaceful coexistence with the rest of the Arab world. In Ezra's day Jews and Muslims were often friends and neighbors. They ran businesses together, sent their children to the same schools, helped one another out in times of trouble, and held a language and culture in common. Whereas Arab-Jewish communities in Yemen and Jerba continued to write primarily in Hebrew, and many Jews in Egypt and North Africa adopted French as their lingua franca, the Jews of Iraq spoke a Baghdadi-Jewish Arabic dialect at home and elected to use standard Arabic as their language of culture.

By the end of the nineteenth century Jews were so thoroughly integrated into Baghdadi society, eating the same food, wearing the same clothes, and cherishing the same local customs as their Muslim peers that often the only way to tell the Jews apart was by their headgear: they wore the red fez, while Muslims favored the turban.

This is not to say that no pecking order was observed. Baghdadi society was religiously and ethnically stratified, with the Sunni minority at the top of the heap, filling all the offices of local government and behaving as if they were representatives of the caliph himself. Many high-ranking Sunnis were Istanbul-educated in those days. They spoke Turkish and were loyal to Turkey, the first stirrings of Arab nationalism still a few years away. What's more, they ruled as the Ottomans ruled themselves, through nepotism.

The Shia majority had second billing in Baghdadi society, but because they had been marginalized politically they were forced to compete with the Jews for power and influence, principally through trade. The problem was that Shia merchants lacked overseas connections as well as the fluency in French and English that their Jewish counterparts acquired at school, and so they never managed to claim their rightful share of city commerce. For the Shias, the ultimate humiliation was that business life in Baghdad ground to a complete halt on Saturdays and not on Fridays, which is the traditional Muslim day of rest: the shops were shut, the bazaars empty, the streets silent. "See how the whole city observes the Jewish Sabbath," Ezra would tell his wife, Salha, a flicker of mischief dancing in his eyes. As for the rest of Baghdad's minority groups, the Kurds were not particularly well represented, preferring to exercise their influence in Mosul, while Christians and Yazidis were generally too small in number to bother with.

That left the Jews in a very strong position. And yet for all their commercial prowess—and in spite of Ezra's wishful egalitarian thinking—Jews remained second-class citizens. Under Muslim law Jews existed as a protected minority, or *dhimmi*. *Dhimmi*s belonged neither to the *dar al-Islam*, the domain of Islam, nor to the *dar al-harb*, the domain of war, but to a nebulous place in between that is sometimes referred to as the "domain of conciliation." They were, in short, tolerated. But they were free to practice their faith and administer to the needs of their community without deference to Muslim society as long as they paid a poll tax and land tax, and as long as they observed a number of archaic social rules, such as agreeing to distinguish themselves from Muslims by dress—hence the differing headgear. It was a fair deal by most measures. What's more, the *dhimmi* communities were exempt from military service, which suited the Jews very well, since their Muslim overlords prosecuted few wars that they regarded as their own.

Under the Turkish *millet* system by which *dhimmi* communities were officially recognized, Jewish self-government assumed a more complex form, a paler version of the multiple ranks of officialdom and bureaucracy that characterized the Ottoman hierarchy itself. Numerous religious and lay councils were responsible for the spiritual, moral, and fiscal welfare of the community, for handling judicial matters, and for representing the community's interests to the Turkish authorities. Most important, the Jewish leadership was given free rein both to levy its own taxes and spend the monyes raised as it saw fit. By means of tariffs such as the hefty meat tax known as the *gabelle,* the Jews were able to set aside funds for the running of hospitals, charities and schools, and pay the salaries of the rabbis and shohets, trained experts who slaughtered animals in keeping with the laws of *kashruth*.

This was the world in which Ezra Sehayek operated. It was a world he understood and never questioned, since in all the ways that mattered—that is, with regard to his faith, family, health, and good fortune—life had so far treated him well. By all accounts, my great-grandfather was a mild-mannered soul who was much loved by all who knew him. He had gentle gray eyes and a big droopy mustache, and he spoke in soft, equivocating sentences, insinuating his opinions into conversation rather than asserting them. My mother says that Ezra was clever, bookish, fair-minded, and tolerant, but that beyond all these things he was possessed of an inner contentment that few people on this earth are lucky enough to own. It lit him up from the inside like a beacon.

Ezra Sehayek worked as a moneychanger, which was typically a route to great wealth. But the limit of Ezra's ambition was that his family should simply be comfortable. At the end of the week he would dependably hand over the housekeeping to Salha, and with that duty discharged he would absent himself from his wider responsibilities and retire among his books, leaving the world and his wife to their own devices.

My great-grandmother Salha—the bony and crooked old woman whom Regina tried to impress on me as a child—was a determined and bossy matriarch who ruled her husband, children, and the household servants with an equally firm hand. Whenever she wanted to feel her own power she would finger the large bunch of keys she kept hidden under her skirts—keys to secret chambers and cupboards where she hoarded sweet treats for the children and domestic odds and ends that testified to her yen for organizing and her good sense. An astute and prickly character, Salha seldom disguised her pleasures and disappointments: she could carry the mood of a filled room up or down with her. At the same time, she exuded a quiet strength. In fact, in everything she did she moved with the confident certainty of those born into wealth. She even smoked openly at a time when the activity was largely associated with men.

My mother tells me that for all her bombast Salha was devoted to living a Jewish life and that she took particular delight in the Friday-night ritual that welcomed in the Sabbath each week. On Fridays, Salha would get up early to prepare the evening meal, delegating chores to the servants and instructing them to set the table with her best china. Then she'd take a long bath to wash away the impurities in her heart along with the dust and sweat of her kitchen labors so that she could appear clean before God. She would scent herself with jasmine, search her wardrobe for something special to wear, and smooth reddish-brown henna paste into her shoulder-length hair. Then she'd push into her pierced earlobes the solid gold rings that Ezra had given her after they were betrothed.

Like most Baghdadi Jews, Salha observed communal rites and domestic routines that had remained unchanged for centuries and were thus comfortably predictable from month to month. In March the orange trees blossomed, usually in time for Purim, and giggling children collected the delicate flowers in large reed baskets. April marked the start of the *turab* or dust storm season, when families sleeping outdoors would awake to find themselves coated from head to toe in a fine layer of dust. In June and July the house was full of scorpions, while in August women made the year's supply of tomato paste and date juice, leaving the fruit to dry on the roof terrace under the burning sun. September was Rosh Hashanah, October Succoth, and on it went, with religious holidays and seasonal markers checking off the days and weeks until everyone was back where they had started.

Secure in the cradle of life's cyclical rhythms, Salha was able to manage things exactly as her mother and grandmother had done, and as their mothers and grandmothers had done before them. "What was good enough for my mother and for me is good enough for you," she would later tell Regina, if her daughter ever chased after some new fad or freedom. Above all, there was a reassuring quality to this straightforward replication of traditions handed down from generation to generation, for it meant one thing: continuity.

Everything bowed before the God of continuity and its high priests: ancient ritual, established custom, and time-tested wisdom. The more thickly something came encrusted with the residues of the past, the more respect it commanded, while change was viewed with suspicion, and newness, faddishness, and fickleness were lumped together alongside foolishness and credulity. It was all perfectly logical if you believed that preserving the past was the sure route to guaranteeing the future.

By the end of the first decade of the twentieth century, however, fissures were beginning to open up between progressive and established elements within the community, with one group wanting increasingly to test its values against the wider world as the other clung ever more tightly to tradition. On the side of the tried and true were the rabbis who continued to maintain Mosaic law as a living, breathing entity, impressing every soul in their care with the love and fear of God. They encouraged a life of servility, obedience, and unquestioning orthodoxy, qualities that over the years had worked to isolate the community from the world at large. Indeed, if the rabbis had had their way, the Jews of Baghdad would forever have remained a group apart.

But the community's business leaders were beginning to strain against the restrictiveness of the old life. Many of them had had contact with Europe and with Western Jewry, and along with a number of enlightened families who had reaped the benefits of a largely secular modern education, they were drawn to the ideas of progress and self-improvement. They wanted more for themselves and their children than the blinkered certainties of faith and they believed they could have it without compromising their identities as Jews.

By the time H. D. Shohet prepared his report for the British consulate in 1910, a subtle shift had taken place in the balance of power within the community, giving the lay leadership an upper hand over the Jews, and an influence that exceeded that of the chief rabbi and his religious council. Officially the chief rabbi was head of the community. He drew his salary from the community treasury and his appointment was underwritten by a *firman* from the sultan. He was supposed to be the medium of correspondence between the Turkish authorities and the community, but according to Shohet, this had become merely a matter of form: "The Chief Rabbi is simply a mouthpiece. He exercises no real influence over either the Turkish authorities or the members of his own community."

The true power in the community, wrote Shohet, resided in the hands of its wealthy bankers and merchants, men such as the moneylender Sion Aboudi; Meir Elias, an important stockholder; and Menham Salah Daniel, a landowner who would later become an Iraqi senator. "It is these persons who discuss measures together in cases of emergency, and who form deputations in important questions to the *wali* and other high officials." The chief rabbi, for his part, was "a mere puppet in their hands."

Shohet's report was written two years after the Young Turks swept to power, deposing the sultan and reintroducing a constitution that was intended once and for all to do away with the nepotism, corruption and elitism his position had come to embody. With true revolutionary fervor, the Committee of Union and Progress lost no time in overhauling the vast body of officials in the various Turkish provinces so that their reforms might be speedily implemented across the empire, and in the course of their purging and cleansing Baghdad acquired a string of progressive *walis*, each with a zeal for modernizing that was greater than his predecessor's. The result was that within a few short years the city was yanked into the new century.

A public telephone service was added to Baghdad's existing telegraph system, and the city's incipient press witnessed a remarkable flowering of free speech as competing Arabic- and Turkish-language newspapers came into daily circulation. Baghdad began to attract resident foreigners whose presence, in turn, boosted internal drives to increase literacy, and there was a general revving up in the tempo of life. Parks were created. A zoo was opened. New asphalted roads were built through Baghdad's intricately folded network of alleyways, making it possible for Jawad Pasha, the current *wali,* to ship the first motorcar from Aleppo for his personal use. Whenever this magnificent vehicle appeared on Baghdad's streets it drew spontaneous applause from the crowds, while barefoot children would run after it, hooting in delight and amazement.

Here was the brave new world in which progressive Jews had been longing to participate. And from 1908 onward they could, because with revolution came the abolishment of the *dhimmi* status and the granting of full citizenship to Baghdad's various minorities. For the first time in their history the Jews stood on the same footing as their Muslim peers.

As if to mark this wonderful improvement in their status, in 1909 a Jew named Sasson Hesqail became one of six parliamentarians to represent Baghdad in the new elective chamber at Istanbul. The appointment had an immediate ripple effect throughout the community. Many Jews, in particular the business minded, the educators, and the politically inclined among them, rushed to acquire the Turkish tongue, while the young enrolled in the Turkish military schools, where they might train to become officers in the Ottoman army. All of them studiously ignored the rabbis with their stony faces and endless grumbling and their ominous warnings about wolves in sheep's clothing. None could know that the sweeping reforms of 1908 would be the least of the rude and often sudden changes that the Jews of Iraq would have to face over the coming decades.

Regina Sehayek was born in 1905, the first child of Ezra and Salha. Salha had endured a long and painful labor lasting two days and one gruelling night, yet she well remembered how in the midst of her agonies the midwife had leaned into her ear and whispered that only a boy was capable of generating such torments. Salha had taken the words at face value, as an encouraging confirmation of what she believed she already knew.

Throughout her pregnancy, friends and family alike had continually remarked on the position and movements of the baby inside her. It had to be a boy, they'd said. They told her that her cravings for watermelon and pistachios were really *his* cravings, and that her sudden intolerance of excessive heat owed to *his* sensitivity to warmth. When the baby lunged at her from the inside, they'd cooed that *his* strong kicks spoke of wonderful strength. But then Regina came along and surprised the entire clucking company, turning their guilty hopes upside down.

This preference for male children among the Baghdadi Jews had deep cultural roots. A son would continue the family name and, with any luck, the family business too. He would look after his parents in old age and provide for his siblings if need be. Above all a son would not drain the family resources, since he would not require a dowry. If Ezra had secretly shed a few quiet tears at Regina's birth, he would not have been the first or last Iraqi man to do such a thing. Nor could Salha be blamed if she had not for the merest fraction of an instant felt the bitter sting of disappointment. Yet whatever their early misgivings, Ezra and Salha soon came to love Regina with the peculiar fierceness that parents often feel for their firstborn.

From the beginning Regina was closer to her father. As her brothers recall, she was a caring and thoughtful child who never shirked her responsibilities and always performed the chores her mother set her without complaint. Like most children she had a sweet tooth. But for Regina, sweets remained a lifelong compulsion and her dark eyes would burn intently whenever her radarlike senses detected the proximity of sugar. Even when she was living in the nursing home in England and her hands were perpetually shaking with Parkinson's, she would exert the greatest force of will to work trembling cutlery over the occasional sweet or pastry.

My grandmother's early life was comfortable and secure, unfolding almost entirely within the confines of home. The only outings she enjoyed were visits to cousins and aunts, and her only exposure to the outside world involved peering at it from behind her mother's skirts. Against this backdrop of fussing and cosseting, it is little wonder that one of Regina's earliest memories was a snapshot of river life at full throttle: the impression stood in such stark contrast to the walled-in experience of her everyday existence that it stayed with her forever.

Regina could never remember how or why she found herself at the water's edge, or even who had taken her there, though it was probably her father, Ezra. Everywhere she looked, a different kind of vessel plied the water, connecting Baghdad to Mosul in the north, Basra in the south, and the larger world beyond for the greater glory of all its citizens. There were British-built steamers, lateen-sailed dhows, high-hulled cargo ships, and gondolalike *bellums*—the larger craft bringing coal from Wales, coffee from Brazil, sugar from Egypt, tobacco from Persia, and tea and spices from India. In the opposite direction traveled dates and rice, wheat, gums, gallnuts, and licorice roots. Arab horses were shipped to India, hides to Constantinople and Europe; local wool went to London, and intestine linings went to the United States for sausage making.

Amid all this traffic large rafts piled high with watermelons bobbed precariously across the river, and passenger ferries operated by the Lynch Brothers chugged and hooted their way back and forth. Most striking of all were the *quffas*, round reed baskets, thickly coated with pitch inside and out. These unique vessels, skillfully propelled by men wielding long paddles and poles, could each carry two donkeys, six sheep, a dozen people, and a thicket of bundles and bales, but they looked their best when they ferried reeds from the southern marshes upstream, the reeds standing tall inside them, displaying their feathery blooms like the plumes of a preening bird.

The nonstop river traffic made for a magnificent sight, especially to young eyes wanting to take in every species of Baghdadi spectacle. My grandmother drank it all in. Standing on the pontoon bridge, looking down at the comings and goings below, listening to the water swishing and the oarsmen shouting, and with the big steamboats blowing their horns, she felt as though she lived at the center of the world.

Three
JEWS AND POMEGRANATES

When Regina was growing up, the vast bulk of Baghdad's Jewish population lived in the city's Jewish quarter, or *mahallah,* a compact, airless neighborhood in the north of town where the houses were so densely packed together inside a maze of twisting streets that they constituted an almost solid mass. Salha used to say that the houses clung together just like the people who inhabited them: large and small, they were wedged alongside synagogues, community halls, schools, ateliers, and workshops, wall pressed against adjacent wall, while shops were jammed into market streets like too many teeth in a crooked smile. Each building seemed to jostle its neighbor as if competing for a piece of the sky. Each family needed only to glance across the roof terraces to learn another family's business.

Since there were no parks or garden squares in the Jewish quarter to open things up a little and make the air more breathable, nor any easy means of navigating your way from one place to another except by memorizing the local landmarks, the area tended not to attract outsiders, which the Jews thought was just as well. Indeed, aerial photographs of the Jewish quarter snapped from British reconnaissance planes during World War I reveal a neighborhood that was intricately folded in on itself, like a clenched fist.

That the Jews of Baghdad chose to live this way is telling, since they wished to preserve their ethnic and communal identity at all costs. It was as if they believed that the closer they were bound together the more concentrated their essence would be.

The same instinct for self-preservation meant that wherever possible, Baghdadi Jews married other Baghdadi Jews, cousins and uncles included if not preferred. It was not uncommon for a young man raised in one of the expat communities in India or Burma to return to Baghdad in order to find himself a bride. Likewise, families settled across the border in Iran would often send their daughters home, charging a guardian with the task of getting them wed. One way or another everyone in the community was related to everyone else.

Among the matriarchs of Salha's generation, tracing the various threads of marital and blood connection was a popular pastime. "Of course Gourji Battat is related to me," Salha might exclaim to a friend at one of her weekly gatherings. "His mother, Violet, is my maternal grandfather's sister-in-law, because Farah, my grandmother, and Violet are sisters." Duly impressed by Salha's genealogical skills, the friend would shake her head, saying *"Israel ghamana"*—Israel is a pomegranate—while Salha savored the small stab of satisfaction that came from having done her bit to prove that the Baghdadi Jews, like the individual seeds of this unusual fruit, were wrapped within a single skin.

It was self-preservation, too, that informed the design of the classic Jewish house. An enigma of windowless brick on the outside, the typical Jewish house was a personal fortress against the clamor and chaos of daily life in Baghdad. The impregnable facades that faced the street were meant to be uninviting. The hulking wooden doors bolted tightly shut. The thick walls rebuffed the most ingenious of thieves. Even the ornamental casements that allowed light and air into the upper story protruded like angry chins. On the inside, however, home was an oasis of colonnaded walkways and inner courtyards that opened to the sky and rang with the sound of footsteps and laughter.

Some of my mother's most vivid recollections of childhood celebrate the almost nomadic mode of living that took place within Baghdadi homes and kept pace with the changing seasons. In summer, mornings and evenings were spent outdoors in the central courtyard eating, gossiping, sewing, and washing, with the children constantly tearing around the adults' feet. On stiflingly hot afternoons everyone relocated indoors, while at night the family carried mattresses and bedding up to the roof terrace and slept under the star-flecked sky. Bedrooms were used only in winter. Yet even then parents, grandparents, and children would gather nightly in the courtyard, where a brazier would be lit and, like Bedouins seated round a campfire, they'd tell each other stories until the air chilled and the sky became nearly black with night.

A generation earlier my grandmother Regina led the same simple existence within a classic Baghdad house on Abu Sa'ad Street, in the Torat area of the *mahallah*. The house was arranged over three floors, if you counted the basement, and it had an ample-size roof terrace, where Ezra and Salha often set a table for dinner. Typically three or more generations would share a house such as this, cooking in one kitchen and eating around one table. But Regina's parents presided over a family that was Western in its nuclearity thanks to the generosity of Salha's father, who was a wealthy property holder. Salman Nissan owned several houses in the area, including a mansion on Torat Street where Salha grew up and where she acquired an early conviction that life worked in happy concordance with her will. Signing over one of these houses to Salha on the occasion of her marriage was nothing to Salman Nissan, though it was a handsome dowry by any standard, and Ezra Sehayek considered himself a fortunate man. As a result the Sehayeks lived in relative luxury, having plenty of room for visitors and guests and no one from the older generation to cater to.

Regina and her younger siblings, Nessim and Josephine, had the run of the house during the day, principally because Salha was too busy always to be on their backs. While she moved between the kitchen and storerooms, making sure there was enough oil and sugar for the week, counting the rice bags and arguing with the cook, they romped around the roof terrace and bickered constantly. There were household chores the children couldn't escape, of course, and at

Passover, Salha put them to work scrubbing the kitchen clean and sifting through kilos of rice, grain by grain, to remove all traces of the five forbidden grains that had to be disposed of by 10 a.m. on Passover eve: wheat, spelt, barley, rye, and oats. Regina looked forward to the matzo they would eat for a week, and especially to dipping it in thick, sweet date juice mixed with chopped walnuts, the Iraqi version of the Ashkenazi haroseth.

Occasionally Regina accompanied Ezra on local errands, and in the process of doing so she fixed a rudimentary map of the area in her head. If they left the house in one direction, they would arrive at the Shorja, where veiled matriarchs gathered in the hazy light of dawn to scrutinize squawking hens waiting for their throats to be slit. In the opposite direction they'd alight at souk Hanuni, the all-purpose open-air market whose vegetable stalls were piled with precarious stacks of sweet-smelling melons, shiny blue-black eggplants, and succulent tomatoes. Beyond the souk a short wide street housed the religious school, or yeshiva, the Jewish Institute for the Blind, the Laura Kadoorie School for Girls, and the Great Synagogue with its high walls, marble columns, and priceless foundation stone, rumored to date from the reign of Jehoiakim, last king of Judah.

Regina loved to walk past the synagogue, which she attended with her parents every Sabbath, dressed up in frills and flounces like the other little Jewish girls. But on weekdays the building seemed somehow more inviting, home to a secret confab of learned men in white robes and coiled cloth turbans, and the mysterious source of a sonorous murmur of low prayer that rose into the street from deep within the building to cast a lyrical spell over passersby.

The outer limits of the Baghdad Regina knew as a child were located at the end of this street, where a knot of winding lanes brought together several boys' schools and made a rich man of old Fattal, who owned the only bookshop in the vicinity, and who, at the start of each school term, presided over a barely controlled run on his stock. The pharmacy could also be found here, as could Yehazkel Abu al-Anba's shop, which was deluged by school children buying *samun* and *anba,* a sandwich of crusty bread filled with mango pickle. There was always a line outside Abu al-Anba's shop, which gratified its owner no end because it filled his cash till with silver *qurush*.

Regina's life had a simple rhythm. It revolved around food and family, Sabbath and high holidays, and the weekly open house, or *k'bul*, which Salha determined would be held on Wednesdays. Preparations for this social event, when up to thirty people might descend on the Sehayek household expecting to be fed, would begin days before. It was a precision operation. Dozens of pitchers of orange juice and lemonade, made from hundreds of fruits that Ezra had carted home from the market by donkey, would be lined up on the pantry shelves like soldiers awaiting deployment. Crockery would be dusted and prettily stacked, and napkins would be starched, ironed, and folded.

The next task was to make fillings for the pastries. Almonds had to be ground, sweetened, and then spiked with crushed cardamom; dates had to be pummeled into a sticky paste, and cheese needed to fill the soft pastry pouches known as *sambuseks* had to be grated, salted, and mixed with eggs. When the baker set to work at a big table in the courtyard, everything would be waiting for him, including homemade dough prepared the night before and already risen. Over the course of a day he would make the week's supply of biscuits and flat breads as well as dozens of *sambuseks*. Regina remembered the baker as the roughest man she had ever seen, with his burly arms, coarse aprons, and sweating brow. She liked to watch him at work as he bent over the clay oven or *tannour*, pulling out trays of cooked pastries and exchanging them for unbaked ones, and she'd wince as the heat singed the hair on his forearms and turned his cheeks a raw shade of pink. It was a marvel to her that someone so rough could produce something so sweet, for the baker made the finest treats she'd ever tasted.

When my mother and I gaze back together at the lost world of the Baghdadi Jews, her memories lighting my way into the dim chambers and dusty corridors of the abandoned past, the feature that stands out above all others is a quality of innocence that is almost too pure, too shining, to be believed. "Life was good," "Life was simple": these are summary pronouncements my mother makes over and over as she describes various scenes, while I struggle with the idea that things might really have been that uncomplicated.

In 1913, when Regina was eight, she began attending the Laura Kadoorie School for Girls, which had been opened twenty years earlier by the *Alliance Universelle Israélite*, a charity formed by a group of French intellectuals in order to provide a top-notch secular education to Jews in the Levant. The school proved instantly popular with the community's middle classes, and aspiring Jewish parents across Baghdad flocked to enroll their daughters there in the hope that they would acquire European refinements.

Thumbing through a handful of surviving photographs of the first generations of pupils to graduate from the Laura Kadoorie School, my mother and I squint at neat rows of young girls standing tall and proud before the camera. They are entirely covered up in floor-length dresses with long sleeves and lacy white collars, and they wear their dark, oiled hair twisted into shiny buns. They have names such as Albertine and Suzette and Irene and Clare, as if they had just stepped off the boat from Marseilles. And they have a knowing look about them that hints at knowledge beyond their years.

What strange hybrids these girls must have been. Dark-skinned beauties who, thanks to the schooling they received at the hands of the *Alliance,* could chatter away gaily in fluent French; Arabized princesses who delighted in the francophone names that separated them from the Sayeedas and Khatouns of their mothers' generation. Previously they had scarcely been exposed to the light of day, let alone the ways of the world. Yet at the instigation of the *Alliance,* they learned to play the piano, to play tennis, and to smoke cigarettes from long tortoiseshell holders when they thought no one was looking.

My mother is adamant that despite such pretensions to sophistication, girls such as these—girls "from good families"—had no real Western freedoms. They had no careers to dream of or travels to plan, no power to shorten their hemlines in keeping with the latest fashions, and almost no say in whom they would marry. Although the *Alliance's* charitable founders espoused a *mission civilisatrice,* its schoolmasters and mistresses stopped short of spoiling a generation of girls destined to become good Baghdadi wives.

By my mother's reckoning, almost nothing in Regina's early experience prepared her for what was to come. There were no ominous warnings or dark foreshadowings, no secret communication from the world of spirits. More important, there was no formative event or sudden test of her worth to show her what she was really capable of. Any tensions in the management of the Jewish community sparked and crackled unnoticed overhead, like lightning from a distant storm, while the world she knew, encompassing school and home, was safe and warm, closed off for the most part from society at large.

In 1913, with additional funds from Shanghai banker Sir Elly Kadoorie, the school's original backer, the Laura Kadoorie School moved into imposing premises in the heart of the *mahallah*. The new red-brick building was laid out in grand proportions over two floors, each lined with tall arched windows separated by thin pilasters, and it contained an enormous courtyard filled with light. The courtyard was ringed with white columns like a Roman senate building, while behind the columns ran a wide corridor leading to assembly rooms, cloakrooms, and also the water room, lined with metal faucets that dispensed fresh drinking water. On the upper story, where girls leaned over iron filigree railings to talk to fellow pupils in the courtyard below, there were large airy classrooms with sliding glass-paneled doors.

The year that Regina joined the school, it already had 788 pupils aged between four and seventeen. Salha had sailed into Madame Bassan's office, fully expecting that the new principal, like everyone else she encountered in life, would accommodate her wishes, but Salha had had to fight even to get her daughter into the school. Madame Bassan had said the school was full and there was nothing she could do for Regina that year. At least that is what she would have said had she spoken any Arabic, or Salha any French. Instead she had taken a water glass and filled it to the brimming point, thereby presenting the matter to her determined visitor as clearly as she could. But Salha was not so easily deterred. She had plucked a single rose petal from the vase on Madame Bassan's desk and floated it in the water glass, as if to say "What difference would one more girl make?" Madame Bassan had been so delighted with Salha's quick wit that she admitted Regina into the school.

At first Regina struggled with a new regime that was more taxing than anything she was used to at home, when Ezra might spend the evening teaching her to read and write. She endured hours of French and Arabic and more long hours of Hebrew and history, before struggling down Torat Street, her schoolbag loaded with homework. Thus was she encouraged and prodded into learning, and all because the *Alliance*'s representatives in Baghdad wanted to civilize her. Not least, they were determined to combat with solid, secular, and provable fact, the irrational superstition that cloaked the entire community from its respectable head right down to its uneducated toes.

Not long before Regina started school, one of the English teachers at the *Alliance*'s boys' school wrote to the Anglo-Jewish Association in London complaining that he was at his wit's end over the level of credulity among the Baghdadi Jews. He related an incident involving an old trapdoor that had blown off the roof of his school in strong winds and landed in a neighboring courtyard, fortunately without injuring anyone. "It was soon rumoured," he reported, "that a door had fallen from heaven, and hundreds of persons crowded to the house to see it. Barren women rushed eagerly to see and touch the door from heaven, and it was only after two or three days that our trap-door was recognized as something earthly and finally restored to us."

It never occurred to the English teacher, or to any of the other instructors for that matter, that among Baghdad's Jews reason and superstition might coexist quite happily. Or that it was perfectly possible for a pupil like Regina to have tucked into her clothes all sorts of amulets designed to protect her from baleful spirits and evil eyes and yet still comprehend the causes of the French Revolution.

Nor, as an outsider, could the English teacher ever appreciate what a rich selection of superstitions there was to choose from. Believing in djinns and devils and in the mystical power of kabbalistic passages; in the value of strange potions and herbal infusions; in the touch of a learned rabbi's hand; in the power of invoking the name of a famous sage; in kissing the stones of holy shrines; in abstaining from particular foods on particular days; in the runic qualities of birthmarks and moles; in throwing water on the ground after visitors left the house; and in the idea that sickness, miscarriages, personal injury, barrenness, reversals of fortune, and even death could all be attributed to jealousy's evil eye.

Regina subscribed wholeheartedly to every one of these superstitions. She knew when to mumble a protective incantation and when to avoid crossing the threshold of a house where a woman had recently given birth. She had seen Salha light a candle to Rabbi Meir on many occasions, and she trembled whenever she remembered the story of how her grandfather once stopped to pick up a baby that had been abandoned on his doorstep only for it to turn into a grinning demon that leaped from his arms as he bent to embrace it. She had even accompanied her mother to the shrine of Ezekiel in el-Kiffel, so that the auspicious occasion of Nessim's first haircut might have the prophet's blessing. She had teased Nessim all the way there, telling him that he would lose whatever strength he possessed once his hair was snipped, just like Samson. And she had teased him all the way back, saying that his fallen locks would make a fine lady's wig.

But of all the superstitions that lurked unquestioned within the dark cushioned folds of my grandmother's private belief system, the one she both feared and respected most was the reading of people's futures in their coffee cups. To doubt the powers of this particular art would have been to doubt her very self, since within the community her own mother was generally acknowledged as having a remarkable gift for it.

Many of the visitors who came to the Sehayek household on Wednesdays came primarily to have their *finjans* read and only secondarily to savor Salha's equally famed *sambuseks*. Regina took a perverse pleasure in watching these guests dissimulate. They would nibble at pastries, complain about the weather, nod at other women they recognized across the courtyard, and laugh as if they hadn't a care in the world, all the while keeping one eye studiously fixed on the *fin-jan* they had just upturned on its saucer, lest a careless servant should mistakenly clear it from the table. When Salha finally offered to read for them, they feigned exaggerated surprise and then grew flushed at their own deceit. All the same, they'd trot off after Salha to a quiet corner of the courtyard where the sound of their private business wouldn't flutter about everyone else's ears.

As inconspicuously as she could, Regina would slip over and sit by her mother's feet so that she could hear people's fortunes unfold and participate in a familiar ritual that her mother commanded from beginning to end. Salha would don her reading glasses, purse her lips, and, holding the *finjan* under her nose, proceed to turn it this way and that, examining the powdery brown rills the coffee dregs silted in their wake once they'd slid into the saucer. Over the years Salha had learned how to draw out the suspense of a reading by taking her time over these silent appraisals. Without lifting her eyes from the dregs, she would nod her head slowly as though she were listening to an invisible sprite whisper in her ear. Then she would blow her breath out measuredly as she weighed what she had to say. Only when the coffee drinker could wait no more to learn what fate had in store for her would Salha begin.

"I see another baby," she told Lizette Battat one time. "Definitely a girl." And she held out the *finjan* for Lizette to see, pointing to an inscrutable cluster of granules along one side of its rim. Often when Salha saw children in a cup she was only confirming what the coffee drinker already knew, and so it was with Lizette. Already three months gone and with two girls already at school, Lizette was anxious that her third child should be a boy. She'd been holding off telling her husband because she knew only too well what his reaction would be. Another girl and he'd cry like a baby, complaining that his finances would never squeeze out another dowry. Salha reassured her friend that all would go well, and that mother and baby would be happy and healthy. But about the sex of the child she could do nothing. Six months later Lizette had a girl.

Sometimes Salha only revealed her hand after the fact, when she foresaw a miscarriage or bankruptcy, or had intimations of someone's

death. At the time of the reading she would pretend that the dregs refused to speak to her, or that they'd dripped down the *finjan* in such a
way as to be unreadable. But once the tragedy struck she would turn
to Ezra with her eyes burning, and say, "I saw it."

In Salha's capable hands the future seemed an orderly place to
Regina. Events followed one another in much the same regular pro-
cession as they did in the present. Marriages were arranged, business
deals forged, trips undertaken, children were born, money came and
went. Even if the future held a calamity or two, it usually held few surprises. This wasn't at all like the past that Regina was learning about at
school from *istadh* Shahmoon, where events took on the overblown
proportions of high drama and calamities seemed to be the order of
the day.

Until she went to school Regina had no inkling that with the exception of Abraham the Jews had begun their long history in
Mesopotamia as little more than slaves. Shackled in chains, they'd
been forced in their thousands to trek nine hundred kilometers across
the desert from Judah to Babylon, where Nebuchadnezzar set them to
work building and fortifying irrigation canals. *Istadh* Shahmoon said
that you could trace an unbroken line from those exiled Jews, torn
from their homeland in 586 B.C., and the Jews who lived in
Mesopotamia today, and that those Jews of old were the same ones
who had laid down their harps on the banks of the Euphrates and
wept for Zion. They had seen Jerusalem plundered and watched the
Temple of Solomon burn to the ground, and they had nothing to sus-
tain them but the belief that God would engineer their eventual return.

Regina was taken with the notion of direct lineage, the idea that by
dropping a plumb line into the murky depths of the past, you could
actually fish out an ancestor, a kind of original Jew who served as a
template for those who followed and who defined the experience of
the Diaspora. She wondered why no one bothered to talk much about
the Holy Land these days. They only said "next year in Jerusalem"
every Passover, and even then it was just a matter of form. No one actually hoped that they'd be spirited away from Baghdad to witness

some grand restoration. Except a handful of Jews her parents used to laugh at, the ones who bought cemetery plots in Palestine, thinking that even if they didn't get buried in them their certificates of purchase would guarantee them a place in Jerusalem in the afterlife.

When it came to learning about the medieval academies at Sura and Pedumbeditha, where famous *gaons* labored to produce the Babylonian Talmud, or how temporal authority over the Jews passed from father to son through the royal office of the Exilarch, Regina would switch off. Especially when *istadh* Shahmoon rolled his eyes and spoke in breathless hyberbole about the Jews' great prosperity and high social standing. The glory days of Babylonian Jewry bored her the same way *baba* Nissan bored her when he sat her down and recited all the properties he owned in Baghdad until he was punch-pleased with himself. When *istadh* Shahmoon read out the letters of Benjamin of Tuelda, who traveled to Baghdad in the eleventh century and goggled at the Elixarch's visible wealth, Regina would stifle a yawn. And when he spoke in whispered respect of Sa'ad al-Dawla, Baghdad's legendary Jewish governor, she'd buck herself to attention. Only Hulagu's bloodcurdling conquest of Mesopotamia had her sitting on the edge of her seat.

Hulagu Khan, grandson of Ghengis and king of the Mongols, is the man history holds responsible for bringing centuries of enlightened Abbasid rule to a conclusive end. It is said that his savage armies butchered so many people in Baghdad in 1258 that the Tigris ran red with their blood, and that they built gory victory mounds out of the decapitated heads of their victims. As for the caliph himself, Hulagu had him trampled to death after rolling him up inside a carpet. Within weeks of the Mongol invasion, the material and artistic production of an entire era was ruthlessly swept away. Baghdad was ransacked and burned, its inhabitants slaughtered, and the splendor for which the city was renowned the world over was never again recovered.

When war came to Baghdad in 1914, Regina kept asking Ezra if the city would again be invaded. Would another Hulagu bloody their waters? Or would an army from the West snatch Baghdad for its own greedy ends, just as Sultan Murad had claimed it for the Ottomans in

1638? Her father reassured her that their beloved city was safe from invading forces and power-mad conquerors, even though he wasn't at all sure he was right. Full mobilization had been quickly declared in the province of Baghdad, where the Ottomans' Sixth Army Division was headquartered, and hundreds of Jews with inadequate training were hastily dispatched to fight the Russians on the Caucasian front only to perish there or be taken prisoner.

Ezra himself was too old to be called up for military service, and he thanked God that Nessim was too young—never more so than when he saw Jewish boys marching through Baghdad's streets in their smart new uniforms, puffed up with their newfound nationalism, and he found himself standing to one side to let them pass, looking like a relic from the last century in his cotton *ziboon*, and wondering how many would return.

The Sehayek household, like many others belonging to Baghdad's better-off classes, was perpetually ablaze with rumors at this time. Each week someone else's son seemed to disappear, apparently without a trace, only for the grapevine to provide word several weeks later that the boy in question had made it to the Iranian border and crossed safely into Khorramshahr, successfully avoiding conscription. The most frequent discussions revolved around trying to recall precisely how old this or that boy was, or how wealthy a given patriarch was, since a brisk but covert trade had sprung up in forged birth certificates, which by lowering a boy's true age by a year or two placed him just outside the call up window. At the same time many prosperous Jews dangled bribes before the Turkish authorities, hoping to get their sons out of active service and into administrative positions in the telegraph office or the military stores. Amid all the frantic draft-dodging, barely anyone had time to ponder the irony that it had taken a war to make many a Baghdad family for once grateful that they'd had girls and not boys.

Regina continued to attend school, war or no war, but she was not blind to the many changes that had befallen Baghdad. The new Samarra railway was kept busy day and night with movements of men and supplies. The streets were congested with military personnel and army vehicles, and there were always scuffles in the souks over goods that had rapidly grown scarce. On the river the *kelleks*, large brushwood rafts mounted on inflated goatskins, which usually floated down from Mosul laden with grain, now carried an amazing assortment of unheard-of cargoes: rifles, ammunition, automobiles and even light field guns. But it was the blond nurses who worked for the German Red Crescent who intrigued Regina the most. They were the palest creatures she had ever seen, and their hair was like spun gold. Had they not walked with the heavy gait of hospital matrons, she might have believed them to be angels sent from heaven.

Then, without any warning, in October 1915 the Laura Kadoorie School was closed down. It had been requisitioned by the Turkish authorities for use as a war hospital, along with several other private buildings in the city, including the *Alliance*'s boys' school. Henceforth its classrooms would be host to the wounded and the dying, while its displaced inmates would be forced to keep up with their French and English studies at home. Ezra and Salha were relieved to have their children at home again, especially when the city suffered an outbreak of smallpox and hunkering down seemed the best way of avoiding the contagion. Besides, Salha, now pregnant for a fifth time with her son Solomon, was in the mood for nesting. And yet, having battened down the hatches, the family felt more powerless than ever in the face of new Turkish aggressions.

As the British advanced upriver toward Baghdad late in 1916, the Turks began to feel victory slip from their grasp, and they resorted to ever-more-desperate means of bolstering the war effort. They confiscated dozens of warehouses belonging to Jewish merchants and plundered them for anything that might be of military use: stocks of paper, iron, and steel; tea and coffee; typewriters and telephones. Those caught trying to hide their goods or their gold were tortured and killed, leaving families clueless as to the fate of their defiant loved ones, until one by one they began finding the maimed bodies of their husbands, fathers, sons, and brothers floating in the Tigris. Ezra knew he had escaped the worst when he managed to avoid the wrath of the deputy *wali* Faik Bey, who, in order to force the Turkish paper money at its nominal value on Baghdad's unwilling moneychangers, had several of them imprisoned in the cellar of a police station, from which they never again emerged.

The Turks succeeded in extinguishing whatever spark of nationalism the revolution of 1908 had stirred in Jewish hearts. The Jews had been embraced as citizens, but they turned out to be dispensable ones. Once again, the Jews concluded, they'd been embroiled in a war that was not theirs to fight. Seeing more clearly than ever that they had nothing to gain from a Turkish victory, they began counting the days till the British arrived. Except for Regina. Much to her own surprise, she was counting the days until she could go back to school.

Four

VERY NICE
TO MEET YOU

On a bright November morning in 1917, a hush fell over the whole of Baghdad, muting and stilling everything. The air had a residual chill to it from the night before, when the boom of Minute guns had rolled across the city like low rumbling thunder, causing Salha to practically jump out of her skin. Now everyone was jittery, waiting for the next act to begin.

Regina and Ezra were standing in New Street alongside what seemed to be the entire population of Baghdad. All around them lay the detritus of hasty construction, broken-down houses and shops, some with paintings still hanging forlornly from their walls, and alleyways piled high with rubble. New Street itself had not yet been asphalted, and without its usual cargo of horse-drawn carts, milling pedestrians, and motorcars, it looked as raw and gritty as an unhealed wound, reminding Ezra of the desperation that had prompted its cutting when the Turks finally understood that victory was going to elude them.

For much of the war the lack of a proper main street through the city had been painfully felt by troops forced to move artillery and supplies across town and by officers fed up with delays in communication. At first Khalil Pasha had resisted calls from his German staff officers to cut a wide thoroughfare through the heart of the city, knowing that such a crudely conceived project would entail tearing down large blocks of private housing as well as two bazaars, one of them held in trust by the religious authorities, or *waqf,* and therefore not his to dispose of. But as the pressure of the Turkish campaign mounted, the *wali* at last acted, and engaged a demolition gang to undertake much of the work by night, thus presenting the *waqf* and the city's wealthy landowners with a *fait accompli.* Almost a year later the evidence of the blunt and shoddy labor of these hired thugs remained for all to see.

Unused to crowds, Regina glued herself to Ezra's side. From there she took stock of the magnificent ethnic mélange she and her father were part of. Mingled together on either side of the street and on platforms and balconies that banked it up to the rooftops, she picked out Jews in red fezzes, Kurds in distinctive black pot hats, lordly turbaned Muslim elders, Persians in tall lamb's wool caps, tribal sheikhs, Christians, Syrians, and Sabaeans. All had gathered on Baghdad's sole thoroughfare to pay their last respects to the man who'd finally succeeded in driving the Turks out of the city, General Sir Stanley Maude. Or, as Regina would say it: "Stan-er-ley Mod." He had died suddenly the night before, the victim of a brief but virulent attack of cholera.

Only a week earlier Ezra had been among hundreds of guests attending an evening's entertainment at a Jewish school at which the general had been guest of honor. It was the first time Maude had agreed to attend a public function since he entered the city, victorious, some eight months earlier. A deeply religious man with pale, almond-shaped eyes and a long, pious face that seemed to radiate devotion, a nonsmoker and nondrinker, Maude was famous for retiring to bed before ten and for shunning any social obligation that required him to break with form. The Jewish community had been beside itself with excitement when it received word that Maude was actually coming, and it went to great lengths to impress him.

Maude had sat enthroned in the school's courtyard looking like a Viking king. He'd laughed wholeheartedly at the guileless performances of Jewish children who danced and curtsied before him on a platform that had been specially erected for the occasion. The courtyard was ablaze with color. Dazzling Persian carpets hung from the upper balcony alongside homemade banners proclaiming welcome, and bright electric lights were strung up like bunting. All of Baghdad's high society was in attendance, with many of the women unveiled as a sign of their trust. Sitting next to Maude was the chief rabbi, in his ceremonial white silk robes and gold-edged turban, who was solicitous in making introductions, while the school's headmaster, a picture of suaveness in his tight-fitting European suit, fussed over the general, smiling profusely and chattering away in French.

During a short intermission in the program, a low table was placed in front of the general and coffee was served. With a polite nod to his hosts, Maude helped himself to the coffee and poured into it a large quantity of cold, fresh milk—contaminated milk, as it turned out. He was taken ill the following afternoon. The next day Sir William Marshall was called in from the Eastern Front to assume Maude's duties. On the evening of the third day Maude was dead.

Instantly dark rumors flew about town intimating that Maude had been poisoned. But the facts of the case leave little room for intrigue. Baghdad had suffered a terrible cholera epidemic that summer and Maude had ordered that all his men be inoculated. He, meanwhile, had persistently refused the prophylactic, claiming that he was too old to be struck down. This vein of recklessness in the man puzzled Ezra, who found himself wondering whether all English people possessed a wild and unpredictable streak, their ostentatious love of discipline and order being just so much camouflage disguising the true national character.

Ezra and Regina watched Maude's coffin pass in front of them, draped in the folds of the Union Jack and carried aloft on the shoulders of grief-stricken British soldiers. As it sailed slowly through the crowds toward the Muadham Gate, beyond which lay a wasteland containing the new British war cemetery and the ugly north terminal of the Baghdad railway, the heavy silence that had hung so portentously over the city all morning was broken by a smart clipping sound rippling along New Street in a continuous wave, as Indian troops lining the road clicked their heels together, snapped their rifles to their shoulders, and stood to attention.

Regina felt a shiver run along her spine. She had never attended a funeral before, and it moved her. Had she been party to the private scene that followed at the cemetery, when Maude was gently lowered into his grave amid a low murmur of prayer and a volley of rifle fire, with the blare of trumpets rolling out across the desert wastes the haunting wail of "The Last Post," who knows what desolate feelings she might have tapped within herself: grief for all those boys who went to war and never came home, for the fathers of her friends who had been arrested never to reappear, for the loss of so much promise and so many innocent lives.

It would be years before Baghdad's population fully recovered from the war. For many people, however, bidding farewell to General Maude was the first step in putting their suffering behind them.

General Maude had arrived in Mesopotamia in the summer of 1916 to take charge of British troops in the field. His appointment marked the transfer of supreme command from Simla, in India, to London, where government officials were determined to reverse the downturn in Britain's fortunes in the region.

The eastern campaign against the Turks (Germany's allies throughout WWI) had begun well for the British, whose Indian Expeditionary Force had swiftly occupied Basra in 1914. Although the occupation was a largely unplanned affair, motivated by a desire to protect the oil installations at Abadan and maintain British control of Gulf waters, it created a sense of momentum, a feeling that there ought to be some follow-up. And so the British had hastily embarked on an ill-conceived land-grab campaign that had no real objective beyond driving the Turks northward. Only later did they set their sights on Baghdad. Somewhat predictably, things quickly began to go wrong. It was a classic case of underestimating the enemy. Whenever the British least expected it, "Johnny Turk" rallied his forces and put up a good fight, so that for every gain the British made, there followed a compensatory loss. The low point of the campaign came after a British thrust took His Majesty's Army to within fifty miles of Baghdad, only for an Ottoman counterattack to drive them back to Kut: and at Kut they were besieged for five long months.

This dreadful siege, which ended in the unconditional surrender of field commander Gen. Sir Charles Townshend and eight thousand troops, mostly Indian, lasted an entire winter, from November 1915 to April 1916, and it ranks as one of Britain's most abject military humiliations. Inside Kut the men endured terrible starvation. They were forced to eat their donkeys and horses. Then, when the horses were gone, they were reduced to probing the ground for "battered tins of potato meal, bully beef or sacks of flour" and to shooting down starlings from the sky. The local hospital groaned with the sick and dying. The bodies of the dead were thickly plastered over "Corpse Hill." Meanwhile the men suffered relentless bombardment by Turkish forces fresh from their Gallipoli victory. They were picked off by snipers whenever an attempt was made to acquire water from the river, assailed by cold, floods, heavy rains, flies, vermin, and an array of exotic diseases, and regularly betrayed by a hostile local population bent on giving away to the Turks the garrison's every plan and movement. It was a wonder so many survived.

In the middle of December 1916 Maude took the offensive, driving the Turks steadily upstream. By February 1917 he had reoccupied Kut, and by the beginning of March his forces were threatening the outlying defenses of Baghdad. Anticipating a British attack, the Turks had prepared five lines of defense around the city, but they proved incapable of holding any of them for more than a few hours. On the night of March 10, 1917, with the British less than four miles from the city, an emergency council of war was held at Baghdad's Khirr Pavilion. There, in the presence of his field commanders, Khalil Pasha paced the floor nervously, knowing that Istanbul wanted him to make a dignified stand. His generals, meanwhile, urged an immediate withdrawal. Hesitant as ever, the *wali* retired to another room with his chief of staff in order to deliberate his next move, but he returned just ten minutes later to sanction a withdrawal. To Istanbul, he telegraphed: "I am faced with the sorrowful necessity of abandoning Baghdad." Then, without further ado, he left for Kadhimain.

As they retreated, the Turks attempted a wholesale destruction of Baghdad. They exploded dynamite around the pillars and wall chambers of the ancient citadel and in the flagstones that paved its floor. They destroyed important military positions in the city. The new radio station near the Baghdad West railway terminal was blasted to pieces, and the historic Talisman Gate with its bricked-up passage and writhing dragon carvings was blown up, together with the ammunition stored in it. The pontoon bridge across the Tigris was broken up, and the individual pontoons destroyed. Then, at midnight, the military commandant of Baghdad left his post, taking with him the city police and officials and issuing orders for all official records to be destroyed or removed.

The subsequent occupation of Baghdad by the British must qualify as one of the most bizarre events in military history. As members of the King's Own Regiment approached the city in the early morning hours of March 11 they encountered a ghostly quiet. Advancing cautiously, arms at the ready, the men anticipated resistance. But as they reached the outskirts of town, unaware that the Turks had vacated their stations the night before, they were confronted instead with the mournful sight of land littered with corpses and the bones of dead animals. Within the mud embankments that circled Baghdad, they found thousands of makeshift Muslim graves, while inside the city an eerie stillness prevailed. The filthy streets, entirely empty of people, had been given over to the roaming opportunism of diseased and half-starved dogs. Fires smoldered everywhere. And broken-down houses spilling rubble into the streets and alleyways spoke eloquently of the city's broken spirit.

In sharp contrast, the face Baghdad revealed later that morning bore a jubilant smile. Once the Union Jack had been hoisted in the citadel and British and Indian troops had finished patrolling the bazaars and dispersing bands of looters who'd poured into the city as the Turks left, the city's natives, who had barricaded themselves inside their houses the night before, bounded into the streets and celebrated. Men clapped their hands and clicked their fingers, women ululated, children danced. Armenians who'd been hiding in the city's churches for days, fearing for their lives, came out cheering, and Muslims who had secretly begun dreaming of Arab self-rule warmly shook the hands of the khaki-clad officers: perhaps now they would have some chance of steering national affairs. To British troops, unaware how much Baghdad had suffered over the past year as a result of food shortages, a dead economy, and the total lack of public services, it was a bewildering reception.

Even more baffling, the honeymoon was to last almost two years. That was how long it took the British finally to decide what they wanted to do with Mesopotamia. Were they liberating the Arabs? Expanding their own empire? Preparing to prospect for oil? Or protecting existing commercial interests and trade routes? No one seemed able to say, and in the absence of any definitive answer, the politically expedient solution was for the British to emphasize their support of Arab self-rule.

The British had promised the Sharif Hussein of Mecca that in return for raising an army against the Turks and aiding the Allied war effort the Arabs would have their own kingdom. In turn, this noble warrior king had set his heart on Mesopotamia, and in and impassioned correspondence with Sir Henry McMahon, Britain's high commissioner in Egypt, he romanced the land and its potential, referring to it by its ancient cartographic name: Iraq. The problem was that through the Sykes-Picot Agreement of 1916, Britain had simultaneously entered into a secret deal with France to carve up the ex-Ottoman territories between them, with control of Mesopotamia and Palestine going to Britain and that of Syria going to France.

Maude had to tread a careful line. In a proclamation made as soon as he entered Baghdad (largely written by Sir Mark Sykes at the War Office in London), the general downplayed any differences between British and Arab expectations. In words that would be reproduced almost verbatim by the Americans in 2003, he claimed: "Our armies do not come into your cities and lands as conquerors or enemies but as liberators" who desire nothing more than that "the Arab race may rise once more to greatness and renown among the peoples of the earth." Maude promised that the British would not impose "alien institutions" on the land. Instead, he intoned, "I am commanded to invite you, through your nobles and elders and representatives, to participate in the management of your own civil affairs in collaboration with the political representatives of Great Britain who accompany the British Army, so that you may be united with your kinsmen in the north, east, south and west in realizing the aspirations of your race."

It sounded like the promise of self-determination. But the British didn't know what they were doing. In a compromise that fooled nobody, and that ultimately proved a recipe for disaster, they would attempt to rule indirectly.

Along with the rest of Baghdad's Jewish community, Ezra and Salha welcomed the arrival of the British as liberators and protectors. Within weeks of Maude's occupation of the city they acquired new neighbors. Salha delighted in the fact that next door to them there now resided British officers. It gave her a certain social cachet. Privately, though, she couldn't help giggling at the tall, gangling creatures with knobby knees and red faces who picked their deliberate way through Baghdad's streets like exotic flamingos staking out a sandbank. She'd seen nothing like them before, and each time she encountered the British anew she'd shake her head in silent wonderment at how these strange men in khaki shorts and solar topis had come to rule the world. Yet for all her chariness, if she chanced to be out on the roof terrace when her new neighbors were on theirs, she lost no time in inviting them over and offering them a cold drink, proudly getting her children to show off their best English.

Though Salha was loath to admit it, a number of changes stealthily made their way into the Sehayek household. She began offering her guests milk with their tea, and instead of serving it in small hourglass-shaped tumblers, as was the Baghdadi custom, she dusted off her virtually unused china and began using that instead. She started buying Lyon's biscuits and tea cakes from the new shops that had sprung up to cater to British tastes, ignoring Ezra's complaint that they were flavorless. Oblivious to its utter uselessness in Baghdad, she began extolling the virtues of double glazing, an invention she associated with the marvelous ingenuity of the newcomers. Although many of the Jewish women rushed to discard their long gowns and *abayas* in favor of European dress, Salha at first drew the line at such obvious aping. Yet she too succumbed, telling herself that one couldn't very well show up at one of the new British officers' clubs or YMCAs in an *abaya*.

"Do you know what they're calling Baghdad?" Ezra asked his wife one day. "The city of Haroun al-Rothschild," he said, a note of triumph in his voice. It was true that in the business sphere the British viewed the Jews as competitors who had a stranglehold on the city's trade. Yet, as an occupying force that needed to restore the working life of the city and rebuild the apparatus of civil government, the British relied heavily on the Jews, whom they recruited en masse into the new commercial and administrative leadership. Because the Jews were able linguists, fluent for the most part in Arabic, English, and French, they proved indispensable. The result was that most of the men hired by the British to work in finance, the postal service, the telegraph offices, telephone exchanges, railroads, and ports and customs houses were Jews, as were the clerks who worked alongside British political officers in what would later become local councils and government ministries.

For their part the Jews admired the energy and determination of the British. In the immediate aftermath of the war they watched in awe as the British embarked on a furious round of activity: restoring security, opening banks, introducing the sound currency of the Indian rupee, re-establishing public services, restocking bazaars, improving sanitation and bringing employment. Salha said they reminded her of worker bees, pulling together to achieve the common goal of cleaning, mapping, and tidying Baghdad so that it might once again attract business and bounty to its queenly lair.

Within two years Baghdad had not only been restored but improved. The British had replaced the pontoon bridge across the Tigris and built a fine modern boat bridge named after Maude. They had unpacked their tripods and theodolites and cut straight new roads that ran parallel and perpendicular to New Street, and they'd hatched plans to extend Baghdad to the north and south with modern suburbs built on a grid system. They had also introduced a new method of mapping the city by quarters, or *mahallahs*, so that in each district, every house, *khan*, souk, and community hall now had a unique and exact address denoted in both English and Arabic numerals. Whenever Regina or her friends were denied permission to go out alone, which was most of the time, they would vainly protest that it was now quite impossible for them to get lost.

The British did not stop at mapping. The city's flood protection dyke was widened and strengthened, a power station that gave Baghdad streetlighting for the first time was thrown up in the suburbs, and work was begun on a water purification plant that would soon provide Baghdad's inhabitants with a clean and regular water supply. Railway lines began sprouting in every direction. The Kut line now crept along the eastern side of town to the Muadham Gate, where it threw off a branch to the river. Baghdad East station became the junction for a long branch to Baquba, Shahraban, and the Persian frontier, and, to the south, the railway was extended first to Hillah and then, later, to Basra.

On the back of all this industry the Jewish merchant community was flourishing. Ezra was coming home and reporting to Salha that business had never been better. Everyone wanted to open a shop or hotel or taxi concern to capitalize on the boom in trade, and there wasn't an entrepreneur in town who had not approached the money-changers with talk of new schemes and developments. Amid the flurry of commercial activity, a handful of Ezra's contemporaries, such as Khedouri Zilcha, managed to parlay their businesses into full-fledged banking concerns that eventually grew to rival such established institutions as the Ottoman Bank and the Eastern Bank.

Profit, it seemed, was to be made everywhere. These were the palmy days of 1918 and 1919, when many a wily businessman rose to fortune by furnishing the British with supplies and raw materials, or else made his name by reselling British army and air force surplus acquired on the cheap. The coffeehouses became scenes of eager speculation, as one deal after another was struck between new and unlikely business partners—Muslims and Jews, *effendis* and rogues, *Alliance*-educated gentlemen and street traders. Meanwhile Baghdadi Jews who had sat out the war in America or the Far East began trickling back to the city to participate in the commercial jamboree. After the economic collapse Baghdad had suffered during the war years, the British seemed to have effected nothing short of a miracle.

From the middle of 1917 Regina was back at school, with Madame Bassan at the helm once again and *istadh* Shahmoon droning on about history as if nothing had changed, even though, as he spoke, a new Baghdad was taking shape outside the classroom window. Older if not very much wiser, Regina was also getting her first taste of personal freedom, even if all it meant was dawdling with classmates outside the school gates once lessons were over, or taking a detour to Taht al-Takia on the way home to indulge her sweet tooth.

She was part of a clique now, along with Claire Dellal, Violet Masri, Farah Nissan, and Louise Fattal, all of them girls from good families; an advantage that, had they been born in the West, might have given them more of a footing in the world than their peers. But in the East, girls from good families were kept ignorant of life. They were protected by their parents, and their liberty was severely curtailed. The example of "bad girls" and the sorry fate that usually awaited them was perpetually held up before them as an object lesson in the consequences of having too much license. In spite of such cosseting, the girls in Regina's clique were possessed of a confidence that came from knowing that they belonged to the upper ranks of the community. They knew how to look after themselves. Especially Louise Fattal, Regina's best friend.

Though only fourteen, the same age as Regina, Louise already had the body of a woman: she was the same hourglass shape as the glasses in which Baghdadis used to serve hot sweet tea. Every day as she walked home from school, an old Arab with dirty robes and craggy features would be waiting for her on the corner of Torat Street, tugging at his moustache and grinning like a monkey. As she passed he would squeeze one of her breasts, clinically, proficiently, as though he were checking fruit for ripeness at a market stall, and then he'd dart off guiltily. No matter how many girls accompanied Louise on her way home, the same thing would always happen, and

Louise felt powerless to prevent it. Until one day she hit on an ingenious plan. Determined to put a stop to the Arab's unwelcome
maulings, she turned her bra cups into prickly porcupines by sticking dozens of pins through them. Then, after her tormentor made
his customary grab, she ran away as fast as her feet would carry her,
leaving him shaking down his arm furiously as if his hand were on
fire and cursing to the four winds like the *fellahin,* or peasant, that he
was. He never troubled Louise again.

At the candy store on Taht al-Takia to which the girls repaired,
Regina found a unique exhibition of mouthwatering sweets. There
were syrupy *baklawas*—stuffed full of chopped nuts, cut into diamond
shapes, and piled into tall, sticky heaps—and trays of deep-fried, bright
orange *zingoolas*, which dripped syrup and were shaped like scribbles.
On the sales counter, star-shaped *masafans* made from honeyed
ground almonds sat beside crunchy sesame snaps, and trays stacked
with coconut macaroons jostled cardboard boxes brimming with pale
sugared almonds and powdery cubes of Turkish delight. But it was the
aloocha that Regina eyed greedily. These were sticky toffee stars that
stuck to your teeth and had to be sucked off slowly. Regina seldom got
to eat them. Whenever Ezra brought home a bag of *aloocha* as a treat,
Salha would confiscate them, lecturing everyone about miserable den-
tists and rotting teeth.

In those days one rupee went a long way, and after the girls had
bought all they could eat from the candy store they moved on, following the intoxicating aroma of freshly baked goods that extended from
the bakery and into the street like a beckoning finger. The pastries
from Taht al-Takia were sought after all over Baghdad; warm date
cookies that crumbled as you put them in your mouth, pillowy *sambuseks* and chewy *malfoof.* Beyond the bakery was the pickle shop,
which boasted brightly colored turnips, beets, cucumbers, carrots, and
eggplant, packed into bottles that lined the shop's vitrine. Outside the
pickle shop an old man dressed in rags sold sweet hot beets, freshly
baked on burning charcoal. He would peel each one neatly, his crin-
kled face a picture of quiet concentration, and present them to his customers wrapped in clean paper torn from a notebook. A few yards on,

a red-faced vendor spent all day slow roasting salted nuts, while farther along another street cook sold *kubba burghul,* deep-fried balls of bulgur wheat filled with spiced ground meat.

Walking along Taht al-Takia, Regina would lose herself in a sensory reverie as the sharp smell of pickles mingled with the inviting aroma of pastries baking and *kubba*s frying and with the whiff of smoke from the barbecue restaurants nearby. Sometimes it was too much for her, and she would feel heady and light. At suppertime, after they had settled like dead weights in her stomach and she could not eat a thing, she was reminded of all the pastries she'd consumed. Quickly she'd excuse herself from the table, claiming that some chore needed seeing to. In this manner she managed to exit all the talk of politics that had come to dominate family discussions.

Ezra Sehayek never cared for politics. "Power appeals to those denied it: money to those who have it. But politics appeals only to rascals," he would say. He climbed off the fence quickly enough, however, after the British announced that they intended to unite the former Turkish territories of Baghdad, Basra, and Mosul under a single crown, and that this crown would be worn by an Arab king. Surely the British knew that the various peoples of these regions did not seek unity. Or that when it came to the future of the proposed new nation, they held passionately opposed views. Only Sunni nationalists wanted an Arab kingdom, Ezra and his friends observed. The Shia majority wanted an Islamic state, the Kurds sought independence, and the intelligentsia wanted a return to the Turks. The Jews, meanwhile, favored continued British rule, and for reasons that ought not to be sniffed at: the British had been good to them.

Fearing for their security under Arab kingship, between 1918 and 1921 the Jews of Baghdad made three separate appeals to the British, asking for British citizenship. All were perfunctorily denied. "What will become of us?" Salha beseeched her husband at each rejection. "Without the British to protect us we'll be at the mercy of tribal leaders, nationalists, and petty despots." Ezra viewed matters differently. "Why should we have to forfeit our hard-won freedom," he told his wife. "We were citizens under the Ottomans, and we'll be citizens in the new kingdom, perhaps even nationalists."

In the short term Ezra was proved right. The British went to great lengths to guarantee the Jews of Baghdad protection of life, liberty, and property, and they encouraged their "royal" candidate Faisal, son of Hussein, the Sharif of Mecca, to do the same. Prodded by the British into giving Faisal a fair hearing, the chief rabbi held a historic reception for Faisal at his private house. There the man destined to become Iraq's first king famously declared: "There is no meaning in the words Jews, Muslims and Christians in the terminology of patriotism, there is simply a country called Iraq and all are Iraqis." These were fine words, and they succeeded in winning over the bulk of Baghdad's Jews. More important, they were words that Faisal would stand by.

Throughout his tenure as king, Faisal respected Jewish rights and freedoms. In fact he went out of his way to befriend the Jewish community, visiting schools and hospitals and holding meetings with the chief rabbi and his council to discuss national and communal affairs. At the risk of raising eyebrows among the Sunni elite, Faisal held receptions for Jewish business leaders, consulted Jewish financial advisers, and, on the recommendation of Miss Bell, he appointed a Jewish minister to his first parliamentary cabinet. Modern historians who have remarked on Faisal's strange affinity for the Jews generally refer to the king's "enlightened" perspective on matters of religious difference. But perhaps the king's closeness to the Jewish community stemmed from something less cerebral and more instinctive: namely, that as an outsider he identified with them. In particular, he was every bit as reliant on British protection as they were.

Although Faisal won respect in Iraq as the scion of an ancient and venerable family that could trace its lineage directly back to the Prophet, he had no real connection to the land. He'd been brought up in the desert and educated in Istanbul, and to Arab eyes, at least, his fondness for things Western lent him the air of a stranger. He had the advantage, as an outsider, of not being associated with any particular group or faction. However, as an Arab he did not have much support among the Kurds, and as a Sunni he found little favor with the Shia

majority. For their part the old, established, and landed Sunni families
in Iraq tended to regard him as an interloper. Only the ex-Ottoman officials who'd supported him during the Arab revolt and who themselves were mostly of Mesopotamian origin, gave him their
wholehearted support. These were the men who, for better or worse,
would dominate Iraqi politics for the next thirty-seven years, propped
up by British muscle.

It was with deep reservations that Faisal had agreed to become
king in the first place, knowing the weakness of his position in a
country on which he had no genuine claim and that was not even
truly independent, but held in a kind of trusteeship, or "mandate," by
the British. Nor was he fool enough to be encouraged by a bogus
referendum held by the British, which showed that 96 percent of the
public backed him. Worse still, having become king, he had no choice
but to bolster his strength through an increasingly centralized government and to turn to the British whenever tribal insubordination
threatened the stability of his monarchy. With British help, Shiite
agitators in the south, who had stirred up a full-blown revolt against
the foreign occupation of the country in 1920, were deported to Iran
on the grounds that they were Persian subjects. And it was the RAF
that bombed the Kurds into submission when they refused to swear
allegiance to Faisal in 1921, and again when they rebelled sporadically
thereafter, in protest against plans to bring the still-disputed Mosul
region within Iraqi borders.

All this gerrymandering and coercion famously led veteran political
scientist Elie Kedourie to complain that Iraq was never more than an
emanation of British foreign policy, "a make-believe kingdom, built on
false pretenses and kept going by a British design and for a British purpose." Ironically, more than any other Iraqi group, it was the Jews who
invested themselves in the idea of Iraq and attempted to become
model Iraqi citizens.

Five

WOMEN'S SECRETS

Regina was sixteen when her class-mate Agnes disappeared.

The day had begun like any other, with Regina sitting in class, struggling through a lesson in Arabic poetry and inking her fingers exchanging notes with Louise. *Istadh* Obadiah stood at the front of the room, pondering aloud the many-textured meanings of the word *watan*, homeland, as it figured in the various writings of the nationalist poet Maruf al-Rusafi. Big fans whirred overhead, doing little to relieve the already stifling heat, and on the large clock mounted above the blackboard the minutes ticked by with painful slowness.

Not quite an adult in the eyes of the West, at age sixteen Regina, like Agnes, was to Eastern eyes already a woman. She knew that some subtle alteration in her status had occurred after a number of telling restrictions had worked their way into her everyday routine. She was no longer allowed to swim, Salha saying it was shameful for her to display her body in a swimsuit, and she was forbidden to ride a bicycle, lest she lose something—she'd forgotten what—she was meant to keep for her future husband. She had also, finally, been inducted into the bloody monthly purges that Louise had been complaining about for several years, but which Regina had been too shocked to believe until she had experienced them herself.

By the time she had turned sixteen, Regina had had enough clues to understand that there was no turning back. Yet in spite of these various initiations into adulthood, she did not yet feel like a woman. Not until Agnes disappeared.

Madame Bassan had interrupted the class, walking officiously to the front of the room with her skirts rustling behind her. She nodded to the *istadh*, who stepped to one side, and pivoted around so that she could clearly see the faces of all her girls. Clasping her hands together in front of her, like someone addressing a small child, she announced: "Agnes Shahshou', your father wants you." Then she waited.

Instantly forty pairs of eyes were on Agnes, who quietly began to pack away her notebooks. No one tittered as Agnes filled her school-bag and no one uttered a word when she got up and, hanging her head in what Regina and her friends subsequently discovered was misery, meekly left the room with Madame Bassan. She would never return.

Later, when the tip, tap, and clack of gossip had telegraphed itself along the community grapevine, Regina learned that Agnes had been engaged that night to an Iraqi businessman who lived in Iran, and that upon her marriage she had gone to live with her husband's parents in Tehran, a city she'd never seen, in a country she'd only read about.

Agnes was not a particularly close friend of Regina's; she had never been part of the in-crowd. But she was enough of a fixture in the life of the class for her absence to be keenly felt. In the days following her removal, her empty chair seemed to dominate the room, drawing anxious sidelong glances from every girl. For Regina it was as if something in the karmic energy of the classroom had been disturbed and could not be repaired.

Regina drew two short lessons from what happened to her classmate: the first was that girls were made to be disposed of, handed over from father to husband as soon as decency would allow; the second was that soon it would be her turn.

For my grandmother, as for all Iraqi Jewish women of her generation, life possessed little of the appetizing sizzle that Westerners relish when pondering the possibilities of a personal future built bit by bit through chance, choice, and impulse. Life was rather something that unfolded mechanically according to a preset plan from which there was little option to deviate without suffering the strictest censure. Instead of choices, one had duties. In exchange for possibilities there were certainties.

There was never any question of Regina seizing her life for herself and making of it what she chose, of her traveling the world in search of adventure or devoting herself to study. And it was unthinkable that she should have a profession or career. She would become a devoted wife and mother; she would cook and keep house, entertain guests, and care for her elders. She would always practice the art of self-denial, never acknowledging a need that sprang from her own heart. Then, in old age, she would throw herself on the generosity of her children, at last reaping the rewards of a lifetime's hard labor.

Regina accepted the Baghdadi Jews' societal decrees with an almost preternaturally calm resignation. The only hint that there was perhaps more for a woman like her to aspire to was that, every so often, she had the overwhelming sensation that her life had somehow already been lived. If she felt any sense of creeping horror when, not long after Agnes's departure for Tehran, the marriage broker began paying regular visits to her father's house, she never thought to articulate that feeling as dread. All she was conscious of was that she loved her family, and she didn't want to leave its bosom for the dubious freedom of being able to run her own household under the watchful eye of any strange man who might become her spouse.

Regina took against the *dellalah* from the first, as she watched the woman inveigle herself into Salha's good graces using a mixture of flattery and deference. Even before she'd been formally introduced, Regina decided that she didn't care for the *dellalah*'s face, which was disfigured by the *ukht*, or Rose of Baghdad, a deep sallow lesion caused by parasite-carrying sand flies. Most Baghdadis have an *ukht* somewhere about their person, but only the unlucky ones have an *ukht* on their face. Regina further disliked the way the *dellalah* conspired with her mother, whispering things in her ear, then pulling back and smiling, satisfied that some seed she had planted in Salha's head would take root there. When Regina came home from school to find the two women locked in consultation, Salha would lift her head and peer at her daughter through a haze of cigarette smoke. "Haven't you got some sewing to be getting on with?" she'd ask.

Most of all Regina feared the *dellalah*. She was incredibly well informed, knowing exactly which boy was in need of a wife and exactly which girl would suit him. Though she was compensated for her efforts by the two families for whom she'd arranged a match—a mark of her trade that put her, along with singers, nurses, and teachers, in the barely reputable category of female earners—the *dellalah* was nonetheless considered a woman of many talents. She knew how to spot good breeding and how to recognize an educated mind and she understood the necessity of having an equality of wealth and social standing between the families involved in any given union. More discreetly, the *dellalah* could be relied upon to uncover anything unseemly that lurked hidden in the past of a prospective bride or groom. As if this were not reason enough for Regina to be on her guard, she had a surprising knack for finding husbands and wives for those generally believed to be lost causes: the ugly, the lame, the impoverished, and the simple-minded.

Most of the time the *dellalah* herself would instigate the long chain of events that eventually led to marriage. She would visit a family of wealth and renown, say, and venture the opinion that one of their sons appeared ready to settle down. Then, if his parents were agreeable, she might suggest one or two girls who would make a suitable bride. It went without saying that the girls had to come from highly respected families, ones whose ancestors were well known and whose achievements were celebrated in the community. The question of a dowry was more delicate. Often it was simply expected that when money married money a fat dowry was fair due. But sometimes a boy's parents were amenable to negotiation, especially if their son was less of a catch than he might be—if he wasn't all that bright or if he was considered too old. Then again, occasionally a girl was found of such unparalleled beauty that the very question of a dowry became irrelevant.

Salha liked to keep on top of the local gossip, mainly to hear of the *dellalah*'s successes with other families, but also to learn of the latest scandal. Louise's mother, Rosie Fattal, was a veritable repository of such information. According to Ezra, the woman could talk the ears off a donkey. But Salha enjoyed her trysts with Rosie, when a furious exchange of whispered confidences would take place over the coffee table. At the end of these energetic sessions, she'd leave Rosie's house in a state of excited agitation, and then she'd hurry along the street, impatient to get home and brief Ezra on her findings. "They say that Anwar Kedoori's boy is no good," she'd tell him. "He drinks and he gambles. His poor father is at his wit's end. But the silly man keeps covering his son's debts." And: "Apparently Abraham Masri has been taking money out of funds he was meant to be collecting for the synagogue. He denies it, of course, but no one believes him." Ezra, only half listening, would make suitable noises indicating surprise or interest. Yet he seldom gave Salha his full attention, even when she had a full-blown scandal to relate, such as that surrounding the family of Salima Joury.

Salima came from an educated family that had lost its money, and so her father had no dowry to bestow on her. Still, Salima was beautiful. All her cousins were in love with her and ready to wed her at the drop of a hat. But Salima's father wanted the *dellalah* to find an older man of wealth and high standing who could give his daughter the financial security that he could no longer give her himself. When the *dellalah* did as she was bid, Salima's cousins were horrified. They pleaded with her father for Salima's hand and swore on their mother's lives to provide for her. But Salima's father was immovable. Meanwhile Salima herself had fallen hopelessly in love with a neighbor's son, an admirable boy and a lawyer of some note, but also a devout Muslim. It was a secret and illicit attachment. But it became public soon enough, after Salima's father announced her impending engagement to a community elder only to have the young lovers elope to Mosul.

In the wake of a scandal it was never just the errant boy or wayward girl who faced ruin: the entire family was tainted with shame. None of the children of the house was considered remotely eligible, and the marriage prospects of their cousins were blighted as well. Not even the grandchildren escaped the ignominy of a scandalous past. What's more, it was always worse for the family of a girl.

In Regina's day it was universally understood in Arab culture that a woman was not an independent being but came under the authority of her husband or father. She had no rights. Her will was regarded as something to be broken, and her intelligence an asset only if she had no ambition to use it. It followed that her chief attribute was her person and specifically her chasteness, this being an almost sacred thing that her father had to safeguard. What every father feared beyond all else was that his daughter would disgrace herself on his watch, for then he'd be obliged to administer the traditional Bedouin punishment and preserve the family honor by killing her.

The Baghdadi Jews adhered to a somewhat watered down version of these beliefs. Honor killings were unheard-of in the community, although they occurred from time to time among rural Jewish populations that were "Bedouinized." Yet even among educated Jews in the cities it remained a given that a woman's chastity was everything, the principal item of worth she was deemed to possess and, therefore, everything she had to lose.

Regina knew that the most innocent contact with the opposite sex contained within it the potential seeds of her destruction. She took care not to speak to the English officers next door without one of her parents present. She wouldn't mix with boys her own age and, just to be on the safe side, she did her best to avoid looking at them. There were plenty of opportunities for her to trip up, especially in synagogue, where women, herded into an upstairs gallery so that their presence would not distract the men, spent much of their time, in turn, surveying those same men praying below. Unlike Louise, Regina never smiled at a boy in synagogue.

This self-control was something she managed to exercise with relative ease, since her opinion of the opposite sex wasn't very high to begin with. Regina lived her life among women. The only boys she knew at all well were her brothers and cousins and they, for the most part, were mere irritants. If she ever left the house, for whatever reason, one of these male relatives was required to chaperone her. And if anyone addressed her in the street, they, not she, would reply.

It irked Regina that things were different for boys. They had rights and freedoms that she could only dream of, which they exercised in the coffeehouses and casinos that were present in such number in the Old City that entire streets were off-bounds to women. Indeed, Regina had heard of Jewish boys who went so far as to date Muslim girls. But when she asked Salha how that was possible, her mother was less than helpful. "A boy is a boy," were her final words on the matter. Louise proved a better source of information. She told Regina that boys couldn't very well be left ignorant of life. They needed *experience*, she said, pronouncing the word "experience" in a drawn-out, affected manner. Louise and Regina giggled about the multitude of sins that this worldly word was designed to cover.

According to the Infinite Wisdom of Louise Fattal, which Regina was beginning to discover was quite extensive as far as the affairs of the heart were concerned, fathers just want to get rid of their daughters. "They can't wait to be free of them," said Louise, "and they'll marry them to anyone: old, ugly, or bald." Regina felt herself squirm just imagining being near such an ogre. But what alternative was there? "Well," said Louise, "you could marry a cousin. That way you'd already know that your match came from a good family and all the family's wealth would remain concentrated in one spot . . . Alternatively," she offered, "if that isn't an option, you could always marry an uncle." Neither girl relished this suggestion very much, and shrugged off any feelings of discomfort they'd unearthed by resolving there and then to remain spinsters.

Long before the *dellalah* had been invited into the Sehayek household, Salha had been privately scheming. When it came to the selection of a husband for her eldest daughter, she found it hard to relinquish maternal control. Besides, she had ideas of her own. Ideas above her station, Ezra would quip, annoying his wife no end. But he had a point. He was no Salman Nissan, with properties dotted across Baghdad and huge landholdings in Sulaimaniyah and Kirkuk. Although he and Salha were comfortably off, wealthy in the estimations of some, by Ezra's own reckoning they were out of the running when it came to the families that Salha had placed on her short list. Among these families it was not unusual for astonishing fortunes to be traded on the head of a bride. While it was all very well for those families who could afford it, Ezra did not belong to one of them. In a bid to console his wife, he argued that the sad sons and daughters of wealth and privilege had even less choice in their betrothal than their otherwise less fortunate peers. Within reason Regina would at least have some right of veto.

This right was something Regina exercised liberally in the months and years to come as she rejected one candidate after another, to her mother's growing consternation. On one memorable occasion, when she and her brother Nessim were invited to join the family of a prospective groom for tea, Regina took fright at the mere sight of the man her parents had sunk to considering. He had rheumy eyes, rotten teeth, and breath so oniony Regina thought she would faint. Not knowing quite what to do, she began sticking her tongue out at him when no one was looking, and when she got up to leave she did her best to cross the room with a distinct limp. Another poor soul by the name of Maurice was treated to a display of such petulant virtuosity—everything from eye rolling to facial twitching—that he practically ran from the Sehayek household.

"And what, might I ask, was wrong with Maurice?" Salha demanded of her daughter.

"Everything," said Regina.

"But he comes from a good family; his parents are lovely people. They are educated. They are kind. And they have money."

"He's not for me," said Regina, flatly.

"Well, someone will have to be. And soon," said her mother, and with that she turned and stomped out of the room, uncertain of how to bring her surprisingly willful daughter to heel.

Alone in the living room, safe in the comfort of the world she knew, Regina was at last willing to face a home truth: that as limited as her freedom was at home, this was the freest she would ever be. Little wonder, then, that she was doing everything in her power to preserve it.

Only when Salha took her troubles to Ezra did she allow herself to break down and cry. She could feel the weeks and months flying by, blowing right through her, and her younger daughters getting older with each passing one. "That girl is going to turn my head gray," she told him. Ezra did his best to soothe his wife, reminding her that a couple of prospects had asked for dowries so extravagant that he could only chuckle. Yet even he admitted that Regina was clearly reluctant to leave the nest on Abu Sa'ad Street.

As time went on, Salha redoubled the rigor of her investigations, tiring out the *dellalah* with her endless demands. Was the boy healthy? What childhood diseases had he had? Did he suffer from allergies or laziness? Did he drink? Did he have a temper? What were his business prospects? Did he have debts? Was he honorable and trustworthy? Well educated and fine mannered? Did he respect his elders? Offer charity to the poor? And would he look after their eldest girl the way he ought? The more she knew, she believed, the harder she could press her case.

With Regina standing obstinate, the whole family was at an impasse. Unattached, she was fast becoming a liability. The moment she turned twenty she would no longer be able to pick and choose according to her fancy. She would have to settle for someone her parents deemed suitable—and fast, because by twenty-five she might as well consider her life over. The idea that Regina might enter her mid-twenties unmarried appalled Salha. In her more anxious moments she had nightmare visions of her daughter having to work as a dressmaker or teacher and of her growing old and miserable under their roof. She wanted more for Regina than that.

Eventually it was Ezra who persuaded his daughter, but not before Salha had exhausted every possibility. Convinced, at one point, that Louise had put ideas of courtship and romance into Regina's innocent head, she decided to sit Regina down for a heart-to-heart. "Love is not lasting, *habibi*," she began, addressing an embarrassed and rather bewildered Regina. "And, in any case, the aim of marriage is altogether different. In marriage a woman is given protection and security, while the man gains the comfort and pleasure of a good wife." Each has duties to perform, she explained: he to work all day to bring home money, she to raise the children and prepare the family meals. Days, months, even years go by in this fashion. A whole lifetime spent in harmony, with husband and wife working together like the well-oiled parts of a finely crafted timepiece. How can love or personal fulfillment compare with this, with the satisfaction of discharging one's duty with honor and pride? Regina had to admit that they couldn't. But then, what did she know about such things?

In the end Regina did submit to duty. She was twenty-three years old and became engaged to a man nearly thirty years her senior. The *dellalah* had presented Elazar Levy as quite a catch. He was mature, yes, but didn't he still have a full head of thick and shiny hair? And wasn't he well respected in the community, not just as a businessman but as a dutiful brother and son? Every way you looked at it, Elazar was highly eligible. He came from a long line of learned and professional men, all of them educated and held in high esteem by their contemporaries. And he was wealthy enough not to care whether his wife arrived on his doorstep bearing caskets of gold. What he wanted was an educated woman from a good family. If she was pleasing to the eye as well as the soul, then that was a bonus, and he saw no reason why a match with Regina should be anything other than successful. Like Salha, Elazar Levy was realistic about marriage. He knew that passion was something that might never exist between himself and Regina. But there would be an enduring mutual respect between them that in the long run was worth far more.

Engagements in Baghdad were typically short, lasting no more than a few months—in other words, as long as it took to organize the wedding. They were also binding, the way any contract is legally binding. But, as Regina discovered, an engagement is also a state of mind. For the duration of hers she could see nothing anywhere except marital unions, not just between people but in the realms of nature, art, and politics. The relationship between Britain and Iraq looked like such a partnership, one cemented by oil. Even Faisal's relationship to the country was spouselike, to judge by the number of portraits of the king one would ordinarily encounter on a day out shopping—in business establishments, coffeehouses, and public buildings, as a spontaneous show of love. Then there were the Jews, bound to the emerging nation by the new Iraqi constitution, which, even as it pronounced Islam to be the religion of state, promised equality before the law to all of Iraq's minorities regardless of race and creed. Everywhere she looked Regina saw improving unions forged out of pragmatic self-interest.

Regina spent most of her engagement sewing furiously. A more pointless preparation for her future as a married citizen is surely hard to conceive. But in keeping with the Baghdadi Jews' deference to life's niceties, the assembling of a proper trousseau took precedence over her making other, more immediate adjustments to the fact that her life would soon be inexorably changed. No doubt Regina would have derived far more benefit from some basic advice on how to conduct herself as the mistress of her own domain, how to manage maids and servants, and how to hold her ground in the all too inevitable run-ins with her future mother-in-law. Some knowledge about the nature of intimacy between a man and a woman would also not have gone amiss.

As it was, Regina went to her wedding ignorant of all of it. She met Elazar only once prior to their betrothal, and between then and her wedding night, she saw him just a handful of times, each of them supervised by her parents. On one occasion they sipped tea together at the Sehayek house, with Regina scarcely able to look Elazar in the eye. In the past she'd been bold with her suitors, determined in her efforts to put them off. But now shyness caught her off guard, smothering her with the appearance of virtue, making her blush, quelling her speech. The difference, Regina realized, was that this time it was for real.

On another occasion, she and Elazar walked side by side in the park exchanging pleasantries, while Nessim and Salha walked a few paces behind them. Regina glanced back at her brother from time to time, trying to ascertain what he made of the union, but Nessim gave little away. What did her brother think of Elazar's open features, she won-

dered, his wide nose, bushy eyebrows, and graying, wiry hair? Did he
feel, as she did, that Elazar's face was kind, trustworthy?

As the park opened up onto the riverbank, Elazar quizzed Regina
about her upbringing and schooling as though he were a kindly uncle.
Who were her closest friends? Her favorite poets? Her most memorable teachers? Regina noticed that Elazar moved his hands in large
arcs as he spoke, as if gesturing his generosity to the world. She decided that he had nice hands, hands that were smooth and well looked
after. Yet for all her clever guesswork, at the end of the day Regina
hardly felt that the two of them were better acquainted. And she was
wholly unaware that there was anything else she ought to know.

A deep-rooted cultural reticence about discussing private bodily
matters more or less proscribed any frankness between women, so
that women tended to eye one another knowingly without a word of
mutual confidence passing among them. Regina had already been left
to discover the ordeals of menstruation for herself. At the first bleeding she had run to her mother, convinced she was dying. But Salha
had only cradled her head in her hands and begun softly intoning,
"May your mother die," which, roughly translated, meant she would
rather expire on the spot than carry the burden of a daughter who was
now capable of getting pregnant. Once she'd recovered herself, Salha
had shown Regina how to wind a cloth into a sturdy belt that went
around her waist, leaving a large piece of fabric dangling like a tail, to
be pulled up between her legs and then knotted at the front. Each day,
said Salha, the soiled cloths had to be put in a big pot, whose contents
would be washed at the end of the week.

Salha would never have dreamed of sharing with Regina the
trauma of her own marriage experience. She would have delivered
homilies and sermons aplenty, the wisdom of the world tripping off
her tongue with ease and assurance. But the idea of confiding intimacies to her daughter would have struck her as inappropriate. In fact, it
was practically a matter of policy to keep girls ignorant of anything to
do with sex on the grounds that when all was said and done, *knowledge*
was as corrupting as *experience*.

Salha, it turns out, had been married at twelve. She had spent her own wedding party running around her father's courtyard, playing with the other children. When she'd wanted to see the musicians and dancers perform, Salman Nissan had hoisted her up onto his shoulders. The seriousness of the occasion was entirely lost on her. Until she was obliged to leave for her in-laws' home, and then she had cried bitterly for her parents, her brothers, her sisters, and for the house she would have liked to have finished growing up in. She was terrified of her new husband's still unformed appetites. He was only just out of his teens and clumsy in his expressions of affection. Salha was happy enough to play with him by day, but at night she tried her best to avoid him. She'd hide from him, or else she picked arguments that allowed her to storm off in a theatrical huff. She even slept in her mother-in-law's bed, taking the extra precaution of latching herself to the older woman's dozing form with a large safety pin. Years later she could laugh about it, but only with other married women—and Regina did not yet belong to that club.

As the wedding approached, Salha was as twitchy as her daughter, her nerves jangling apace with her gold bracelets as she threw herself into a flurry of activity: ordering the flowers that the male guests would be given, superintending the preparation of the wedding banquet, hiring the *daqaqas* who would serenade the new bride, not to mention finding the right dress for Regina. Ordinarily it was up to the groom's parents to throw the wedding party, but Elazar's mother had asked Salha to relieve her of this duty, because she was old and all alone in the world and, she had protested, hopelessly out of touch with what the young were all about. Salha had jumped at the chance to take up the reins. But now she was beginning to regret it, fearing that her constitution would cave in under the stress. To calm her nerves she read Regina's *finjan*, which augured well for the union and pleased her daughter no end.

In keeping with Baghdadi custom, two days before his marriage Elazar Levy sent a huge platter to the Sehayek residence. Made of hand-beaten silver, it was round and thick-lipped and laden with white sugared almonds. Two men were needed to carry it through the front door. The women of the house ah-ed and cooed as the men set it down, and even Ezra confessed to being impressed. In keeping with another custom, Elazar had hidden a silk pouch among the sweets, which one of Regina's sisters managed to fish out. It contained a pair of carved earings, made from the purest gold, which were meant, and were taken as, a sign of affection.

Later, alone in her room, Regina blushed as she pushed the golden rings into her ears. Standing before the mirror, she patted down the pale silk dress she'd chosen for her henna party and allowed herself for a brief moment to take pleasure in the woman that she had become: it was time, she decided, to move on, to embrace adult hopes and cares, to rely on herself to have the right instincts about things. While she was in this almost somnambulant state, Nessim knocked at the door and startled her. How grown up he looked in his dark suit and shiny shoes, she thought. Clearly it was not only she who was changing.

Settling himself on the chair next to the squashed oval of the stand-alone mirror, Nessim cleared his throat. "You know, you don't have to go through with this," he said, his voice croaky with muffled emotion.

"Yes I do," said Regina. It must have been hard for him to confront her like this.

"Don't get me wrong, because I'm genuinely fond of Elazar. But he's too old for you, Regina."

"What if I told you that the age difference was immaterial?" she said.

"Then I'd believe you," said Nessim.

"Well then, it is immaterial. Besides, I like him."

Looking back at pictures of my grandfather today, I see an attractive older man, with a high forehead, intelligent eyes, and a smile that ran the gamut from warm to wry. There was a softness to his features, and I can understand how Regina would have found him appealing.

Nessim, however, remained perplexed by his sister's choice. But if Elazar was good enough for Regina than he would be good enough for Nessim too. He got up and kissed his sister on the forehead. Then he stepped back, smiled broadly, and raised an imaginary glass to toast her future happiness.

After Nessim left, Regina took several deep breaths to steady her nerves. Then she headed downstairs to join her parents' guests at the prenuptial feast.

The next day was traditionally set aside for ritual cleansing. Salha accompanied Regina to the local Jewish baths, where she was dunked and scrubbed and scraped, her skin practically peeled off her. Then, following a picnic that Salha had prepared to mark the occasion, they returned home to await a visit from the *heffafa,* whose unique skill was to glide a piece of cotton sewing thread over the surface of Regina's skin, twisting it sharply as her hands moved, so that with each twirl a number of fine hairs would get caught and pulled out. In this manner Regina was plucked clean as a chicken. Not even the thicket of hairs which concealed the part of her body that was most foreign to her remained.

As for the wedding itself, the simple synagogue ceremony was followed by a party at the bridegroom's house. By all accounts it was a wonderful affair, and Salha acquitted herself in front of everyone whose opinion mattered, not least her new son-in-law. For Regina, however, the wedding was a blur, any detailed recollection she had of it eclipsed by what came after. She thought she remembered a sea of smiling faces, hot and flushed in the evening heat. And then she was dancing, and the sweet and pungent smell of sweat pervaded the air. There was music too, and singers, the *daqaqas,* who sang to her from the perspective of the groom's mother. "Bravo. Bravo. Look at what you've achieved," they chanted. She remembered that she hadn't really eaten, although there'd been a banquet fit for royalty and a cake inscribed in sugared icing with the date of her marriage: March 28, 1928. "I tired myself out. I exhausted myself, and you took him ready made." But she thought she could still smell the delicate aromas of the *kubba, arouk, tibit, ingriyi,* and other savory dishes that their guests had enjoyed.

It had been late when everyone departed and Elazar, his mother, and her parents had retired indoors. Regina felt lightheaded. Did she actually drink the wine that Elazar handed her as everyone toasted the happy couple's health? She couldn't remember. She knew that Elazar had led her to a bedroom and that his mother, Salha, and Ezra had all seated themselves outside it. But what happened next? A tussle? A rude clashing of bodies and limbs? Regina had been shocked by the feel of another so close to her, and she didn't like the smell of Elazar's expensive cologne. She felt unable to breathe. Then there was the pain in the most private and delicate part of her body: sharp, intense, and somehow internal, accompanied by bleeding. Regina looked to her husband for an explanation, but Elazar had already left the room to assure his in-laws of Regina's virginity.

Regina's generation was the last to suffer the indignities of semi-public deflowering, since the practice was slowly phased out of Baghdadi Jewish culture in the 1930s. Nonetheless, my grandmother never lost sight of the fact that her married life had begun as it was meant to continue—with a test.

Six

INDEPENDENCE

Baghdad had changed in the years since Regina was a schoolgirl. Like some laboratory experiment gone awry, it had mutated madly throughout the 1920s, adapting to the ever-changing and often contradictory demands of its resident mandatory rulers, its imported monarch, and its growing native populace. Several new suburbs had sprung up in the south, built to Western particulars, with spacious villas and bungalows lining wide leafy streets and hugging the curve of the river. Automobile services now linked the city to centers of population as far-flung as Damascus and Beirut, shortening the traveling time from London to Baghdad by weeks to just nine days. A maze of industry had built itself in and around New Street, now the commercial hub of old Baghdad. There were printing presses and bookshops, silversmiths and watchmakers, specialty bakers, and fabric stores stocking the latest patterns from the *Ladies' Home Journal*. The king, meanwhile, had acquired a brand-new royal pavilion.

There was no disputing that Baghdad was a better place, boasting several new hospitals, half a dozen new colleges of higher education specializing in law, medicine, engineering, pharmacy, and teacher training, and a modern parliament whose first constitutional assembly resembled a model of representative authority; no fewer than five Jews and four Christians were members of this august body, and it was they who succeeded in securing equal rights under the law for Iraq's minorities. Nor could anyone complain about the city's modern fire service, the smart row of Western-style hotels that had shot up along the riverbank, its municipal court, chamber of commerce, or its high-minded governor, who served as president of an elected city council. With the architecture of civic society in place Baghdad began more and more to resemble a modern European metropolis.

All the same there remained an air of artifice about it all, stemming from a sense that so much window dressing functioned chiefly to disguise Britain's raw imperial designs on the country. With the exception perhaps of the Jews, everyone suspected the British. Beneath the visible sheen on almost every aspect of daily life, all manner of discontent was brewing.

There was widespread disaffection among the Shia majority. It was unprepared to tolerate the continued presence of a Christian power in the land but was prevented from organizing any effective opposition to that power as its own spiritual leaders had been deported to Iran after inciting a wide spread rebellion against the British in 1920. Nor did the Shia have much time for the Sunni-dominated government, which looked to them to be no more than a dancing bear, hopping unhappily from one leg to the other with each crack of the British whip.

The Sunni elite itself resented the mandatory arrangement that bound Iraq to British interests and kept the government from assuming full control of national affairs, chief among them the defense of the realm. With King Faisal's quiet encouragement, many Sunnis in high positions began looking to strengthen their ties to Arab nationalist elements that wished to deliver Iraq to the Iraqis without delay. Among businessmen and city leaders who had done well under the Ottomans there was little appreciation for the stiff-collared propriety that symbolized British industriousness and placed such a high premium on plain talk and plain dealing. Free to choose, many of them would gladly have returned to a comfort zone where justice could be bought, local politicians owned, and plans for every kind of municipal improvement kept flexible through the liberal application of palm grease.

The British leadership, under no illusions about its popularity in Iraq, labored under additional pressures from home, where a "Quit Mesopotamia" campaign was waged by the national press throughout much of the 1920s. Iraq was costing the British government millions, and although the government remained committed to protecting the overland route to India as well as the newly discovered oil fields near Kirkuk in the north, a certain amount of postwar retrenchment was inevitable. Projects started early in the decade were abandoned, departments restricted, and military expenditure greatly reduced. At the same time funds promised to schools failed to materialize and those set aside for experiments in agriculture and irrigation were hastily capped. To top it off, a draconian system of tax assessment and collection came into effect, punishing alike to rich and poor, both of whom found themselves paying more taxes than ever before and wishing that the British had left the inherently corrupt system of old alone.

Yet in spite of Iraqi frustrations with British rule, a precarious peace prevailed. People adopted a wait-and-see approach to the future, knowing that the League of Nations Mandate obliged Britain to give the country up to self-rule in due course; or, as the official terminology phrased it, "until such time as they [the mandated territories] could stand on their own." Besides, out of bald curiosity as much as anything else, most Iraqis seemed willing to give Faisal a chance.

King Faisal desperately wanted to be seen as the figurehead of a free Iraq. But with the direct channels of influence closed to him, he became a deft double-dealer, placating the British one day and making rash promises to Arab nationalists the next. When his inveigling got him nowhere, he would throw a tantrum and agitate for more rope, only for the British to tie it promptly around his neck. The British, of course, held the trump card in this process, and each time Faisal got uppity they used it, threatening to withdraw to Basra or else altogether. Both sides knew that Faisal would always back down since he was well aware that his monarchy could not survive without British support. As Colonial Secretary Winston Churchill wryly observed, in a letter to Iraq's first high commissioner, Sir Percy Cox: "All the time he [Faisal] takes our money he will have to take our directions." Be that as it may, Faisal was only prepared to accept the Mandate for as long as it took to hammer out a treaty of alliance that would replace it.

The king had shrewdly calculated that although there was little feeling of national identity in Iraq, with most people remaining loyal to tribe, town, and family before state, there was sufficient support for the idea of a sovereign Iraq for his demands for autonomy to bear fruit. There was overwhelming support for the formation of an Iraqi army that would eventually render a British military presence in Iraq redundant, even among the younger generation of Jews who were now being accepted into the new military academy to be trained as officers. And there were great hopes that oil revenues from the rechristened Iraq Petroleum Company would soon underwrite a new Iraqi currency. Just as important, there was enough goodwill about the whole nationalist enterprise for thousands of Iraqis to discard the traditional fez and, in a spontaneously patriotic gesture, take up the uniquely Mesopotamian *sidara* instead. In these small signs Faisal divined that his legacy in Iraq would be assured if only he could be seen to have sent the British packing.

In the midst of Baghdad's physical and political transformation, Regina was adjusting to the fact that she was moving up in the world. A married woman now, with wealth, status, a new house, and a new name, she had cast off her old skin and climbed into a newer and more promisingly elastic one. Even so, Regina felt hopelessly out of her depth.

After their wedding Elazar had taken her to his family home, a sprawling mansion on Taht al-Takia that had once belonged to his grandfather and namesake and which now hungered for inhabitants the way a coffeehouse begged for customers. In the past the house had been a joyful place, home to Elazar senior, his seven sons, their seven wives, and their many children. It was bustling and chaotic, with people constantly coming and going and the servants running around trying to meet everyone's needs. On Elazar senior's death, the house passed to his son Haron, who himself had a sizable brood, and he in turn left it to Elazar. With each generation's passing the house grew emptier, until Regina appeared on the scene and only Elazar and his mother were living there, their footsteps ringing through lonely corridors, their meals eaten quietly in an echoing dining room.

Regina had been so overwhelmed by the scale, not to mention the bareness, of her new home that Elazar hired builders to divide the house in two before he moved his new wife into one half and rented out the other to a man who converted it into a furniture factory. While half the house was more manageable, it still qualified as grand, and as Regina paced its empty rooms, she reflected that it would be some years yet before it would once again be filled with people and laughter and food.

The house was entered via a huge, high-ceilinged hall that doubled as a sitting room. It was cool and cavelike, with a stone floor and bare plastered walls, and it was lined with narrow divans, casually overlaid with Persian carpets. Beyond it lay a large tiled courtyard, which, unlike the house on Abu Sa'ad, contained a freshwater well. Such a well was a prized feature, and a whole apparatus of water purifiers was dedicated to showing it off, the centerpiece of which was a rickety wooden edifice that supported a number of earthenware pots. At the top were large roughly worked pots that received water from the well, while beneath these was a series of smaller, smoother pots into which the water would drip, drop by precious drop. This was the drinking water. In summer, as Regina soon discovered, a big snake invariably coiled itself around the lower pots trying to keep cool. At first she was terrified, but she soon saw that the snake minded its own business as long as she minded hers.

To one side of the water room, as one circled the courtyard, was a kitchen, a toilet, a string of servants' rooms, the dining room, the storeroom, and a corridor leading to a set of stairs. The stairs descended to the basement in one direction and, in the other, climbed all the way to the muddy roof terrace. There, beautiful wildflowers would sprout in springtime, creating a colorful carpet that Regina preferred to any number of the valuable Persian varietals that skulked indoors, hanging heavily on the plaster walls and, in winter, smothering the flagstone floors as well. Elazar traded in upmarket carpets, as well as in tea, coffee, and leathers, and every now and then all the carpets in the house would disappear to be replaced by a new lot, as dismal, to Regina's mind, as the previous set. That said, she valued the carpets as armchair covers, when it was their warmth that mattered and not their aesthetic qualities.

The most daunting fixture in the house was Regina's mother-in-law, a formidable woman who could recite whole books of the Bible by heart and who doted on her only son like an Old Testament matriarch. Simha Levy had been born into a powerful banking family and her general sense of entitlement, honed over decades that had left her gnarled and creaky, was something she emanated from her core. Like her walking stick, gray head, and black robes, her prerogative was something tangible. People said that on any given Sabbath, you could hear her tut-tutting from the synagogue gallery if one of the rabbis made the slightest mistake in his reading, while the sharper tongued among them intimated that her five daughters couldn't wait to get married and leave the house.

Under Simha's wise-owl glare Regina constantly felt as though she were being appraised, as though each day contained hidden traps and pitfalls that her mother-in-law had planted to see how she would fare. Was she firm enough with the servants? Kind enough to the neighbors? Sufficiently solicitous of her husband's needs? A good cook? An able household economist? Regina had expected to be the mistress of her domain, as Salha so clearly was of hers, and yet most of the time she felt like a daughter of the house.

Regina's way was to tackle things gently. Rather than lock antlers with her mother-in-law, she would try to win Simha over by showing her her worth: she would woo her as one might woo an admirer. And so Regina lovingly prepared the most delectable Sabbath feasts, setting the table with platters of rice, one spiced with saffron and garnished with grated egg, one mixed with red lentils and cumin, and another decorated with tender pieces of slivered lamb. She cooked chicken stuffed with fried giblets inside a poultice of rice that had been gently sautéed with onions, herbs, and tomato paste, and she made delicate pastry fingers filled with spiced chicken, parsley, raisins, and pine nuts. To finish things off, she served a large plate of fruit, with melons, apricots, pears, pomegranate seeds, orange slices, and fresh dates fanned across it in colorful bands.

Regina had a flair for cooking. She liked nothing better than to spend the morning at work in the womblike kitchen, warmed by the heat of the *tannour* and the smells of fresh food baking and frying. It filled her with simple, unquestioning contentment. She was also at her most confident in the kitchen, allowing herself a measure of experimentation and whimsy. At the house on Taht al-Takia she gave new twists to dishes she'd learned at Salha's shoulder, using paprika in one chicken dish instead of tomato, and she asked the butcher for cuts of lamb she'd never cooked with before. It seemed to Regina that if she could impress Simha anywhere, it would be here, in the engine room of her new domestic life. But while Elazar was full of praise for his wife's culinary creations, Simha preferred to eat her meals in contemplative silence. At those early Sabbath dinners Regina had taken such trouble over, she scarcely looked up from her plate, and when she did it was usually only to say: "It needs more salt."

Owing to the profoundly patriarchal character of Baghdadi Jewish society, my grandfather's forebears loom much larger in family memory than my grandmother's, whose recoverable lineage seems to stop abruptly with Salman Nissan's grandfather, Yehesqail Nissan, on the maternal side and with Ezra Sehayek, the grandfather of Regina's father, on the paternal side. Beyond the names, there's nothing substantive to grab hold of, no dates, professions, or anecdotes, only the bald fact of their Baghdad births. It could be argued that my grandfather's more illustrious ancestors left their stories to posterity because their achievements were more worthy of record. But whatever the reason, on paper, I have a lopsided genealogy that leans heavily toward men of note, rather than toward the women who propped them up. What interests me most about this line of descent is that it offers a typical trajectory of an Iraqi Jewish family and also demonstrates the fluidity of movement that existed with the Jewish community in Persia.

The great patriarch of the Levy clan was Agha Elazar Levy, a Persian Jew who practiced medicine at the shah's court in the middle of the eighteenth century, and whose skill was valued highly enough for him to be ennobled for his services: the title *Agha*—pronounced *ar-rah*—is loosely equivalent to the British "Sir." After uncovering a plot to take his life, Agha Elazar relocated to Baghdad, where he took up manual work but continued to treat patients at home in the evenings. For this service to the community he refused all pay. It is said that he was a very humble man and that he dedicated himself to medicine until the end of his days.

About Agha Elazar's only son, Yaeer, the records are curiously silent. It is known that he had seven sons and that the eldest of these, my great-great-grandfather, was born in Hamadan, which suggests that at some stage Yaeer moved back to Persia. In some papers his profession is given as "doctor." Yaeer's eldest son, also Elazar, was born in Hamadan in 1803, and moved to Baghdad as a young man. A jeweler by profession, he is at the center of a marvelous story that has been handed down the generations, fictionalized by a well-known British author and turned into a court case of such proportions that literally hundreds of litigants were involved.

The story begins in the 1820s when Elazar and his brother Shimoun were operating an antique-dealing business with branches in Mesopotamia and Persia. One day, while sorting through stock purchased in a small Persian town, the brothers stumbled across a dusty earthenware kettle, a curious-looking thing that was parched, cracked, and heavy. Passing the kettle back and forth between them, the brothers accidentally dropped it, spilling thousands of precious gemstones onto the floor, and then they panicked, convinced that the authorities would come after them and confiscate their lucky find. In the heat of the moment they decided to transport the jewels to England, where they gave them up to the Bank of England for safekeeping. Not long after, they returned to Baghdad and drew up a will dividing the fortune evenly among their children.

Another version of the story has the brothers selling the jewels for a small fortune, and a rumor has long circulated in some family circles that one of these jewels ended up decorating Queen Victoria's coronation crown. Both versions claim that some investment, whether of money or jewels, was made with the Bank of England, and much of the family believes that the original deposit remains untouched to this day.

In 1956 a group of Levy descendents living in Israel, many of them destitute immigrants from Iraq, banded together to press their claim with the Bank of England, even though the receipt for the original deposit had long ago been destroyed. Reporting on the legal proceedings a year later, the *New York Times* said that more than two hundred Jews were locked in a "bitter struggle" with the bank over a reported $392 million inheritance, though the paper did not reveal how it had arrived at such a sensational sum. Needless to say, the claimants saw nothing of this fabulous fortune, which, according to one Ruth Montefiore, who received a personal notice from the Bank of England in 1992, had been "distributed" in 1856. Since Elazar and Shimoun were still very much alive in 1856, it seems possible that they secretly cashed in on their investment.

Like his father, Yaeer, Elazar Levy senior also had seven sons, though for good measure he had a daughter as well. One son, Haron, took up the Levy mantle by becoming a doctor, and, like his great-grandfather, he treated the community free of charge. Haron apparently became expert at pulling teeth, which in the days before anesthesia was notoriously painful. It is said that he performed this operation with such patience and empathy that patients in need of extractions would line up outside his house for hours.

When Haron inherited the big house on Taht al-Takia, he had already married Simha, who bore him his only son and heir—my grandfather—followed by five daughters. Therein lies the explanation as to why my grandfather had to wait until he was in his mid-fifties before he began searching for a wife. Haron died young, leaving Elazar responsible for his mother and sisters, and thus it fell upon my grandfather to marry each of his sisters off before he was entitled to a bride of his own. It was a point of pride with him that he gave every one of his sisters a sizable dowry.

My mother, aunt, and uncle knew my grandfather only as children, and so all they recall is Elazar the disciplinarian, the stern father who gave them little leeway and whom even Regina tiptoed around. They tell me their father was a quiet man who let others do the talking, that he was educated and deep thinking, that he liked to read, that he abhorred dirty jokes, and that he scorned gambling—although he drew the line at backgammon, or *towli,* a game he often won at. Apparently, he saw himself as something of a storyteller. But his taste was for mean little parables. One that has stayed with my aunt to this day tells of a French count who chastened his son for climbing so high into a tree that he was too frightened to come down again. "Jump son, and I will catch you," said the count, and so the son jumped. But the count did not move to catch him. Instead he let his son fall to the ground with a painful thud. "I wanted to teach you a lesson," cautioned the count. "Never trust anyone, not even your own father."

My grandfather owned a *khan* in the commercial part of town, and there he stored his imported wares. The *khan* was as big as Aladdin's cave, and as well stocked. It was lined and floored with fine Persian carpets and piled high with stacks of wooden crates filled with coffee beans and teetering towers of intriguingly stamped boxes packed full of tea. It smelled of must and damp and leather and rubber—another of the materials in which Elazar traded—and my grandfather liked nothing better than to bury himself in its dark depths.

Removed from the flurry and hum of life on Baghdad's streets, Elazar would spend many pleasant hours walking up and down the narrow isles, checking off stock lists and inspecting crates for damage, or else he would snatch a quiet moment to run his hand over the latest silken piles he'd picked up in Isfahan or Kermanshah and mull over which ones he might take home for a spell. Most of the time, however, he was stationed at his writing desk at the mouth of the cavernous *khan,* the only evidence in it of a civilized presence. On top of the desk sat a clunky old typewriter and a telephone with a handset that looked like a seashell—two of Elazar's few concessions to modernity—and with these bare tools my grandfather would gaily connect Bombay and Basra to Paris, London, and Milan, turning his stock to profit before it had even left his care.

A man of habit as much as principle, Elazar never gave up wearing the fez, even as the rest of Baghdad took up the *sidara* in the 1920s. This reluctance to move with the times had nothing to do with political atavism, for, like every other enterprising Jew of his generation, Elazar was glad to have washed his hands of the Turks and eager to participate in the new Iraq. Instead, his failure to fall in with the sweeping trend boiled down to his innate resistance to change: when he looked in the mirror at his befezzed head, he recognized himself. When he wore a *sidara* he did not.

Habit, tradition, custom, and routine: these were the household gods on Taht al-Takia, and Regina was expected to fall in with their unvarying pattern. Elazar would breakfast with his wife in the mornings before heading out to work, leaving Regina to her domestic chores, her shopping and cooking, her banter with neighbors, and meetings with various friends. Then he would return at dusk, eat a freshly prepared meal and retire to his study to read for the remainder of the evening. A few times a week an *arabana* would pull up at the door and transport Elazar and Regina to their social club, where Elazar played *towli* and Regina met her friends. And on feast days, the Levy and Sehayek clans would come together to celebrate. That was the sum total of their life together. It was ordered and predictable, evenly paced and comfortable.

To someone of my generation who believes in marrying for love this arrangement might appear lacking, but Regina was far from unhappy with her lot. She and Elazar had an understanding: they had signed up to share their lives together, and they would accommodate each other accordingly. Besides, unlike his mother, Elazar had offered Regina many small proofs of his appreciation.

Insofar as the outside world impinged on life at Taht al-Takia, it was only to ruffle Elazar's feathers. He had been slow to warm to the British, and their whirlwind transformation of Baghdad had for a long time left him bemused and uncertain. Then, once he'd finally adjusted to the British presence in Iraq, Elazar's peace of mind was again disturbed, this time by Arab nationalist demands for independence. Flustered and annoyed, he would tell Regina that the Jews had successfully survived a succession of overlords far less scrupulous about their rights and obligations than the British were: "So why can't the Arabs figure out a way to coexist with *their* new masters?"

Nor was Elazar's own community free from strife, caused, as he saw it, by the endless appetite for reforms of every kind, in education, manners, dress, even in the institutions meant to provide spiritual guidance. More and more Elazar found himself longing for the days when a man knew where he stood, which, in his case, was in direct continuity with the past.

My grandfather was not especially religious, but he was not among those in the community who approved of the way in which the lay council was trying to unseat Chief Rabbi Ezra Dangoor in order to replace him with their own candidate, Rabbi Sassoon Khedouri, who they believed would be more sympathetic to their progressive views. At the time of my grandparents' marriage in 1928, this long-drawn-out dispute had reached a stalemate: the lay council had succeeded in securing Rabbi Dangoor's resignation, but the spiritual council had swiftly retaliated by disordaining Rabbi Khedouri, thereby disqualifying him from assuming the vacant office. Elazar hated to see the community so bitterly divided, but he concluded that the tide of change was unstoppable and that it was only a matter of time before the reformists would get their way.

He was right. The lay council eventually appealed to the government to enter the dispute on its behalf. The Iraqi government duly interceded in 1931, enacting a new law governing Jewish affairs under which a layman was allowed to preside over the community as chief rabbi so long as his election was ratified by a royal decree. Thus, after a long struggle that caused an irreparable rift in the community, Rabbi Sassoon Khedouri was appointed chief rabbi in 1933.

The long-term result of this top-down intervention was negative, weakening the community's power to manage its own affairs. The new chief rabbi, beholden to the Iraqi government for obtaining his seat and equally reliant to retain it, became little more than a government tool. In the turbulent decades that followed, he was more inclined to toe the official line than to represent the interests of his community to the Iraqi authorities. Disillusioned, the reformists severed their connections with an institution they considered decrepit and anachronistic. In search of a new direction, many of them began identifying more overtly with Iraqi society, and an every-man-for-himself ethos began to work its fragmenting influence on the community.

Regina had an easier time adapting to wholesale change than her husband did. In getting married, moving into a new home, and then becoming a mother, she had in short order experienced such a torrent of change that she had no choice but to flow with it. The arrival of her daughter Bertha in 1929 was a landmark event that sealed her fate to Elazar's in a more concrete way than their marriage alone had done. Motherhood also brought Regina back to herself again, rekindling the self-confidence that had lain dormant for too long. It gave her purpose and opinions, vision and values, and it sparked in her a keener interest in the affairs of state.

Up until the point when Regina committed herself to an independent Iraq, she had had few political inclinations. She didn't follow the frequent comings and goings of prime ministers and their cabinets. Nor did King Faisal's love-hate relationship with the British capture her interest day by day, as it did a large portion of Iraqi society's. Now, however, she believed that she had grasped a few simple truths: chiefly, that Iraq needed to wean itself from its dependence on British support. In order for Iraq to become a mature and responsible nation, it had to stand up on its own, learn from its mistakes, harness its indigenous talents, and exploit its natural assets. Only then could it bid farewell to the imperial power that had given it birth.

By the time Bertha came into the world, Faisal had extracted a promise from Britain to sponsor Iraq's entry into the League of Nations in 1932 in return for safeguarding British interests. But nothing official had been signed because the king was still a long way from realizing the kind of separation he dreamed of. In particular, Britain's disproportionate control over the Iraqi army remained a running sore.

After a great deal of acrimonious bargaining, a treaty of alliance was signed in 1930. It asserted that Iraq would be responsible for its own defense come independence, but that British troops would nevertheless be stationed in the country. This was a paradox acceptable to both sides.

The precise details of disengagement were worked out over the next three years, during which time Faisal and Nuri as-Said, the politician most closely associated with the views of the monarch, consolidated their power base, knowing that the British would do nothing to stop them. Thus they marginalized opposition parties and Shiites, persecuted the Kurds, ignored Assyrian pleas for greater autonomy, and appointed to key ministerial positions Arab nationalists who immediately took measures to erode the rights of minorities, even as the constitution enshrined them.

By the time independence arrived in 1932, the government in Iraq was virtually autocratic, which explains why the general population was not much inclined to celebrate the nation's freedom. To dampen the spirit of independence further, it was clear to everyone but the self-deluding Faisal that the British had used the treaty as a means of formalizing their indirect rule. They retained air force bases in the country, at Habbaniya and Shu'ayba, and they maintained a stranglehold on foreign policy, with many officials occupying the same advisory positions after independence as they had before it. Thus there was no eruption of joy, no dancing in the streets, no heartrending public declarations. Just a quiet accommodation to overwhelming disappointment.

Although Regina's views on Iraqi independence would sour over time, the actual moment of Iraq's official release from the mandate was heightened for her by coinciding with the birth of her second child: my mother. Marcelle would be one of the first native citizens of the new Iraq, and in the initial flush of excitement that attended her birth, it was almost impossible for Regina, now twenty-seven, to separate the hope she invested in her daughter from the hope she invested in the country.

Part Two

CHANGING TIMES

Seven

ARABS BEFORE MUSLIMS

Once children entered her life, Regina experienced that familiar dissonance that all new parents feel between the cocooned world of home, where time seems almost to stand still, and the world outside, which recedes so that you no longer hear its din or feel its heat and which remains out of reach, mysteriously muted, until your children begin to participate in it.

With endless chores eating up the better part of her days, Regina had little time to reflect on anything much beyond her literal reach. As a rule her hands did the thinking for her: grabbing a child, stocking supplies, reaching for fresh linens or foods, mending, cleaning, clearing, tidying. In all this, Regina moved from one thing to the next with speed and efficiency, clocking on and clocking off like a productive pieceworker. And yet the cumulative value of her efforts seemed to elude her. It was as if she had somehow gotten stuck on the factory floor, with its dim vantage point and bad air, instead of directing operations from the light-filled manager's office, where she believed, on her promotion to motherhood, she ought to have been installed.

Salha took a perverse satisfaction in Regina's mired circumstances. "Now she finally understands," she would say to Ezra. Elazar did his bit to help, making a point of pushing the daily paper his wife's way once he'd read it. But Regina seldom found time to register the headlines, much less delve into the details behind them, and before long her window on the world disappeared altogether. You could argue—and Salha often did—that it hardly mattered, since when Regina's head wasn't full of lists, it was as if she had cotton for brains. It was all she could do just to keep up with friends like Louise and participate in family gatherings. Where anything more taxing was concerned, she simply checked out.

The brief blinkered period when child care proves all-consuming usually represents no more than a blink of an eye in the life of a nation-state; at most one might miss a change of government, a corporate scandal or two, a small tectonic shift in the cultural makeup of things. But in Iraq, when Regina was adjusting to her new role as a mother, events moved at such a pace, restructuring the face of Iraqi society so completely, that by time she emerged from her chrysalis she hardly recognized where she was. In particular, the two rival forces of Arab nationalism and Zionism, previously confined to the fringes of regional politics, had stepped boldly forward onto center stage.

A more seasoned political observer than Regina, or even Elazar, might have predicted that as soon as Iraq broke free from its mandatory shackles the Arab nationalists would seize the upper hand in running the country. But few could have foreseen the speed with which this stealthy takeover would occur. Across the Arab world there was a revival of respect and love for Arab history that was fundamentally secular in character and that drew its support from across tribal, regional, and religious divides. Although there was no specific rallying cry associated with the movement, a phrase Faisal often used sums up its ethos: "We are Arabs before being Muslims, and Muhammed was an Arab before being a prophet."

The principal theme behind Arab nationalism was Arab unity. The idea was that the Arabs were one people, or "one body," but this historical fact had effectively been obscured by centuries of colonial conquest that had fostered division where once there was harmony. The nationalists believed that only by casting off the imperial yoke and reuniting once again could the Arabs become a true nation.

In pursuit of this national ideal—effectively a brotherhood that transcended normal state boundaries—the Arab nationalists rejected

French models of nationalism, which predicated the existence of the nation on that of the state, and looked instead to the Germans for inspiration. In particular, the idea of Johann Gottlieb Fichte (1762–1814) that what defined a people was their shared language and culture struck a chord. Many commentators have pointed to the irony of this Arab identification with Germany at a time when the Nazi racial scale ranked Arabs over Jews by just the barest of margins. But Germany was far less aggressive about imposing its colonial designs on the Arab world than either Britain or France. Nor had it had a hand in fragmenting the region. Moreover, under Prussia's militarized leadership, Germany had succeeded in uniting its own disparate parts to become a seemingly model state: disciplined, strong, purposeful, and thereby worthy of imitation.

Arab nationalism's leading ideologue, Sati' al-Husri, likewise distinguished the vital Arab nation from the legal or mechanical entity of the state. Language, he wrote, was "the soul and life of the nation," and history was "its memory and its consciousness." When Faisal ascended the throne, he plucked al-Husri from the ossified Ottoman bureaucracy in Istanbul, where he had served as an educational reformer, and installed him in Iraq in the impregnable position of director general of education, an appointment immune from the usual vicissitudes of electoral politics. From there al-Husri exercised a singular influence on Iraqi thinking. He overhauled the entire education system, bringing it into line with the precepts of Arab nationalist ideology. A rigorous grounding in classical Arabic was ensconced at the core of the school curriculum and all students, from primary level up, were instilled with new pride in their cultural heritage through a history program that lovingly toured the pantheon of Arab heroism. The idea was to trumpet the importance of the Arabs' shared civilization over that of their shared racial profile and common territory.

The question of where the Arab nation would exist geographically was nonetheless important. After World War I, the entire region, released from Ottoman rule, was subdivided into separate prospective states ruled by imperial mandates, but with governments like Egypt's, Jordan's, or Iraq's that looked forward to becoming fully independent.

None of these emerging states, however, could be called an Arab state in the sense that they embraced the whole Arab nation as defined by the nationalists. In their eyes none of the states was destined for permanence; sooner or later they would have to merge to form a united Arab superstate. This aspiration is known as Pan-Arabism, and Iraq in the 1930s became its leading proponent, although not under Faisal's inspired direction.

Just a year after Iraq's admittance into the League of Nations in 1932, the king died and the Iraqi throne passed to his only son, Ghazi, an enthusiastic Pan-Arabist with a passion for all things German. Ghazi was an immature king, whose inexperience on the battlefield was matched only by his political naïveté. Unlike Faisal, who had enjoyed a cosmopolitan upbringing and an Istanbul-based education, and who came to the throne bearing military scars and political wounds earned through long years of battling for what he believed in, Ghazi arrived in Iraq still wet behind the ears, having spent his childhood moving back and forth between the provincial expanses of the Hejaz and the ivory towers of Harrow, in England.

A spoiled son of privilege, the twenty-one-year-old Ghazi was more interested in sharp suits, fast cars, and casual womanizing than in managing the affairs of state. And when he did show an interest in national politics, he fancied himself an autocrat manqué, like his hero, Mussolini, who by way of acknowledging the king's fawning attentions shipped a sleek new Italian sportscar over to Iraq, pleasing Ghazi no end. If the people loved him—and they did—it was on account of his pan-Arabism, for there was little else to recommend him.

Given these handicaps, Ghazi had a hard time retaining the loyalty of those around him and he proved incapable of curbing the increasing influence of the army. Nuri as-Said and Yasin al-Hashimi, the two most powerful politicians in Iraq, briefly vied for his allegiance, but when they realized that Ghazi was not his father, they diverted their energies to concentrating power in their own rival camps and to building strategic alliances in the army. Left to his own devices, the king fell under the sway of Dr. Fritz Grobba, Hitler's ambassador to Iraq, who arrived in the country in 1932 and immediately began to intrigue behind the scenes, stoking the flames of Arab nationalism and sowing seeds of popular discontent that would weaken Britain's hold on Iraq.

An erudite Orientalist, fluent in both Turkish and Arabic, Grobba was quick to make friends in high places and establish a base of influence that gave him the necessary leverage to negotiate arms deals between Iraq and Germany in contravention of the treaty with Britain. But he had an ideological agenda, too, and after buying up the noted daily paper, *al-Alam al-Arabi,* he began serializing *Mein Kampf* in Arabic translation. Grobba could always be relied upon to find a receptive ear into which he could mutter complaints about growing Jewish influence in Baghdad—an influence that surely hindered the Arab agenda of self-determination—and he spent a good deal of energy cultivating the army officers who ranked among the fiercest nationalists in the country.

With the aid of his glamorous and sociable wife, Grobba threw regular parties at the German legation, some of which Ghazi attended as guest of honor. These parties were boisterous affairs, where champagne and beer imported from Munich flowed freely, and the Grobbas screened films such as *Deutschland Erwacht,* which vividly portrayed the strength and unanimity of the Nazi movement. They also extended their hospitality to student leaders and minor civil servants, thereby taking the lessons of national socialism directly to the centers of activism.

Rumor had it that it was Grobba who gave Ghazi the radio transmitter that the king, dazzled by a sense of his own importance, later used to broadcast seditious messages to the Kuwaitis, inciting them to revolt against their British-backed leaders and to join Iraq in building an Arab union. At one point he even ordered the army to annex Kuwait, foreshadowing actions Saddam Hussein would take in 1990. Fortunately, Ghazi was talked out of his expansionist ambitions by the army's top brass before any real damage was done. But it was clear even then that the young king was something of a firebrand when it came to nationalism, and Grobba was not the only prominent figure in Iraq to exploit this trait.

Ghazi surrounded himself with like-minded patriots who wished to do more than merely pontificate their creed from the podium. One of these was Sami Shawkat, the physician and educational ideologue who succeeded al-Husri as director general of education, and who, within a few short years, would take Arab nationalism to new extremes within the school system. A broad hint of what he intended came at the end of 1933, when, in the royal presence, Shawkat addressed students of the Central Secondary School: "Sixty years ago, Prussia used to dream of uniting the German people," he said. "What is there to prevent Iraq . . . from dreaming to unite all the Arab countries?"

For Shawkat and his comrade in arms, Muhammed Fadhil al-Jamali, who together dominated the Ministry of Education throughout the 1930s; for the members of the nationalist Muthanna Club—ostensibly a forum of ideas for Iraqi intellectuals but effectively a propaganda machine for the Arab cause; and for the bulk of senior army officers fed up with being kept out of the power loop by pro-British politicians, Ghazi was—in spite of his failings—someone who could be groomed to be the figurehead of Arab unity. And so they began their campaign. Photographs of Ghazi decked out in full military regalia were inserted into every school textbook. His life story, along with that of his father and grandfather, was taught alongside the life stories of the great Abbasid caliphs. And he was paraded before the people on every state occasion, sitting bolt upright in his uniform as he rode a white stallion through the cheering Baghdad crowds, the feather plume in his hat fluttering gently in the soft breeze. Hail Ghazi.

Even Nuri as-Said, who had so promptly abandoned the king and who was caricatured as a British stooge, rallied to the pan-Arabists' vision of a nation free and proud, united under the Hashemite crown.

Unlike Arab nationalism, which focused on a unifying culture that acknowledged no borders, Zionism was obsessed with land. And the land at issue was God's own kingdom: Palestine. From the end of the nineteenth century, European Jews had been settling in Palestine and buying property from wealthy Arab landowners, many of whom had settled abroad and were more than happy to sell. They never sus-pected that the buyers of their estates nurtured visions of building a national home for the Jews in the land of their ancestors.

By the 1920s Palestine's future hung in the balance. The region was caught between its British mandatory rulers, who, via the Balfour Declaration of 1917, had committed themselves to supporting the cre-ation of a Jewish national home in Palestine, and the territory's rela-tively powerless Arab population, who, for the most part, wanted to unite with their brothers in the north in order to create an indepen-dent Greater Syria. To the extent that the boundaries of the dispute over Palestine were at this stage merely political and not racial or reli-gious, in 1919 King Faisal was able to express his formal support of a Jewish home in a letter to Chaim Weizmann, the acknowledged leader of the Zionist movement, without rocking the boat at home. At the time Faisal believed that his support of Zionism might help further Arab nationalism's own cause, especially in the eyes of his British pro-tectors, who had invented the concept of self-determination.

But the Jewish obsession with land proved contagious, and by the beginning of the 1930s the Arabs of Palestine, now styling themselves Palestinians, were also calling for national independence: rather than become part of Syria, they had decided that they wanted a country of their own. The trouble was that both the Zionists and the Palestinians had their sights set on the same bit of land, and so their dispute be-came narrowly territorial, eventually—and inevitably—erupting into violent conflict. The romance of mutual accommodation, even as Faisal had envisaged it, which involved incorporating an autonomous Jewish enclave within the larger Arab nation, was over.

The Jews of Iraq had little time for Zionism. The Balfour Declara-tion, which stirred so much excitement in Europe, left barely a ripple on the surface of local political thought in Baghdad. Arnold Wilson, Mesopotamia's postwar high commissioner, recalled discussing the declaration with the city's Jewish leaders, who told him that for them Mesopotamia was a "national home"—a "paradise" no less—to which the Jews of Bombay, Persia, and Turkey would be glad to come. "Give us a good government and we will make this country flourish," they said.

The Iraqi Jewish experience in the Diaspora differed fundamentally from that of European Jews. For the most part the Iraqi Jews had not been victims of pogroms or state persecution. They were an educated and urbane population, long established in Iraq, and for the first time in centuries they were enjoying the advantages of greater civic freedoms. They were even being courted as fellow Semites, sons of Shem and, therefore, as brothers, by Arab nationalists who espoused an inclusive and broad-based nationalist ideology. From the Jews' integrated and patriotic perspective, Zionism looked like an upstart foreign movement, irrelevant to their everyday concerns.

Neither Regina nor Elazar nor any other member of their family had the least interest in Zionism. Before she was married, Regina had gone to see a film about Jewish pioneers in Palestine and another about the building of Jerusalem's new Hadassah Hospital. But she had not sought out the films themselves as much as an opportunity to hunker down inside Baghdad's first movie theater, which was called the National. Sinking into the deep red velvet seats with Louise next to her, a bottle of cold lemonade propped up on the armrest between them and the sound of the projector whirring in her ears, she couldn't have cared less about the images on the screen—or indeed the younger brother she was obliged to take along as chaperone. She had made a point of advertising the films' lofty subject matter to Salha beforehand, but only because otherwise her mother would never have permitted her to go.

Elazar had even less interest in the new ideology, which he regarded with some distaste as a hubristic way of thinking: after all, it was nobody's place but God's to restore Israel to the Jewish people. "Try telling that to the poor, however," he would complain to Regina, "because it only takes one provocateur, one crazed local zealot or earnest missionary from the Jewish Agency to agitate among them, and suddenly they're in a Messianic frenzy, every day hoping for their miraculous salvation and thinking that by magic the tables will be turned and the downtrodden will become overlords."

Besides, he reasoned, his merchant's mind picturing a hefty ledger book fat with credits, the Jews were doing just fine in Iraq. One had only to look along Rashid Street (the name given to New Street after independence) to see that. There were at least two pharmacies belonging to Jews there, as well as Dellal's department store, Bata shoes, the Loya brothers' American Watch Company and, most imposing of all, the Lawee Brothers building, which served as the gateway into Iraq for companies such as Chrysler and Buick. "Who would want to uproot themselves from this?" he told Regina whenever the subject of Zionism came up. "And for what? A plot of parched land on which you'd have to build everything from scratch, while hostile Arabs looked on, laughing at the stupidity of your purchase if they weren't lamenting the loss of their tenancies?"

The Jews of Iraq were doing conspicuously well. Elazar was right about that. The overwhelming majority of the Chamber of Commerce's first-class members was Jewish, which meant that they owned businesses with assets worth more than 75,000 dinars ($300,000). And thanks to British patronage, the number of Jews filling the ministries and the civil service, managing the railways and the national telegraph service, staffing the port authority at Basra and running the banks far exceeded the number of Arabs in similar positions. As Elazar saw it, only a fool would turn his back on these achievements to chase after pipe dreams of a Jewish national home.

While Elazar's views were typical of the community as a whole, they did not represent everyone. The lower classes were periodically prone to a popular Messianism that enraged him. But equally, among the educated classes, Zionism was inevitably making converts. One such convert was Aaron Sassoon, who took it upon himself to distribute the Zionist English-language weekly *Ha-'Olam* around Baghdad. By families like the Sehayeks and the Levys, men like these were considered nuisances. Indeed, Salha practically slammed the door in Sassoon's face when he turned up uninvited at her house and began lecturing her on why she should emigrate to Palestine forthwith.

In 1920 Aaron Sassoon established Iraq's first Zionist Association and dedicated it to "re-establish[ing] the ancient glory of Israel." The association had its work cut out for it, however, and in 1924 its secretary wrote to the World Zionist Organization, complaining of the "virulent antipathy of the high class" in Baghdad, who were "indifferent to national redemption" and who preferred to express their "love of the motherland . . . in prayers only." Still, with dogged optimism the Zionist Association assured the WZO that the future held more promise. "Mesopotamian Jews will not stay behind forever deaf and dumb admirers in front of the activities displayed abroad," he said.

A more accurate prediction came from Menahem Daniel, who represented the Jews in the twenty-member Iraqi Senate throughout the mandate period, and who was as pessimistic about Zionism's prospects in Iraq as Sassoon and his associates were optimistic. According to Daniel, the Zionist movement posed a serious threat to Arab national life. "It is the feeling of every Arab," he explained to the Zionist Organization in London in 1922, "that it [Zionism] is a violation of his legitimate rights, which it is his duty to denounce and fight to the best of his ability," and that "any sympathy with the Zionist Movement is nothing short of a betrayal of the Arab cause."

Daniel anticipated that Zionism would soon encounter "active resistance" among the Arabs and envisaged that the average Jew would find himself in a very "delicate situation," whereby "unless he gives proof of an unimpeachable loyalty to his country and avoids with care any action that may be misconstrued," he will be unable to "maintain himself" in the advantageous position he has been lucky enough to enjoy in Iraq.

After all the discussion and speculation, anti-Jewish feeling finally erupted in Iraq in 1928. The occasion was an official state visit by Sir Alfred Mond, a British industrialist and Zionist who was in Iraq to study the effects of using fertilizer in Iraqi agriculture. A mass demonstration was staged in Baghdad. Hundreds of Muslims took to the streets, chanting against Zionism and brandishing placards that demanded an end to British control of Palestine. The mullahs called for a minute's silence to be observed in the mosques, and the nationalist papers appeared with black borders to signify national mourning. The Jews had intended to welcome Mond to the city by holding a magnificent reception in his honor, but in the face of the protest the celebration was called off.

A year later Baghdad was again convulsed by a wave of anti-Jewish feeling, this time in direct response to events in Palestine. The inciting incident was the killing in Jerusalem of more than one hundred Arab rioters by local police and British troops. The rioters had been set upon after months of escalating violence between Arabs and Jews culminated in the massacre of 129 Orthodox Jews attempting to pray at the Western Wall. The reaction in Iraq was instant. More than one hundred thousand demonstrators gathered at Baghdad's Haiderkhannah mosque to hear prayers recited for the victims of Zionist aggression. But with so many people present, spilling out into Rashid Street, disrupting business and holding up traffic, the situation soon got out of control. Predictably, there were violent clashes with the city police. But the mob prevailed. A number of violent attacks on Jews took place, and Jewish property in and around Rashid Street was stormed. This was much more serious than the protests of 1928.

Regina heard the demonstrations from the house on Taht al-Takia and felt utterly immobilized. Bertha, just one month old, was crying. Simha, who'd been frightened by the noise, had disappeared into her room to mumble prayers, and there was no way of contacting Elazar, who was shut up in his *khan*. Regina listened to the shouts and cries, trying to determine whether the demonstrators were getting nearer, though she had no plan of action if they did end up pouring into Taht al-Takia. In this state of heightened preparedness, she practically hit the ceiling when someone started banging loudly at the front door. Without thinking, she picked up a heavy candlestick from the dining room and crept up behind the heavy door. "Who is it?" she demanded. "It's me," came the reply, "Solomon."

Regina opened the door, and there was her brother, not yet fifteen and still in short trousers, panting and sweaty from running. Solomon tumbled into the house, shut the door behind him, then fell back against it to catch his breath.

"I've just been in Rashid Street," he said, gulping air between every few words, "Father sent me out for something, but I got caught up in the riots. They're shouting, 'Down with the Jews!' and I saw people kick an old man to the ground."

Regina brought her brother a glass of water and tried to get him to sit down. But there was too much anxious energy in Solomon for sitting. Besides, he didn't want to be pampered by Regina. He had enough of that at home, with Salha calling him her "war baby" and fussing over him as if he were still a small boy. Pulling himself up to his full height, which was already greater than Ezra's, he instead put an arm around Regina's shoulders and announced, "I've come to protect you."

Regina did her best to conceal a smile. As solemnly as she could, she thanked Solomon for coming. Then she told him that even men needed refreshment. An hour later, with the demonstrators dispersing, she, Solomon, and Simha were sitting around the dining room table, tucking into an early supper, while Bertha was asleep in the next room. This is how Elazar found them when he arrived home. Later he could never remember which feeling was the greater, the rush of relief he felt to find that his family was safe or his pride in Regina for having handled the situation so capably.

Like thousands of other successful and integrated Jews, Regina and her family underestimated the strength of Iraqi feeling over the Palestine question. They misjudged where Iraqis would draw the line at embracing the country's indigenous Jews as brothers. Forced to choose between defending the rights of the country's loyal Jewish citizens or taking up the Palestinians' escalating grievances against Zionists, there was, for most Iraqis, simply no contest, and it didn't matter how much Iraqi Jews bent over backwards to repudiate the Zionist program.

From the eve of Iraqi independence onward, anti-Zionist feelings in Iraq steadily gathered steam, aided by the influx of refugees from Palestine, Syria, Lebanon, and Egypt. These refugees preached a particularly hard-line brand of Arab nationalism that was intolerant of minorities: just as the Zionists in Palestine were banishing Arabs from their land, it argued, the Arab nations ought deliberately to expel Jews and other minorities from their midst. In 1933 it became clear just how weak the position of minorities in independent Iraq really was when, with tacit approval from the prime minister and no more provocation than a skirmish along the Syrian border, the army massacred the country's Assyrian population, killing every male among them. The Assyrian Christians were settled in Iraq by the British, who employed them as Levies in the army. Their great crime, as the Iraqis saw it, was that they then had the temerity to agitate for autonomy within the country. Afterward the government claimed that the massacre represented a victory against the British, whose clients it considered the Assyrians to be: "Ghazi shook London and made it cry," was the rhetoric sung out across Baghdad.

The Assyrian massacre made a mockery of the "Declaration on the Subject of Minorities," a document that Iraq had presented to the League of Nations as part of its bid for independence. The declaration had boasted ideals of equality between Iraq's different races, creeds and linguistic groups, claiming that each was entitled to "full and complete protection of life and liberty" under Iraqi law. Now it was worthless. So, too, it appeared, was the League of Nations, which could no more enforce the high-minded promises it extracted from its member states than it could mobilize a coalition force to protect the minorities on whose rights Iraq had trespassed.

The Jews of Iraq understood the Assyrian massacre correctly: as a warning. They knew that they were protected from overt hostility and formal discrimination by a government whose official alliance with Britain prevented it from expressing any antipathy toward Zionism too loudly. Still, they had every confidence that the Iraqis would find novel ways of making them pay.

The first discriminatory provisions against Jews came into effect in 1934, making it mandatory for Jews wishing to travel abroad to "deposit" fifty dinars with the authorities. The provision infuriated Elazar, who needed to travel to Persia on a regular basis in order to buy carpets. But there was no way around it. Nor could community leaders formally protest when dozens of Jewish officials were dismissed from their jobs at the Ministry of Transport in 1935, or when strict quotas were unofficially imposed on the number of Jews admitted into higher education.

In addition all Zionist activities and publications were officially banned and the importing of Jewish papers and periodicals, even non-partisan ones, was embargoed. At Jewish schools the teaching of Hebrew was forbidden, teachers with Zionist connections were deported, and Bible study was limited to reading aloud in Arabic. With much fuss and fanfare, Aaron Sassoon, the activist who founded the Zionist Association of Baghdad in 1920, was summarily sent packing.

Jews with a mind to do so could dismiss the punitive measures taken against the community as a by-product of mounting tensions between pan-Arab nationalists in the army and in Ghazi's court, and the pro-British ruling class in government office, which was under pressure to make some concession to popular feeling by baiting the Jews. A little bloodletting, they told themselves, was a tried and tested way of satisfying any immediate thirst for vengeance. But for all their sober-minded rationalizations, they could not alter the fact that Jewish life in Iraq had begun to feel uncomfortably pinched.

In 1936 the situation in Palestine reached new crisis levels after Arab nationalist parties called a general strike. The strike lasted six months, during which time transport workers, national guard units, labor societies, shopkeepers and artisans, the Arab Chamber of Commerce, the port workers in Jaffa, and schools shut down all operations. Among the strikers' key demands—which the British authorities in Palestine had no intention of meeting—was the suspension of Jewish immigration and the prohibiting of land sales by Arabs to Jews. Midway through the strike Foreign Secretary Nuri as-Said visited Jerusalem and attempted to negotiate the peace by persuading the British to accept a suspension of Jewish immigration, in return for which the Arabs would end the strike. But the colonial secretary rejected this proposal out of hand, and Nuri's efforts collapsed.

In Iraq, this rare diplomatic failure on the part of Nuri Pasha was seen as a Zionist victory for which the Jews of Baghdad, Basra, and Mosul would have to pay. Meanwhile, in Palestine, the failure of the strike led to an all-out revolt, directed by the Mufti of Jerusalem.

There followed a rash of violent incidents against the Jews. On the eve of Rosh Hashanah 1936, two Jews were shot and killed as they were leaving their club. When the community took to the streets in protest, two more Jews were assaulted. Then, on Yom Kippur, a crudely assembled homemade bomb was thrown into a crowded Baghdad synagogue, where, as luck would have it, it failed to explode.

The street violence that week by week was claiming Jewish lives was far more disturbing to the community than any actions the government had hitherto taken against Jews. Motivated by anti-Semitism pure and simple, it was mindless, raw, and livid, and it was probably not unrelated to the fact that Said Thabit's Society for the Defense of Palestine had been distributing thousands of anti-Jewish pamphlets around the city. Thabit, a member of the Chamber of Deputies, had been voluble about his dislike of Jews ever since he denounced them at the World Islamic Conference in 1931, which he'd attended as an official Iraqi delegate. Then, he had been something of a lone voice in a climate that was generally tolerant of Jews. But by 1936 popular sentiment in the Arab world had moved to meet him and, with the encouragement of Fritz Grobba, he was making the most of his moment. The irony was that most of the two million dinars that the Society for the Defense of Palestine had collected for Palestinian strikers earlier in the year came from Iraqi Jews eager to impress their loyalty on their fellow Iraqis.

After three more Jews were murdered in October, several Jewish leaders called on the prime minister to ask for greater police protection. As a result extra detachments of police were stationed in the Jewish quarter and in all mixed quarters. At the same time, Chief Rabbi Sassoon Khedouri issued a public declaration dissociating Iraqi Jews from Zionist designs in Palestine. "The Jews of Iraq are Iraqis, bound to the people of Iraq," he said, "and they participate with their brethren, the Iraqis, in their times of prosperity and trial. They are animated by the same feelings, sympathize with the Iraqis in their difficulties and share their affections."

Throughout this difficult period most women in the Jewish community lived under a self-imposed curfew and were resigned to passing the long autumn days at home, growing increasingly jumpy. Not knowing how long the troubles would last, Regina swung into an austerity drive and began rationing supplies from the pantry, as if rehearsing for a time of coming scarcity. She also took to mending everyone's old clothes instead of sewing new ones, thereby proving to herself in however symbolic a fashion that the family could make do in adversity. Of course these activities were largely nervous in nature. Like everyone else in the community, Regina would start each time she heard raucous voices in the street. But then she would check herself, take a few deep breaths, and once again resume the role of a responsible wife and mother.

Barely a day went by, however, when she didn't beg Elazar not to go to his *khan,* even after Rabbi Khedouri made his loyalist declaration. But Elazar set out every morning regardless, determined to remain unfazed by the random targeting of individual Jews. Until one day he stayed home. The lay committee, feeling that the chief rabbi had not set the community's grievances before the authorities with sufficient force, had called an immediate strike, and Elazar had decided to participate in it. For three days in late October 1936 business in Baghdad ground to a complete halt. The streets and souks were empty, and the banks and post offices stonily silent. Most of the shops on Rashid Street were shuttered, and river traffic stalled to the point that it was possible to hear the gentle swish-swish of the water, as in days of old. Such was the economic impact of the strike that government ministers speedily called a meeting with Jewish leaders and promised to take all necessary measures to maintain the security of the Jews.

The following week another Jew was killed in Baghdad.

The week after that, Regina and Elazar were awakened at dawn by the sound of bombers in the skies over Baghdad, interspersed with intermittent blasts that lit up different corners of the city in big orange flares. Their first thought was that one of the extremist groups was taking some terrible revenge on the city's Jews. But the explosions did not appear to have struck the Jewish quarter. They peered out through the shutters, only to be confronted with a strangely beautiful sight. Set against a streak of light on the horizon that marked the dawning day were swirling clouds of what looked like confetti fluttering across the skies like a flock of swallows. Dozens of people were in the streets, trying to grab hold of the descending bits of paper, which turned out be leaflets.

Regina dispatched Elazar onto Taht al-Takia in his dressing gown to pick up one of the fallen leaflets. When he returned he announced that the airdrop came courtesy of Gen. Bakr Sidqi, who by this means informed Baghdadis that there had been a government coup. From now on the military would control Iraq.

Eight

WRITING ON
THE WALL

In the months following the coup, another crisis hit the family. It concerned Elazar's health. At the time of his marriage the *delallah* had been coy and noncommittal on the subject. She'd hinted at the presence of one or two allergies, but she'd insisted that there was nothing in the prospective groom's medical history that warranted undue concern. She had lied.

It turned out that asthma was the bane of Elazar's life. Several times each month he would find himself caught unawares, at the mercy of its paralyzing onslaughts. After all these years he was used to it. But everything about the attacks frightened Regina, from the way they burst upon her husband from nowhere to their remarkable violence, which turned him purple as he struggled for air and made his eyes bulge like a sea monster's. Sometimes Regina would come upon Elazar in this state and see him groping with one hand blindly flapping this way and that, searching for a chair into which to collapse, and she would bite her lip, attempting to banish the guilty thought that her husband, at sixty, was an old man.

Lately, Elazar's condition had worsened. He was bedridden for days at a time, his chest whistling and wheezing like a creaky concertina, his eyes glazed with the effort of concealing his pain. On a good day, however, Regina would find him dozing peacefully in a sitting position, with his reading glasses propped up on the very tip of his nose and his bed strewn with paperwork that he'd brought home from his *khan*.

One morning as she was passing his door, Elazar stirred from his rest. "Come, come," he called out to her, beckoning her with one of his long, arcing arms. Once she was near, he motioned her to sit on the edge of the bed. "I think it's time I showed you a few tricks of my trade," he said. Pushing his glasses into place, he proceeded to teach Regina how to write invoices and letters of credit, and how to fill out shipping and insurance forms and prepare bills of transaction. Regina was a fast learner. She understood that Elazar was taking the highly unusual step of grooming her to become surrogate head of the household should anything happen to him, and she wanted to show she was up to the challenge.

Gradually Regina began to assume a more forthright role in managing the family's affairs. She would visit the *khan* and make telephone calls on Elazar's behalf, to chase suppliers or reassure creditors, and every now and then she'd slip on her *abaya* and head out to the Ottoman Bank to deposit a bundle of checks in Elazar's private account. Instinct told her that she ought not to worry Elazar with her own cares. So she played down her fears about their security in the face of continued unrest in Palestine, and as best she could she kept back news about Jews being attacked in the streets of Baghdad.

The remainder of her woes she took to her old school friend Louise. Louise was herself happily married by this time, to a distant cousin who had apparently admired her from afar for many years and who had petitioned the *dellalah* to press his claim with Mr. and Mrs. Fattal. To his great joy Louise's parents had accepted him, and from that day on Freddy Shohet had walked around with a broad grin on his face, unable to quite believe his good fortune. Even now, several years and two children later, he hadn't managed to stop beaming.

Although Regina never had as much time to herself as she would have liked, she tried to see Louise at least once a month. In happier times, the two of them would fritter away an afternoon gossiping and exchanging recipes. But ever since Elazar's health had begun to deteriorate, the tenor of their meetings had changed. Their conversations ranged over everything that Regina was reluctant to confide in her husband, from her worries about attacks on Jews and the weakness of their community leaders, to matters of politics, business, and money. Regina's latest anxiety concerned the nationalist propaganda that was currently passing for history in Baghdad's schools.

"It's my own fault for snooping, I suppose," Regina told Louise, "but you wouldn't believe the books that Bertha has to read." After casually dipping into a selection of these in her elder daughter's schoolbag, Regina had been dismayed to find that one textbook after another was stuffed with hateful diatribes against the British and the Zionists, and with long tub-thumping passages that served as pan-Arab rallying cries. This discovery alone would have sent Elazar's delicate constitution into fresh seizures of agony. But when Regina quizzed Bertha, asking her to name a national hero, she had piped up not with Sa'ad al Dawla, the one-time Jewish governor of Baghdad, or even al-Samaw'al Ibn Adaya, the Jewish poet commemorated for his steadfastness to the Arab prince Imru al Qays. She had named 'Ali bin Abu Talib, the fourth rightly guided caliph of the Islamic faith, who had defeated the Jews of Medina in battle.

Bertha could recite a whole list of such heroes, conquerors of Iraq, Syria, Egypt, and Persia. Even Muhammed, it seemed, was taught less as a prophet than as the historical Muhammed, valiant founder of the Arab nation. Regina had been sufficiently piqued by the complete absence of Jewish personalities that she had paid a visit to Bertha's new history teacher, a Syrian Arab who had been imposed on the Laura Kadoorie School by the Ministry of Education. From him she learned that the history curriculum no longer included Jews. Rather, it was a narrative of military conquest stretching from Spain to China, designed to showcase the glory of the Arab nation. "Aren't you a patriot?" the teacher had had the nerve to ask her.

"Well, at least the Laura Kadoorie School isn't being canvassed by grasping representatives from the Palestine Defense League who regularly solicit money from us," said Louise.

Louise's boys attended government schools, and government schools were an entirely different proposition. Originally the idea had been that in the government schools Jews would blend in, cultural differences would melt away, and together the students would forge a shared Iraqi identity suited to the modern age. For a while this ethnic melding worked. But as soon as Palestine emerged as a divisive issue in Iraq, Jewish students in government schools felt themselves being singled out. They sat squirming as their teachers taught the class to mouth catechisms of hate against the West, and whenever someone was made to stand up and recite anti-Zionist passages from shamelessly partisan textbooks, they willed themselves into invisibility. The worst of it was that Jewish students were routinely harassed by the paramilitary youth, who, as Louise described it, swaggered around with the pompous certainty that the future belonged to them. "I can't stand all that little soldier stuff," she told Regina, "which is why we're moving the boys to another school."

The paramilitaries were a recent development, the inevitable product of a national culture that was in thrall to militarism. Even before the army emerged as a political force in Baghdad, militarism had been heavily promoted within the school system by educators convinced that the inculcation of discipline was the perfect complement to al-Husri's triumphalist curriculum. Before he died Faisal had set the ball rolling by introducing military education directly into schools. Then, between 1932 and 1936, the Ministry of Education joined forces with the Ministry of Defense to run a cooperative program aimed at further honing the military skills of Iraqi youth, and army officers were brought into schools to teach marksmanship, horsemanship, and military history.

There were rumors afoot that the Germans, who quietly encouraged the militarization of the student body, were subsidizing much of this training. In 1937, at the invitation of Fritz Grobba, Hitler Youth leader Baldur von Schirach visited Baghdad with eight of his staff. He had tea with King Ghazi, toured a number of selected schools, and invited a group of students receiving military training to attend the 1938

Nuremberg rally. The visit would be a great success, for the delegation would return to Iraq as enthusiastic Nazi supporters.

Still, the prime movers behind the militarization of Iraqi youth were home grown. Sami Shawkat and Muhammed Fadhil al-Jamali, fanatical statists both, used their position at the Ministry of Education to sanction the formation of a formal paramilitary movement within the school system. Named the Futuwwah, after a medieval society originally formed to unite people around a rejuvenated Abbasid caliphate, this paramilitary movement provided students with the opportunity to act out what the schools had been preaching all along: namely, that the nation's youth represented all the heroic qualities of the Arab people and that as embodiments of the nationalist ideal they would restore the glory of the past.

British observers on the ground in Iraq at the time were alarmed by the Futuwwah, whose student members were called out on parade at every government inauguration, royal birthday, military anniversary, and high holy day on the nationalist calendar. Freya Stark observed that many Iraqi parents were saddened and wearied by the sight of their sons marching on all occasions, "dressed out in uniforms" and "provided with ready-made battle cries and sham enthusiasms." And Harry Sinderson, personal physician first to Faisal and then Ghazi, sneered at the black-shirted youth brigade that allowed Sami Shawkat to act out the role of *Il Duce* and whose motto was "Be Tough, Luxury Stifles Virtue."

Whenever Elazar Levy saw the Futuwwah marching in the streets, he'd clap a hand to his chest, waiting for the asthma to come.

Militarism may have given Iraqi youth discipline and direction, but it did not stabilize Iraqi politics. There were seven *coups d'états* in Iraq in the five years from 1936 to 1941, beginning with the one that brought the unlikely pairing of Bakr Sidqi and reformist politician Hikmat Suleiman to power and ending with the fateful reign of Rashid Ali al-Gaylani, fronting for four pro-German colonels collectively known as the Golden Square. Beyond the constant changing of regimes, what most disturbed Regina about the new militarism was that the army remained the focus of national unity, irrespective of who was in power. Militarism, in other words, had somehow gotten into the bones of the nation.

The army's rapid rise to power began in 1933 after Bakr Sidqi led Iraqi troops to victory against the Assyrians, and became a national hero. A year later the government introduced conscription, and by 1936 the army's size had doubled to 23,000, with the military sucking up more graduates than the teaching profession. This growth was a boon to Sidqi, who began to see the army's role as that of filling the political void created by the death of Faisal and the accession of a weak king. Ghazi, of course, was close to the army, and even politicians had begun courting the officer classes. With this feeling of military indispensability in the air, Bakr Sidqi came to believe that he had a popular mandate, and so he simply seized his chance.

But Sidqi was an anomaly in the army movement. A Kurd rather than an Arab and a much-decorated military elder, he was viewed by the younger generation of upcoming leaders as yesterday's man. This new generation of army officers, which included Colonel Saleh al-Din al-Sabbagh, ringleader of the Golden Square, were also products of the Ottoman military system. But they had come to Istanbul late, after Arab nationalism had taken hold among the officer corps. When they returned to Iraq they were reluctant to acquiesce in British control of the army, and they fought the Anglo-Iraqi Treaty of Alliance to the bitter end. The crisis in Palestine only sharpened their anti-British and pan-Arab sensibilities, so that by time they became a presence on the Iraqi stage, they were loudly calling for the liberation of Syria and Palestine and the overthrow of colonial rule in Arab lands. Because of their impeccable nationalist credentials, they were lionized alongside Ghazi by the army's pro-German rank and file and by the paramilitary youth, and after they ordered the assassination of Bakr Sidqi in 1937, they dominated Iraqi politics. Even a politician as skilled as Nuri as-Said found it impossible to operate without their support.

As soon as it became clear that Bakr Sidqi's star was fading and that a pan-Arab agenda would from now on be dictating domestic affairs, things began to look even bleaker for Iraq's Jews. Just weeks before

Sidqi was assassinated, opposition elements staged a mass demonstration during which two Jewish onlookers were set upon and killed. Then, when the new government professed a renewed commitment to Palestine—thus keeping its military backers happy—attacks on Baghdad's Jewish population intensified, culminating in 1938 in a series of bomb attacks on several Jewish clubs.

This new spate of violence drew loud, defensive declamations from the Jewish community. Thirty-three Jewish dignitaries sent a joint telegram to the British colonial secretary and the League of Nations reiterating the community's opposition to Zionism and pledging its loyalty to Iraq, while the community's more articulate spokesmen got to work once again on the press.

Speaking for the younger generation of Baghdadi Jews, one Ya'qub Balboul penned an article claiming that Iraqi Jews were among the most fervent supporters of the pan-Arab idea. For good measure he added that "a Jewish youth in the Arab countries expects nothing from Zionism except colonialism and domination." But it was left to the renowned lawyer Yusuf Elkabir—a cousin of Elazar's—to deliver the biting critique that the community leaders felt Zionism deserved. In a letter to the English-language newspaper the *Iraq Times*, Elkabir dismissed the Zionist movement as European through and through. Then he hacked apart its philosophical foundations, claiming they were based on a spurious territorial argument that demanded Palestine as a homeland for the Jews simply because it had been their homeland some two thousand years before. As Elkabir saw it: "Reconstructions of historical geography, if accepted as practical theory," were "patently absurd." For if their legal basis was accepted, then we would "presently have the world ruled by militant archaeology."

Beyond the rarefied intellectual circles where reasoned argument might have found an appreciative ear, Elkabir's letter had little impact: in the popular mind, and especially among the junior officers and the Futuwwah, Judaism and Zionism were one. In her less certain moments Regina felt that it was only out of respect for the nation's leading politicians that the army colonels were kept from authorizing out-and-out war on the nation's Jewish population, thinking that if they couldn't vindicate the Palestinians abroad, they could at least avenge them on home ground.

The year 1939 was an ominous one, whose dark forebodings seemed to begin with the sudden death of Ghazi in April. Apparently the king had been carousing with friends at the royal palace, drinking heavily into the early hours of the morning and pontificating on Middle Eastern affairs, when he was seized by a sudden whim to take his friends for a spin in one of his many prized sports cars. To the consternation of these reluctant companions, the inebriated king began speeding across the palace grounds until he lost control and smashed into an electricity pylon. The impact uprooted the pylon from the ground along with its concrete standard, and both of them crashed back into the car. The heavy standard fell squarely on Ghazi's head, crushing his skull. His doctors could do nothing for him.

The next day there was pandemonium, as rumors flew around town attributing Ghazi's death to British machinations. At an impromptu demonstration in Mosul, the British consul was midway through delivering a public speech about the great loss to the nation occasioned by Ghazi's death when he was pounced on by the bloodthirsty crowd. "They behave just like savages," said Elazar after perusing reports of the incident in the paper, half expecting to read that Baghdad's Jews had, along with the British, been implicated in some dastardly plot to kill the king. Relieved to discover that they were not, he delivered his final judgment: "They belong in a zoo."

The week following Ghazi's death had been declared one of national mourning, and so everyone was at home. The schools were shut, the souks closed, and the *khans* deserted. Regina struggled to maintain order, but with Bertha and Marcelle, then aged seven and four, tearing about the place from dawn until dusk, she ended up expending most of her energies scolding them. She didn't want the girls disturbing their elderly grandmother or their father, who was sick much of the time these days, the victim of a mysterious goutlike malady that made his legs swell painfully. And so she hired an *arabana* and whisked them off to visit Salha and Ezra, who had recently bought a house in Bataween, a largely Jewish suburb to the south of the Old City that had been built by the British in the mandate years. Salha had been nagging Ezra to move there for years, complaining about the narrowness of the streets in the old *mahallah*, its overcrowding, its stifling air, until finally he relented and Salha gleefully took possession of the kind of modern European villa she had dreamed of owning ever since the British arrived in Baghdad.

Like the classic Baghdad house, the Sehayeks' large brick villa was built on two stories, but it had no courtyard, and so every room appeared to be joined to every other, which Regina found disconcerting. Worse still, it trapped the heat, turning all the rooms into ovens. Ordinarily there would have been shutters to create shade, but because Salha had installed steel-framed windows, imported especially from England, the whole family was suffering. The house, which Regina would soon come to know better than she might have liked, was nonetheless a lively, bustling place. As well as being home to her parents, it was where Nessim and his new wife also resided; where Solomon, now twenty-three, hung his hat, and where Regina's little sister, Marcelle, waited out her years until marriage. Her other sister, Josephine, had recently married and moved with her husband to Calcutta.

Regina was pleased to find Salha on form, bossing everybody around, clucking mother-henishly, and gossiping about the Jewish refugees newly arrived in Baghdad from Germany—one of them, a doctor, taking a job at the Meir Elias hospital, and another opening a chocolate factory, of all things. Unfortunately Salha could not return the compliment. "You look exhausted," she told her daughter. This, Regina recognized, was a question. But the most she was willing to confide to her mother was that she had been spending a lot of time helping out Elazar at work. He had been overdoing things lately, she explained, and had worn himself out working on the logistics of hiring a ship to transport to England one of the biggest orders his company had ever received. First he had been under pressure to fulfill his end of the bargain, obtaining sufficient quantities of leather, rubber, and tea for the shipment from India. Then he'd been deluged with paperwork. Finally, with the mechanics of the transaction complete, he had settled down to fretting about whether the ship and the massive investment it carried would safely reach Dover, especially given the fervid speculation about the inevitability of war that was on the lips of merchants from Basra to Manchester. The strain had taken its toll on them both.

When war finally began later that year, the Jewish community, like everyone else in Baghdad, wondered whether Iraq would renege on its treaty obligations to Britain and side openly with the Axis powers. The army was resolutely pro-German from top to bottom, and popular sentiment, stirred by radio broadcasts in Arabic beamed directly into Iraq from Berlin, was broadly sympathetic to the Axis cause. On top of this, it was widely known that many of the most powerful people in Iraq had been making covert approaches to the Germans through Fritz Grobba. Chief among these was Haj Amin al-Husseini, the Mufti of Jerusalem, who arrived in Baghdad in 1939 after leading the Palestinian revolt from his exile in Syria. The Mufti was a dominating personality, charming, eloquent, and with mischievous twinkling blue eyes. He hated the British and was devoted to the pan-Arab cause, and as soon as he established himself in Baghdad, he began building a power base there, negotiating with the Germans to deliver arms to Iraq.

But Iraq did not declare itself for Germany. Thanks to the efforts of Nuri as-Said. Nuri, prime minister throughout 1939, was a statesman of unusual skill, someone who understood that politics was about working within the limits of the possible. Yet he never played his hand more astutely than he did at this time, resolving to honor Iraq's treaty with Britain while managing to keep the rabidly anti-British Golden Square colonels in line.

Slight in build and nervous in disposition, Nuri didn't look the part of an elder statesman, and he traveled everywhere with a posse of burly bodyguards who were not above intimidating his opponents with physical threats. But he was clever and quick and he knew that the British were sufficiently worried by Iraq's swing toward Germany to be politically pliable. Thus, Nuri was able to condition Iraq's role in the war on Britain's Palestine policy, nudging the British government into publishing its infamous White Paper of 1939, in which Britain officially turned its back on the Balfour Declaration and proposed to support the creation of an independent Palestinian state within ten years. For this concession Britain won Nuri's backing in the war, while Nuri established his pan-Arab credentials in the eyes of the army.

Wasting no time, Nuri immediately deported Fritz Grobba and other Axis operatives from Iraq. But dealing with the Mufti and his court of Nazi sympathizers was another matter. Indeed, one might say that as far as Iraq was concerned the war was ultimately about who would win the power struggle at home, Nuri as-Said or Haj Amin al-Husseini.

For Elazar and Regina, war came at exactly the wrong time. Elazar's ship arrived in Dover as intended, but with hostilities about to commence, his British clients refused to a man to pay for the goods they had ordered. Elazar endeavored to negotiate with them, offering them knockdown prices that cut deep into his profits, and stretching his own finances to breaking point in order to extend them further credit. But he was firing his telegrams into the void. In the meantime he was paying rent on the ship, the salaries of the crew, port duties, and berthing fees. Unable to see a way out of further loss, he instructed the crew to dump his precious cargo into the sea, and with that dramatic gesture he lost everything. Before the year was out Elazar and Regina had no choice but to sell their home in the Jewish quarter and move their entire family—including a baby boy, Haron, born eighteen months earlier—in with Salha.

In 1940 Nuri slipped up. Too caught up in his own desire to declare war on Italy, he miscalculated the political temperature within the army and thus the formidable Golden Square colonels were able to force his resignation and propel into power in his place the more malleable Rashid Ali, whose stance toward Italy was determinedly neutral. Over the coming months, the reins of government passed back and forth between Rashid Ali, scion of a hugely respected Sunni dynasty, and the army's commander in chief, Taha al-Hashemi. However, it was clear that the real power behind the throne, as it were, was the Mufti.

Since making Baghdad his base in 1939, the Mufti had rapidly risen to a position of unrivaled power and could count both the Golden Square colonels and the Iraqi movers behind the Muthanna Club and the Palestine Defense League among his closest allies. The government likewise bent over backward to please him, inviting him to state functions as guest of honor and lavishing him with grants, including a stipend drawn from the salaries of government officials, which nicely boosted the funding he was already receiving from Italy, Germany, Saudi Arabia, and Egypt. Because of his priestly standing and his fanatical opposition to the creation of a Jewish home in Palestine, the Mufti commanded tremendous popular support. But it was government he had his eye on.

By the end of 1940 the Mufti had effectively set up his own minigovernment in Iraq and placed numerous Palestinians in the Iraqi bureaucracy. He was greatly feared. It was said that he controlled hirings and firings in government departments and that he decided what went in and what stayed out of the newspapers. It was also believed that he had Hitler's ear, since he had written to the Führer pledging his loyalty to the Axis powers in return for diplomatic recognition and material support for the pan-Arab cause. Because Prince Regent Abd al-Ilah, who held the throne in trust for Ghazi's five-year-old son, Faisal, was seen as pro-British, the Mufti was touted as Ghazi's natural successor as leader of the pan-Arab movement.

In 1941, when France had capitulated and the whole of Europe lay in German hands, Middle Eastern leaders were anxiously asking themselves whether they had perhaps backed the losers. Nowhere was there more handwringing than in Iraq, where Britain's staunchest supporters Nuri as-Said and Abd al-Ilah were all but marginalized. And if they could be sidelined, why not Britain itself? In the mind of the Mufti this was not an unreasonable proposition, and so the plot was hatched to bring British influence in Iraq to a definitive end. The schemers, who included the Golden Square colonels and a handful of other key pan-Arab figures, convened at the Mufti's home. There they swore on the Koran to give no more concessions to Britain, to expel leading pro-British politicians, and to maintain diplomatic relations with Italy. Within just weeks they deposed an uncomplying Taha al-Hashemi and returned the more pliable Rashid Ali to power as their spokesman.

As soon as the rebel government seized power, the regent and his supporters, led by Nuri as-Said, fled Baghdad—and not a moment too soon, since it emerged that rebel agents had searched the royal palace with four doctors in tow and a certificate of death by heart failure already written out. But plotting to kill the regent was the least of the rebels precipitous follies. On April 29, 1941, after falling out with the British over the question of whether or not they had the right to land troops in the country, the rebels ordered Iraqi troops to surround the British air base at Habbaniya and to besiege the British Embassy in Baghdad. In no uncertain terms, this was war.

The fighting that followed lasted only a month, but Baghdad was completely transformed by it. There was a total blackout in the city. Schools were closed, businesses shut, and banks ordered not to pay out any money. The rebels took over the post office and the telephone exchange. At the same time, Baghdad radio blared out martial music all day long in support of the country's heroic forces, and the papers ran articles mocking Britain's imperial might while trumpeting Iraqi victories in the field. Allied broadcasts that might have painted the situation in rather different colors, were jammed. And to crown it all, the Mufti declared a jihad.

Throughout the month of fighting, the Jews were harassed by pro-Nazi elements mobilized by the rebel government. They had to contend with swastikas being crudely daubed all over the Jewish quarter and with direct intimidation by the Futuwwah, whose members brought rather too much enthusiasm to their new role of policing Baghdad. In fact, because the Jews were widely regarded as clients of the British, their position was doubly sensitive. And since actual British people—safely locked up at the British Embassy—were unavailable targets, the Jews served as punching bags in their stead.

In the Sehayek household the mood was initially defiant. Solomon, who had recently started working at the Ottoman Bank, returned home each evening with new stories about Jews who were taking steps to defend themselves. Many Jews, he said, had lined their front doors with sheets of iron or fitted them with bars, and a few people boasted of wiring their premises so that any attacker would instantly be electrocuted. Though he made no mention of it to the family, he had himself resolved to buy a pistol. Nessim, too, made it his business to gather information through the grapevine provided by the coffee-houses. There, several of his Muslim friends, including a sheikh from Diwaniya, offered to help protect him in the event of an attack.

The family's fighting spirit was sapped, however, when it became known that the rebels had applied to Germany to send in an expert at detecting "fifth column" infiltration. The idea was to root out British sympathizers who might be acting as spies, but all too often the finger of suspicion pointed directly to the Jews. Hardly a day passed without some Jew or other being hauled up by the police and accused of signaling to British planes flying overhead, usually on the flimsiest basis. One woman, who by virtue of allowing a glinting silver button to peep through her *abaya,* was detained for signaling to the enemy; another man was charged with concealing a transmitter in his violin case. A few days later the government began announcing over the radio that as soon as Iraq defeated the British it would settle its score with the "internal enemy."

The revenge commenced promptly. On May 6, 1941, a mob armed with knives and cudgels stormed the Meir Elias hospital looking for British agents who had reportedly based themselves there in order to signal to enemy bombers. The vigilantes attacked patients and staff, shooting indiscriminately. They looted hospital buildings and set fire to furniture and medical stores. Within minutes the scene resembled a battlefield: the pharmacist had been shot dead, the hospital accountant gravely wounded, and terrified shrieks rang out from the ransacked wards. Although the police were quickly called in to arrest the rioting mob and restore peace, it was too late for the Jews. They understood their own vulnerability, electrified doors notwithstanding. All they could do now was pull together, strengthening their resolve through unity. To this end the community opened its doors to those patients who had nowhere to go or who were otherwise too weak and shocked by the attack to look after themselves.

Over the next couple of weeks people were too scared to leave their homes. They glued themselves to the radio, hoping to sift grains of truth from the chaff of propaganda, and prayed that their policy of lying low might avert attack. Out in the streets, chaos reigned. Scattergun shooting from anti-aircraft guns on nearby rooftops could be heard all day long, "crackling like thorns under a pot." After curfew fell families resigned themselves to the nightlong onslaught of British bombers attempting to take out military bases and munitions stores on the outskirts of the city. The fate of the Jews seemed to hang by a thread.

Then, when things looked to be at their darkest, a ray of light emerged from an unlikely quarter. A number of Jewish men, who had been ordered to operate a storehouse from the Shamash School for the purpose of stocking supplies for the Iraqi army, began circulating reports that the British had forced the army to retreat from Habbaniya to Fallujah, and that the demoralized Iraqi forces had finally established a front line only miles from the city. This they heard firsthand from the officers who had commandeered the school and who were now busy organizing the defense of Baghdad. From these men the Jews also learned that the Kurdish army in the north had refused to support the rebels and that the Shia tribes in the south were equally reluctant to throw their lot in with Rashid Ali. In the absence of much-needed military backup, the officers were now scrambling to cobble together a civilian defense force by mobilizing workers, students, and the Futuwwah for a valiant last stand—valiant, because it was clear that the war was already lost.

As word of the Iraqi retreat spread, the Jews started wondering if they might allow themselves to believe that relief was at hand. Trapped in their houses for weeks, they were running low on rations and morale, and with nothing but disinformation on the radio, they felt cut off from reality. Then, on May 29, exactly one month after the war began, news came that the British had reached the outskirts of the city and were waiting for word from London about how to proceed. More joyous still were reports that the Golden Square colonels had fled Baghdad, followed by the Mufti and Rashid Ali: too cowardly to face the music, the rebels had sought refuge in Iran. Nuri must have chuckled to himself as he waited from the safety of Amman for the coup to exhaust itself. He had defeated the Mufti without lifting so much as a finger. The obliging British had done his work for him.

Regina, too, was celebrating. "Good riddance," she'd said, when she heard of the Mufti's flight. Every Passover for years to come Regina would curse him by name as red wine representing the spilled blood of Jews was ceremoniously poured into a plastic cup and then coldly discarded. Passover is a feast of remembrance, of good things and of bad, and as long as I knew my grandmother, the name of Haj Amin al-Husseini headed her personal roll call of history's villains.

On May 30 there were British planes overhead, leading Jews and Muslims alike to conclude that a far stronger force was camped beyond the city limits than was actually there. In actuality, the troops that had crossed the desert from Palestine, relieved their comrades at Habbaniya, seized Fallujah, and then dispatched a mobile column to motor its way to Baghdad—all in the space of a month—were a ragtag bunch, consisting of British soldiers from the Household Cavalry Regiment, a battalion of the Essex Regiment, three squadrons of the Transjordan Frontier Force, and the fearsome Bedouin warriors of John Bagot Glubb's Arab Legion. In all, the mobile column was scarcely thirteen hundred strong and far weaker in equipment and resources than the opposing Iraqi units. However, the relative disadvantages of the British were of little consequence to the Iraqis, who were only too willing to negotiate an armistice.

Tired, hungry, and disillusioned, abandoned by the colonels who had lured them astray with sweet promises of self-rule, and as good as betrayed by the Germans, the rebel forces hadn't the heart to fight the British. In the end they more or less surrendered to them. Thus, when the mayor of Baghdad, acting for the hastily formed loyalist body known as the Committee for Internal Security, put his signature to the armistice, the defeated forces were simply broken up and allowed to straggle back to the city in small groups.

With the armistice signed and the specter of Axis rule disappearing in a puff of smoke, the Jews felt they could at last breathe more easily, and they began preparing to celebrate the feast of Pentecost, which spanned the weekend of May 31 and June 1. Tentatively they started to emerge from their homes and hunt for provisions. The synagogue was opened, prayers were offered, and the middle classes embarked on a curtailed round of visits, each family congratulating the next on their happy deliverance.

The Levys and Sehayeks chose to celebrate at home now that most of the family resided under one roof. Salha and Regina pooled whatever food was left in the pantry and somehow produced a feast. Salha had even managed to save a chicken for the occasion, which she rubbed with spices and placed in the *tannour* on Friday so that it would be tender and juicy on the Sabbath. Elazar magicked a bottle of arak from somewhere and the family sat down together to toast the future. "After all," quipped Elazar, "it could hardly be worse than the past."

On Sunday the Jews grew a little bolder, and many of them went out to inhale some fresh air. A few intrepid souls decided to venture across the Tigris to the west bank of the city, where festivities were being held to welcome home the regent and his entourage. Because the day happened to be a Jewish holiday, these Jews were all dressed up in fine suits and hats, which, as details go, ought to have been incidental. However, this small matter of dress was misconstrued by the Muslim populace, who assumed that the Jews were celebrating the nation's defeat at the hands of the hated British. A few Muslim youths began to throw stones at the Jewish celebrants. But trouble began in earnest when a number of Jewish men returning home that afternoon were accosted by a band of demobilized soldiers on the Khurr Bridge. The soldiers flew at them with fists and knives, kicking them to the ground and pummeling them with their boots in a frenzied release of pent-up frustration. Then they ran off, leaving one Jew dead and another sixteen injured.

Soon after, other attacks took place, this time in Jewish areas. One body was found lying in the road, near the movie theater on Ghazi Street. Eight more were found in the poor Abu Sifayn area, while at Bab al-Sheikh, a group of enraged students began dragging Jews off a bus and beating them to death on the street. As dusk fell acts of pillage and murder spread, forcing the Jews, who had so recently come out of hiding, to run straight home and lock their doors. Returning soldiers, Futuwwah members, and youths from other paramilitary brigades perpetrated the bulk of the violence, but the temptation of loot soon led hordes of tribesmen to join the rioters, who now fell hungrily upon the Jewish quarter in huge numbers. A few Jews who anticipated trouble had prepared a crude defense and stood on their rooftops hurling large stones, pitch, and boiling oil at the rioters. But they were vastly outnumbered and quickly forced to flee for their lives by leaping from one rooftop to the next.

In Bataween, cries of horror and suffering could be heard throughout the night, drifting up from the old *mahallah*, where women were being raped, babies crushed, children mutilated. In this free-for-all slaughter, Jews old and young were killed. Some were shot and some stabbed. Houses big and small were broken into and plundered. One story held that after refusing to surrender his savings, an elderly man was dragged into his bathroom by his hair, and there, on the cold tiled floor, he had his throat slit from one side to the other like a goat's.

Bertha was only twelve at the time, but she remembers being awakened by Regina in the middle of the night and hastily bundled down the stairs into the cellar. The family huddled together there, having no idea whether the rioters would eventually reach them. All night long they could hear gunfire cracking intermittently, along with discordant cries and screams emanating from the Jewish quarter. The family maintained its vigil until the light of dawn pierced through the tiny barred windows of their underground hideout and the streets were finally silent. "Hello, hello" they heard a voice calling from outside, and everyone jumped. It was their neighbor Sion Koubi, checking to see if the family was all right.

Later that day, when it became clear that the rioting had resumed and that still neither the Committee for Internal Security nor the police nor the British had taken any disciplinary action, Sion Koubi persuaded the Levys and Sehayeks to take refuge in his house. He had a pistol, he said, and he knew how to use it. I have always found the scene that followed difficult to picture in that Elazar was ill, his mother, Simha, old and frail, and Salha and Ezra no longer young. Nonetheless, one by one, with the younger family members helping the older ones, they climbed over the back wall joining the two houses, using dining tables and chairs that Solomon and Nessim had gerry-rigged into a ladderlike prop. Fortunately no one was hurt in this crazy maneuver, nor did the rioters ever come, even if it wasn't until evening that the governor of the *liwa* of Baghdad finally asked the regent for permission to fire on the mob.

A mere hour after this permission was granted, the streets were eerily quiet, and except for members of the security forces patrolling the city on foot and picking through loot that the rioters had left behind, they were empty. Then began the onerous task of taking stock of the deaths and injuries. Although estimates vary, it is generally believed that around two hundred Jews died in the riots and several hundred more were wounded. Even more Muslims lost their lives, mainly rioters, but also security men and dozens of kind souls who came to the defense of their Jewish friends and neighbors.

As for the looting, much damage was done. Freya Stark, from her besieged position at the British Embassy, watched incredulously as crowds of opportunists poured eastward over the bridges empty-handed and returned hours later weighed down with goods of every sort.

The British doctor who had attended Ghazi's death was also among the victims. His house had been ransacked. Refrigerators, sofas, and garden furniture had been loaded onto trucks by soldiers. His safe was blown open and jewelry and cash were missing; cupboards were smashed in and their contents carried off; and the floor was littered with papers, letters, bottles, broken glass, and china. No curtain, no carpet, no movable item of any kind was to be seen. Even the bathroom and lavatory fittings had been plundered.

The massacre was given the name *farhud* by the Jews, the word connoting a total breakdown of order, and it changed forever their attitude to Iraq. It gave them a renewed sense of their common Jewish identity and cured most of them of the illusion that Iraq was a country to which they could truly belong. No one had come to their aid—not the army, not the police, not the hurriedly formed Committee for Internal Security that had done so much else to restore calm after the fall of Rashid Ali.

Most important, the Jews felt let down by the British. To their lasting discredit, at least in Jewish eyes, the British had made the cold political calculation that it is sometimes necessary to placate one's enemy rather than to help one's friends. In this case they decided that it was vitally important for Iraq's future stability that the regent be seen to reenter the country in triumph and not behind British bayonets. And so they obeyed orders from London not to enter Baghdad and to let the regent restore peace in his own time.

As far as the Jews were concerned, the British were no longer their protectors. From now on they could keep their guarantees of personal safety, their fine speeches about guarding life, liberty, and property, and their overvalued patronage to themselves: the Jews wanted nothing more to do with them.

Nine

BROTHERS

It came from nowhere. One moment Elazar was sitting contentedly in a large armchair in the living room, reading the paper, his bare feet propped up on an ottoman, and his embroidered leather slippers paired neatly to one side of it. The next he was gasping for air and thumping his uncooperative chest with his fist.

Very quickly it became clear to Regina that this was a serious attack. Elazar's asthma had been of secondary concern lately, eclipsed by the constant pain in his swollen legs. Ever since the British marched back into Baghdad in the summer of 1941 he'd barely been able to walk without assistance. Confined to his bed for weeks at a time, he was grumpy and miserable, convinced that the doctors called in to treat him were all charlatans. But this particular morning in April 1942 had the beginnings of a good day. He'd managed to get up and breakfast with the family and then instead of returning to his room he'd decided to sit and read. That was when the asthma struck.

The attack sent the entire household into convulsions of its own. Even though at some unspoken level it had always been understood that such a moment would one day come, the Sehayeks were taken aback by the suddenness of its arrival, the sheer audacity of it, and were thrown into flustered confusion. Amid a great deal of shouting and wailing, Solomon ran off to alert the doctor. But he was too late. Elazar continued to cough and splutter and choke. His skin turned a vivid bluish purple, his tongue lolled outside his mouth, and his eyes rolled in his head. Far beyond the reach of those who loved him, he breathed his last torturous breath just ten minutes after the attack began. He was sixty-seven years old.

My mother, Marcelle, was only ten. All she remembers of the day was that Solomon collected her from school in his new car midway through the school day and explained what had happened to her father as she sat on the backseat inhaling the smell of new leather. The rest of the day's events have been erased, except for one thing: by the time they got home Elazar's body was already gone. Apparently Ezra had taken matters in hand, making all the necessary arrangements, calling the undertaker, and notifying the local rabbi. While his prompt actions spared Regina a complete breakdown, they would not be remembered with much gratitude by my mother, who wished she could have seen her father one more time. As it was, their last encounter was almost painful in its ordinariness. He'd asked her to get him a glass of water before she left for school that morning. *"Arousa, arousa,"* he had murmured in thanks. *Arousa* meant "bride."

Regina's memories were even more disjointed. She remembered that the morning Elazar suffered his fatal attack had been sunny but cold, and that he had eaten flatbread, boiled eggs, and mango pickle for breakfast. She also remembered the onset of her own panic, which had come upon her like a cold sweat and rendered her completely numb. Reduced to blurry shapes, people had moved in and out of her field of vision. Their voices, yelling instructions—"Don't lay him down," "Let him stand up if he wants to"—had echoed pointlessly in her ears. Disoriented, her throat dry, she felt herself float dreamily away from the action, only to be yanked back to earth minutes later with a sudden thud. It was 10:37 a.m. At that moment Elazar passed from this world to the next and Regina's life lurched into a blind left turn. From that minute—that second—onward her future was a blank.

Jewish funerals are speedy affairs. Within twenty-four hours of dying a person will be buried and gone, the ground poured over them and their personal effects hurriedly tidied away. However, the difficult work of remembrance lasts seven days, from morning until night, without break: seven long days filled with sorrow and pain and prayer. When Elazar died his family flung open its doors to the community, and on each of the seven nights of mourning the house was thronged with a large crowd dressed in black, the men rocking on their heels and murmuring softly as they echoed the rabbi's singsong prayers, while the women consoled one another and nibbled on little hard biscuits as desiccated as a widow's lot was presumed to be.

Regina, Elazar's sisters, and other members of the immediate family, who were recognizable from their unshaved faces and their torn clothes, crudely ripped to symbolize the rent in their hearts, sat quietly on the sidelines while the community did its best to fill the immediate void. Regina went through the motions convincingly enough, greeting visitors and thanking them for coming. But the light inside her had been extinguished.

Elazar's seven days were the second time that Regina had been in mourning in the space of a year. The first time was for her mother-in-law, who passed away in July 1941, according to family lore because she couldn't survive the shock of the *farhud*. In the nine intervening months between Simha Levy's death and Elazar's, Regina found herself in step with the Jewish community as it emerged from a period of communal mourning, when it buried its dead, cared for its wounded and dispossessed, and then picked itself up in order to move on.

In the days immediately following the *farhud* of June 1941, the sad and ramshackle sight of Rashid Street seemed to symbolize the violence done to the Jews. Its shops had been vandalized and looted, and broken glass was strewn all over the street. Bricks, blackjacks, and other crude weapons had also been left behind, some of them covered with dried blood. Wooden shutters, half-ripped from their hinges, slapped against violated storefronts, giving Baghdad's prime commercial thoroughfare the air of a ghost town. It was several weeks before anybody opened for business.

The community had been in equal disarray. Hundreds of distraught survivors wandered the streets, searching for missing family members, and returning to their homes to find them ransacked and deliberately flooded. The city's hospitals were filled with the injured. The rebels' storehouse, raided for flour, dates, and oranges, could not yield enough to feed the hungry. And the chief rabbi did not move from his house for eight days while lines of wounded people lined up to petition him for help.

Once they had attended to their immediate, material problems, the Jews began picking over what had happened, searching for some signal moment or action that might explain how and why events overtook them. Would the pogrom have been averted, they asked themselves, had they not gone out to welcome the regent? Could they have put up a better resistance and saved dozens of lives if they had managed a more organized defense? And if the British had returned the regent to Baghdad with a show of airplanes and firepower, as many had hoped, might not the mob have aborted its vengeful plans?

Those who were old enough to remember reminded their fellow Jews that in 1917 the British had marched into Baghdad and fired at whatever resistance they encountered, rapidly establishing both peace and the rule of law. "Those were the days," Ezra told his sons. But everything was different now. Unlike in 1917, the British in 1941 were resoundingly inactive. "Now they want the power," Ezra lamented, "but without the responsibility."

Solomon and Nessim were less inclined toward soul-searching than Ezra's generation. They were angry.

"Did you hear that on the night of June first, just as the Futuwwah was poring into the Jewish quarter, the regent was enjoying a candlelit dinner at the British Embassy? Apparently he played bridge with the British officers," said Solomon.

On this matter Nessim, who much like the chief rabbi himself too often made excuses for the government, was in firm agreement with Solomon. "The Iraqi elite and the British are equally to blame. They chose to look the other way because it suited them to let the mob vent its frustrations on the Jews," he said.

This idea seemed preposterous at first. However, the mayor of Baghdad as good as confirmed it when a delegation of disgruntled Jews peppered him with questions about the lack of policing. He eventually admitted that he'd been restrained by higher powers from acting against the rioters. Fearing repercussions by a contrite administration, the mayor had moaned, "and it will all come down on my head."

There were no repercussions.

Jamil Madfai, whom the regent appointed prime minister on June 2, 1941, proved to be as feckless as the mayor. Although he created a commission to investigate the causes of the *farhud*, he did little to push through its disciplinary recommendations. He offered the Jews only 70,000 dinars ($200,000) in compensation for losses estimated at one and a half million. He also failed to dismantle Iraq's network of pro-Axis officers and officials, who had supported Rashid Ali. To his credit, Midfai did expel the Italian legation, and he repatriated a number of Syrian and Palestinian teachers who had used the schools to sow seeds of pan-Arab discontent. But it took Nuri as-Said's strong-arm tactics to prevail over pro-German elements both within the government and without. Taking office in October, Nuri set up special courts to sentence the Rashid Ali ministry to death in absentia and to impose long terms of imprisonment on dozens of officials who had supported it. Having Iraq embroiled in disaster for the good of Palestine was, he argued, in no one's interests. For once the opposition seemed to agree.

Rashid Ali and the Mufti were never caught. But after the Allies invaded Persia toward the end of 1941, three of the Golden Square colonels were captured by British officers and brought back to Iraq, where they were publicly hanged. The fourth colonel, Saleh al-Din al-Sabbagh, escaped British capture by disguising himself as a dervish and made his way to the Turkish border. But he was arrested in Turkey and interned there for the rest of the war. After the war the Turks agreed to hand him back to Iraq, where he was hanged in front of the gates of the Ministry of Defense. It was an event the army would never forget.

As the weeks and months went by, Jewish leaders persuaded themselves that the *farhud* was a onetime event, a singularly unhappy product of the instability caused by the government changing hands and of no one being willing to assume responsibility for maintaining order in the power vacuum. With Nuri at the helm once more, the Jews felt reassured. The measures he took to thwart rebel sympathizers were decisive, and the discrimination against Jews that was so prevalent in the run up to the Rashid Ali coup had all but evaporated into thin air. For the remainder of the war Iraq enjoyed a spell of prosperity brought on by good harvests and a largely undisturbed flow of oil. The fact that there were close to one-hundred thousand British troops stationed in Iraq once again also meant that there were small fortunes to be made in contracting, and Baghdad's Jews were first in line to amass them. As the nation returned to some sort of normality, the Jews felt they could resume their lives for the foreseeable future without, as the historian Norman Stillman has put it, "being forced to make great existential decisions."

Regina had watched these events unfold with dispassionate interest, so preoccupied was she with the small orbit of her own life, the care of her ailing husband, and the future of her young children. It was not that she didn't care about her community's standing in a country whose hot-and-cold treatment of Jews was profoundly shocking to all but the most fervent Zionists—for they expected nothing less from the Arabs. It was more that she had correctly surmised that the Jews' situation was impossible to predict from one year to the next and that any energy she might expend in speculation would be put to better service at home.

In many ways Regina's life had been turned in on itself by Elazar's illness, though to all outward appearances she was her usual capable self, attending to her chores, her sewing, her children, her cooking, and Elazar's ongoing needs as though she were still the mistress of a big house: as though she were still a woman of means. Inside, however, her anxieties reigned supreme. She worried about her family's future, about money, and about her husband's chances of recovery. No doctor had offered them a reliable diagnosis, and none had succeeded in making him well, in spite of the copious amounts of medicine they had induced him to swallow. Regina by turns accepted and rejected her cruel circumstances. She might find herself weeping at Elazar's bedside while he dozed, but then she would rally and begin to flutter over him, spooning various nostrums and broths into his mouth.

Once, in her desperation to see some improvement in her husband's condition, she invited a Muslim healer into the house. Weatherbeaten and cadaverous-looking, the healer turned up on their doorstep, shrouded in the many layers of light robes that were traditional Bedouin garb, and for an entire afternoon he proceeded to treat Elazar's swollen legs with hot iron nails. The patient screamed blue murder.

Regina had attempted to prepare herself, mentally, for life without Elazar. Indeed, Elazar himself had encouraged her in this regard. "You're going to have to be strong, Regina," he had said. "You're going to have to be the mother and the father of our small family." But the fact of his passing, of her empty bed and empty marriage, affected her profoundly. In the post *farhud* stability, when the rest of Baghdad's Jews seemed to have reestablished their position in society and were feeling solid and beginning to prosper once more, Regina no longer knew where she stood.

In the spring of 1942 a small, stocky man with stubby features and little round frameless spectacles perched on an equally round and largely bald head alighted in Baghdad as a representative of the Palestinian construction company Solel Boneh. The company had been contracted by the British to build some airfields in Iraq and to expand the oil refineries. Its representatives expected to be stationed there for some time. This particular representative checked himself into the Semiramis Hotel on Rashid Street, unpacked his small suitcase, and settled in for the long haul. His name was Enzo Sereni, though he went by the name Ehud. He was Italian—a fact that anyone who heard him speak English or French could hardly fail to notice. He was also engaged in a secret mission.

A month before Sereni's arrival a secret service, or Mossad, agent called Shaul Avigor had come to Baghdad at the behest of the Jewish Agency to discover whether a newly formed secret society known as the Salvation Youth was up to its proclaimed goal of defending Baghdad's Jews from a repeat performance of the previous year's riots. The group had come to the agency's attention after it published a polemical leaflet calling on young Jews to rise up and defend their honor, and arguing that the community could protect itself if it possessed the necessary weapons. Since it was clear that the group as yet had no defined political orientation, Avigor had been dispatched to give it one. In short, his aim was to study the possibility of organizing an underground Zionist movement in Baghdad.

It was Avigor who had called for Sereni and two other emissaries to be sent to Baghdad once he'd discovered that the existing underground, such as it was, consisted of just a few dozen enthusiastic but inexperienced high school students and graduates who rejected the concessionary stance adopted by community leaders. Riven by competition and dissension among their own ranks, the students had managed to collect between them only ten old revolvers, and most of them had no idea how to shoot one.

The movement had a threefold mission: to establish a branch of the *Halutz* movement under Sereni that would take care of Zionist indoctrination and Hebrew instruction; to organize the apparatus of self-defence, the *Shurah,* which would supervise military training and weapons acquisition; and to set up a program of illegal emigration to Palestine. In practice a clear division of labor was seldom observed among the three departments, and the clandestine movement was, in function if not form, a single one.

All the emissaries brought an infectious energy to their work and were convinced that they could offer Iraqi Jews what they needed: a sense of belonging, pride in their Jewish heritage, and hope for a more fulfilling future. That they couldn't get the traction they desired was largely due to the community's old guard, whose resistance to change and political apathy were a constant source of irritation to Enzo. In one of his first reports to the Jewish Agency, Sereni complained about "the lack of enthusiasm among the Baghdadi Jews for Palestine," noting that it would have been better if he had come in the immediate aftermath of the *farhud* before "the Jewish talent for adapting and forgetting" asserted itself. Now, instead of being seen as an angel of deliverance come to release the Jews from bondage, he was received as the European intellectual he was and treated with suspicion from almost every quarter by those he hoped to convert.

Dressing to blend in with the local Jews, Enzo initially tried his luck with the wealthy, hoping to solicit contributions to the Jewish National Fund. Like everything else he would attempt here, this task was an uphill struggle. As Elie Kedourie saltily observed in a seminal essay in *The Chatham House Version,* the Zionist emissaries and the Baghdadi Jews faced one another across multiple barriers of mutual incomprehension. The emissaries argued the Zionist thesis: that Jewish life in the Diaspora was poisonous and impossible and that the only salvation was to become pioneers on the land in the collective of Eretz Israel. This doctrine was frowned upon by Eastern Jews who had not experienced any crisis of identity and to whom collectivism as a political aspiration was wholly alien. The Zionists, meanwhile, knew nothing about Eastern Jewry, except that in the past they had been the object of philanthropy and were now to become the object of proselytism. What's more, they had contempt for the Eastern way of life, which they saw as primitive, feudal, and unprogressive. As a remedy, says Kedourie, they offered trade unions, sanitation, and communal living and they were heartily surprised when these still did not make the population among whom they dwelled friendly to them.

Undeterred by the lukewarm response, Enzo forged on, using his considerable personal charm to win over, one by one, young Jews who could be persuaded to attend his small gatherings. The gatherings were usually held in a private house on a Sabbath morning when the parents were in synagogue and their children were thus able to assemble a small group of friends who could meet "Ehud" undetected.

Enzo would address the group, holding forth about Palestine, talking about Jewish holidays, and explaining their agricultural origins. Then he'd entertain them with tales about Givat Brenner, the kibbutz he called home, and where in spite of his doctorate in philosophy, he was proud to work with his hands, whether in the kitchens, in the factories, or on the land. As he chatted away in English and French, Enzo would simultaneously scan the room, trying to divine whether his smooth talk had gained him any sort of hold on his listener's souls. He never took his leave until he'd distributed specially commissioned Arabic translations of the Zionist classic *Auto-Emancipation* to those who appeared interested.

Written in 1882 by a Polish-born Jew called Leo Pinsker, this slim tract offered a cogent analysis of the Jewish condition. Pinsker argued that among the living nations the Jews were a heterogeneous element that could not be assimilated because they were members of a nation that had long been dead. The Jews were an uncanny apparition, and it was fear of this "Jewish ghost" that created prejudice against them. Civil and political emancipation was not sufficient to raise them in the estimation of other peoples. The only corrective was the creation of a Jewish nationality, of a people living on its own soil. "The Jewish people have no fatherland of their own," wrote Pinsker. "They have no rallying point, no centre of gravity, no government of their own, no accredited representatives. There are everywhere as guests, and are nowhere at home."

Pinsker's ideas did not play well among Baghdadi Jews who were devoted to Iraq. And yet a growing number of younger Jews realized that they could not go on as before. For them, the *farhud* was an awakening. Hadn't the Jews been violently rejected and attacked? Made to feel like unwelcome visitors in a city they believed was home? Hadn't they been scorned, envied, and mistrusted? Maybe Palestine could offer the Jews of Baghdad a new life after all.

Having made an entrée among the activist youth, Enzo turned his attention to making contact with the women of the community. This called for a more delicate approach, since after the riots many women only ventured out veiled like Muslims, and they had all the usual curbs and checks on their behavior to contend with besides. As chance would have it, a relative of the family whose house served as a center for the underground movement agreed to arrange a meeting in her home. It was a brave move on her part, because her family's reputation, not to mention her own hide, was at stake should news of the meeting leak out. Around ten young women turned up. Enzo confidently plunked himself in their midst and talked to them about movies, fashion, the weather, amusing them with stories of his international travels. The *Alliance*-educated women were enthralled and asked if he would meet with them again.

At the next meeting Enzo delivered his Zionist sermon, but he also talked about the importance of the individual in Palestine and about the independent spirit of the Jewish girls there who knew how to defend themselves. Cannily he appealed to their unformed desire for personal fulfillment. Enzo's biographer, Ruth Bondy, makes the point that while the Baghdadi girls did not always understand the ebullient Italian and his sometimes strange choice of terms, he managed to redirect their thinking and provide a focus for all their "vague and concealed" rebelliousness.

In the final analysis Enzo's success was limited. After almost a year in Baghdad, he had managed to recruit no more than 150 to 200 new members to the underground, and of these, only a small portion would follow through and emigrate before he himself was obliged to flee Iraq in May 1943, just days before British intelligence officers in Baghdad blew his cover.

In many ways the *Shurah* was more successful, because rather than attempt to convince people that their only hope lay in emigration, it worked toward the more proximate goal of bolstering the community's means of defending itself. Under Sereni's colleague Ezra Kadoori, a core group of twenty young men and women were trained in various modes of self-defense, in the use of small weapons such as knives, guns, and hand grenades, as well as in hand-to-hand combat and judo. They were also inducted into that small club of militant activists that knew how to manufacture Molotov cocktails. Thus educated, each of them went off to head up a small "cell" of Zionist activists, consisting of seven to ten people who would receive similar training and who were encouraged to acquire arms for the movement, either locally or by smuggling them through Palestinian contacts.

It is estimated that in its first year of operation in 1943 the organization accumulated between seven hundred and one thousand guns, hidden mostly in underground caches in people's homes, but also occasionally, for ease of access, in synagogues. The *Shurah* had further acquired dozens more members, among them Regina's brother Solomon Sehayek.

Throughout the joyless year in which Regina mourned for Elazar, swathing herself in black robes and shunning all social engagements, she had plenty of time to adjust to her new circumstances. The enforced passivity of mourning did not suit her, and behind her sad eyes her pragmatic brain was busy contriving ways in which she might begin to support her three children. Elazar had hardly left her destitute, but there were standards to maintain, and she didn't want her children going without. As a woman alone in the world and, more important, a woman of good breeding, Regina had few options. A distant cousin who had been similarly mired in widowhood with three young mouths to feed had discreetly taken up dressmaking. Women would visit her home to be measured and fitted, bringing pattern books and materials with them, and then the cousin would sew their dresses in her own time, pocketing the small fee owed to her on collection with an embarrassed shrug. But working as a seamstress was out of the question for the wife of Elazar Levy and, in any case, Regina recoiled at the very idea of earning a fee.

She was not averse to dabbling in the commodities markets, however, and to this end she sought the counsel of Elazar's cousin Goorji Levy, assistant director of the Ottoman Bank and a man renowned across Baghdad for his financial acumen. She also called on the expertise of Elazar's nephew Albert Levy, who held the same position at the Rafidain Bank. Between them they helped Regina navigate the commodities markets, advising her on what to buy and when to sell, helping her with the paperwork, and introducing her to reputable brokers who would never dream of taking advantage of a woman. Before long Regina felt quite at home in this abstract world of men, buying and selling sugar, steel, dates, and rubber as though she were a grand merchant moving vast fortunes from one continent to another and not a clever widow learning how to maximize her limited funds.

To her surprise, she also won the respect of the women of the household. "Your mother is a very clever woman," she overheard Salha telling her daughters.

Bertha and Marcelle remember getting a good deal of lecturing from Salha at this time. "Don't bother your mother with your problems," she'd say. "She has enough on her plate already." Or: "You must help Regina whenever you can. Help her with the cooking, help her tidy up, and help her look after your brother. Even if she appears not to need your help, you must offer it."

When Regina emerged from her year of mourning, Bertha was fourteen and Marcelle eleven. Already her girls were miniature models of the women they'd later become. Bertha was outspoken and independent, with a streak of wilfullness that showed itself rather too often for Regina's comfort. Marcelle on the other hand was bookish and shy, the kind of child who preferred a good novel to the distractions of company. Both girls took Salha's lessons to heart. They helped around the house and tried not to trouble Regina with their cares. And so Regina never learned that when her daughters walked home from school, Arab porters smacking laden donkeys through the streets spat in their faces, calling them "dirty Jews," and drove their donkeys into the girls' path, forcing them into the gutter. Dabbing a clean hankie over her younger sister's mud-splattered clothes, Bertha would whisper to a tearful Marcelle: "Be brave. Remember, you are a thousand times better than those horrible men." Then she'd caution, "Whatever you do, don't tell Mom."

Bertha was full of good intentions, even if the strain of being on her best behavior periodically tipped her over the edge. Marcelle remembers Bertha hurling her embroidery across the living room one afternoon and vowing never again to pick up a needle—a promise Bertha as good as kept, judging by the number of times that as a young and fashionable woman she begged her sister to alter her clothes for her. When she was in particularly feisty form, Bertha would come home from school, dump her homework in a closet, and tell Regina, "Now I'm going to fry onions on your ears," which was as good as saying she'd be raising hell. One day, Bertha announced that she wanted to emigrate to Palestine. Regina was furious. "What are you lacking here?" she asked her daughter, who was full of talk of the horror of the death camps in Poland and the utopian ideals of life on the kibbutz. "Work, purpose, fulfillment, dreams," said Bertha. "None of which, as far as I can tell, are to be had in Baghdad."

Although Bertha's passion for Palestine proved short-lived, it was at times like these that Regina missed the disciplinary presence of the girls' father. Even so, she was resolved never to marry again. When a respected community elder who had himself been recently widowed approached her through the *dellalah,* Regina declined his offer. A new husband was too much of an unknown quantity, too much of a risk. If he drank or had debts he'd be little more than an unwelcome burden. And what if he mistreated her children? Besides, Regina liked her independence. She couldn't abide some man making decisions on her behalf, and she could manage both her money and her responsibilities on her own.

Now and again Regina took the need to assert her independence to lengths that baffled those around her. She insisted, for example, that while she lived at her mother's house she would keep her own table. Thus she, Bertha, Marcelle, and Haron would sit down to their own meals at their own dining table in their own corner of the room, while the rest of the Sehayeks dined together, joking, laughing, and discussing the events of the day. "Eat," she'd enjoin her girls whenever she caught them glancing toward the big table and sensing that all the fun in the house was taking place elsewhere.

Upon this one act of independence Regina staked the foundation of her self-respect—perhaps even her very sense of what self was. Almost unconsciously she seemed to have understood that as an island she stood resilient. But if she allowed herself to merge once more into the greater landmass of the family she would somehow lose definition: all her experience as a married woman would be negated and everything she had learned as a wife and mother surrendered to a short-term desire to be nurtured and protected. Intuiting this was as much a survival skill as learning how to juggle bank accounts.

The Sehayeks accommodated Regina's whims without protest.

They rallied around her, offering support, making her laugh, allowing her to cry. If Regina was unable to see a clear future for herself, then with the help of her family she at least felt able to live fully in the present.

Regina herself always said that one of the unmitigated pleasures of living under her parents' roof through this difficult period was discovering that her brothers, once mere irritants, had grown into fine young men. Both Nessim and Solomon were tall and slim, with strong jaws, hairlines that were already noticeably receding, and the kind of aquiline noses more likely to be found on a Roman than an Iraqi. Both of them also appreciated the art of dressing well. Between them, Regina would pretend to complain—waving a theatrically disdainful hand at so much excess—they owned enough suits to stock the menswear section of Orozdibak, Rashid Street's principal department store.

For Regina her brothers were like a breath of fresh air. Around their heads buzzed the energy of passions and disputations, opinions and confrontations, and they enlivened the Sehayek household by bringing the outside world indoors in forceful gusts. At the same time they could be wonderfully affectless, and every now and then, if the mood took them, they would entertain Regina with a made-to-order version of the Lambeth Walk, the two of them looking dapper in tailored jackets and polished leather shoes as they dance-stepped gracefully across the living room floor. And yet, beneath the clowning and the seamless tailoring, Regina's brothers could not have been more different.

Nessim worked as a clerk on the railways. It was a privileged job with flexible hours that allowed him to spend a good deal of time in Baghdad's coffeehouses, socializing with Muslim and Christian colleagues, or mingling with junior ministers and local dignitaries in the casinos on Abu Nuwas Street—a winding riverside promenade linking Bataween and Alwiya that boasted a number of establishments where you could hear musicians and singers perform traditional songs, smoke the nargileh, and fritter away an evening in convivial company. Nessim was an Iraqist who felt comfortable in his skin, a lover of the Arabic language who appreciated the different words and cadences you would find in the way a Muslim, Jew, or Christian spoke. Iraq was a country to which he felt he belonged: it was his fatherland, his motherland, his past, and his future. Not even the *farhud* had shaken his conviction that in time the nation would evolve to embrace all its minorities as equals.

Solomon was a decade younger than Nessim. When Regina rejoined her parents' household he had already given up on a hoped-for medical career, thwarted by strict quotas imposed on Jews, and was busy working his way round the various departments of the Ottoman Bank, from correspondence and drafts through bills and exchanges, determined to excel in each one. Unlike the mixed bag of acquaintances his brother enjoyed dipping into, Solomon's tight social circle was almost entirely Jewish. He had made his friends at school and kept them and then applied an almost religious zeal to the task of maintaining them. It helped that he was an inveterate organizer, always arranging picnics and outings, lectures and musical soirées, to which Bertha and Marcelle longed to be invited so that they could drift dreamily among the older girls of Solomon's acquaintance who owned satin gowns and had their hair smoothed into even waves, like Hedy Lamarr. Bertha in particular was amused by the way so many of these young women swooned over her uncle Solomon.

In Regina's day it had been unthinkable for young men and women to socialize together unchaperoned. But Solomon's generation would tackle the old customs and drag the community's elders into the modern era, kicking and screaming if need be. More politicized and less inward-looking than previous generations of Iraqi Jews, Solomon and his peers displayed an avid interest in public affairs and were committed to some kind of involvement. They joined political parties and took up new causes and ideologies. They were drawn to nationalism, socialism, and the idea of equality between the sexes, all of which probably qualified them as the first generation of Iraqi youth to mystify its parents.

The *farhud* was pivotal to the consciousness of this generation, for which it functioned as a kind of awakening. Solomon had once worn his Jewishness as casually as Nessim wore his, but after the *farhud* shattered the community's confidence, he found himself unable to go on

as before. While Nessim remained an Iraqist and convinced himself
that harmonious relations between Arabs and Jews would soon be restored, Solomon now saw his Jewishness as a badge of essential difference: either you were a member of the club or you weren't. If you
were, then you had a duty to further the cause of your people by
working toward the resurgence of a Jewish nation. This heightened
Jewish consciousness, coupled with a new sense of the Jews' common
destiny, gave Solomon fresh purpose. He seemed more decisive, more
invigorated. It also meant that when his friend Saleh Shammash approached him, urging him to join an underground Zionist cell where
he would learn how to shoot a gun and how to make bombs, he
jumped at the opportunity.

Like all new members of the self-defense units, Solomon was
sworn in on a Bible by candlelight to defend Iraqi Jews, to devote himself to the cause, and to face death rather than forsake it. He had put
his hand on his heart and made his solemn vow. It was the most responsible thing he had ever done, and it made his heart beat faster just
thinking of the difference he might potentially make to the fate of
Iraq's Jews. Perhaps he'd become as valuable to the underground as
Avraham Mordad, the resourceful Baghdadi wireless operator
through whom the Zionist emissaries communicated with Tel Aviv: it
was said that Mordad worked with a revolver on his desk because he'd
resolved not to be taken alive if his operation were ever detected.

In the months that followed, Solomon worked hard at his Hebrew,
took lessons in jujitsu, and every few weeks absconded by night to a
deserted field outside the city for target practice. At last he bought the
pistol that he had promised himself at the time of the Rashid Ali coup.
It was small, tarnished, and surprisingly heavy, and he kept it wrapped
up in rags in a bottom drawer. Every so often, when no one was
around, he would take it out of its hiding place and polish it, peering
down its dark barrel as though straining to discover its history. Then
he'd balance it on his palm, feeling its heft, and ponder whether he
would ever need to use it—especially now that he was pretty sure he
could hit his mark if he had to.

One night, returning home from target practice in the small hours of the morning, Solomon found Nessim waiting up for him. "The question is," said Nessim, carefully enunciating each word, "are we Jews who just happen to live in Iraq or Iraqis who just happen to be Jews?" Before Solomon had a chance to answer his brother, Nessim cut him off. "I know your secret," he said. Solomon hadn't counted on being discovered like this. Should he feign ignorance, deny any involvement with the underground, or attempt to argue Nessim round? He looked at his brother who was now in full flow, berating him for taking extravagant risks without thought for his family's safety, for being foolish and unthinking, not to mention selfish and unrealistic, and he made his decision.

"The Jews are going to found a state," said Solomon. "Just imagine it. The people at the very height of power, the prime minister, the politicians, the judges: all of them will be Jewish and everything will be run by Jews and for Jews. We won't have to cower and hide, always wondering where the next slap in the face will come from, always asking ourselves if the authorities intend to run us into the ground. We will discover our own strength, build our own country, work on our own land."

Nessim was unmoved by Solomon's vision of Jewish nationhood: "The Arab is our brother, we have no other," he said, dredging up an old playground taunt that had lost none of its power to rile. "In any case," he went on, "the so-called Jewish state—if it ever becomes more than a pipe dream—will be run by Jews from Hungary, Poland, Russia, France, and Germany, not by Jews from Iraq or Egypt. Where would you fit in? What would you do? I'd like to see you trade your smart suits and your nice fitted shirts for a pair of dirty overalls and a hoe. Somehow I just can't see it."

Solomon shot right back: "I'm not the one living in a dream world. If all Iraqis were like your friend Abdul Sittar," referring to the Muslim who had brought the family paraffin, fish, flour, and bread the day after the *farhud*, "there'd be no need to contemplate leaving. As it is, the country is full of hidden prejudice. How can you fight that? Where do you begin? I should have gone to medical school. I passed all the exams. But I couldn't get a place because the medical college decided to accept only three Jews a year, and there's nowhere and no one to appeal to against that. This sort of discrimination is everywhere. Open your eyes, Nessim. I can't understand why you're not a nationalist."

"I'm an internationalist," said Nessim, pleased with his own response. "Besides," he argued, "the government isn't anti-Jewish, in spite of taking discriminatory measures against us. Popular opinion is ranged against the government on all sides—right, left, center, and forward. Lashing out at the Jews is just an easy way out of difficulty. It makes the government look powerful and unites the opposition against a common internal enemy, however bogus that enemy actually is. It's pragmatic, not racial."

Now it was Solomon's turn to be unmoved. "And I suppose the mob who attacked us in 1941 was composed of political pragmatists," he said.

Nessim opened his mouth to reply, but Solomon was faster. "Look, Nessim, I'm tired. I'm going to bed. I don't want to argue. You are my brother and I have no other, so let's just let each other be."

As it turned out, the brothers would each adhere to their different paths, Solomon continuing to work with the underground and Nessim trying hard to steer the good ship Personal Conscience on a comfortable middle course between being Jewish and being Iraqi. As a result, events would propel them further and further apart until there was no room in the Sehayek household, in Baghdad, or even in Iraq to reconcile their differing ideologies.

Chapter 10

THREE EVILS

"Jews have no cause other than their surrounding societies," thundered General Secretary Zilkha at the inaugural meeting of the Anti-Zionist League, or AZL. This newly formed protest group had succeeded in drawing a crowd of about one hundred people, mostly Jews, to a small hall in old Baghdad in March 1946 to listen to Zionism being denounced as a "colonialist phenomenon." Standing at a podium at one end of the hall, General Secretary Zilkha delivered an impassioned speech. He called on his fellow Jews to repudiate Zionism and to involve both the Arab masses and the country's popular and democratic institutions in the fight against the British colonial enterprise. Beginning with the Balfour Declaration, he said, British policy makers had sought "to divert the Arab struggle against the colonialists to one against the Jews and to create a rift that would enable them to go on exploiting the Arab people."

This was stirring stuff for Arabs and Jews alike. The Anti-Zionist League was an offshoot of the Iraqi Communist Party. Founded by twenty or so Jewish government employees who worked alongside Nessim Sehayek in managing the country's railroad system, it promulgated the view that Iraqi Jews would be liberated only when the Iraqi people as a whole had thrown off the bonds of oppression and attained full, democratic rights. Its meetings were well attended and, at its peak, the League's daily newspaper Al-Usba [The League] boasted a circulation of six thousand.

Not surprisingly, the rapid growth of the AZL threw the Zionist emissaries working in Baghdad into a state of crisis. In 1947 the leaders of the *Halutz* branch of the Zionist movement complained to their superiors that membership had fallen as a result of Communist and AZL activities and that if nothing was done to counter such defections the trend would worsen. The Jewish Agency, which was responsible for immigration matters, reacted promptly and dispatched several more emissaries to Baghdad to battle things out in the ideological trenches where they could boost morale among the troops and win back apostates.

That Jews were bouncing back and forth between movements that were in every way diametrically opposed underscores the desperation that beset young Jewish activists in the years immediately following the war, when public opinion once again turned against the Jews. The activists wanted to do something to counter vulgar prejudice, but they didn't know which way to turn. Should they adopt an assimilationist ideal or retreat behind the walls of ethnic difference? Work toward the ultimate goal of a workers' revolution or commit themselves to national resurgence? Either way a huge leap of faith was required, because the activists needed to believe in the imminent dawning of a reborn Jewish state or else in a reborn Iraq.

The reappearance of anti-Jewish feeling in Iraq was due to a combination of factors. The economy was in a postwar slump. Oil revenues were down, and severe droughts had occasioned a series of poor harvests. Whenever the Iraqi people felt the noose of austerity tighten around their necks, the conspicuous wealth of the nation's Jews grated. In June 1946 the Arab League adopted a resolution urging Arab governments to take measures against Zionism. The league, which included Egypt, Iraq, Syria, Saudi Arabia, Transjordan, Lebanon, and Yemen, had been founded two years earlier in order to address the need for a united Arab effort on the Palestine question. Meanwhile the Anglo-American Committee of Enquiry, a joint commission set up after the war to investigate conditions in Palestine, was recommending the immediate admission of one-hundred thousand Jewish refugees, mainly death camp survivors. From the Arab perspective, the proposed immigration appeared unfair, as if the Arabs were being held to account for the European Holocaust.

Following years in which the war effort saw hundreds of Jews employed in government departments, Jews were dismissed without notice. Jewish merchants, especially those in the import-export business, were refused essential trading licenses. The number of Jews admitted to state schools and institutions of higher learning was once again drastically cut, while in secondary schools Jewish teachers from Palestine were dismissed and replaced by Muslims. Strict censorship was imposed on all contact between Iraqi Jews and their friends and relatives in Palestine, and any letters exchanged between them were seized and filed, to be used later in a sustained campaign of persecution.

Even the government directed thinly veiled threats at the Jews. Ministers and senior civil servants spoke darkly of the seriousness of their situation, blaming Zionists in Palestine for destabilizing conditions at home. Historian Nissim Rejwan gives the example of Muhammed Fadhil al-Jamali, who testified before the Anglo-American Committee of Enquiry in Cairo in May 1946 as a representative of Iraq's Ministry of Foreign Affairs. Al-Jamali explained that until Zionism had come "to poison the atmosphere" in Iraq, Jews had been living alongside Muslims in "perfect peace and harmony" for "thousands of years." He acknowledged that Iraqi Jews were "embarrassed" by Zionism and "the bitter relationship that exists between us and the Zionist Jews." Nevertheless he pointedly declared: "It is a great burden on the Iraqi government to maintain that peace and harmony which we have enjoyed over a long period in our history."

The Jews understood the nature of such threats. Thus, when the Anglo-American committee rolled into Baghdad later that month to gather evidence for its Palestine investigation, the community leaders who testified before it publicly declared that the Jews were doing just fine, that the handicaps to which they were subjected were of no consequence, and that the community's economic health was generally good.

The Anti-Zionist League campaigned hard to boycott the committee's visit to Iraq on the grounds that it was "useless, aiming at deceiv-

ing the Arabs." In so doing the AZL won government approval. But
because the organization was as resolutely anti-British as it was anti-
Zionist, its leaders simultaneously endeared themselves to the opposition. Thus it was only a matter of time before the AZL was outlawed,
its printing presses seized, and its leaders tried and imprisoned, accused, of all things, of secretly working to promote the Zionist cause.

Around the time that Chairman Zilkha began addressing the anti-
Zionist faithful, Solomon Sehayek assumed responsibility as secretary
of a very different kind of club. Toward the end of the war, he and a
number of Jewish friends had begun holding fund-raising events—fairs
and fêtes mainly, where you could buy arts and crafts, play darts, or
try your luck at games of chance—in order to raise money to purchase land and build facilities that would eventually house a club for
the community's youth. The club opened in 1946. It boasted two tennis courts, a lecture hall, and a tearoom, and it revolutionized Iraqi
Jewish society by bringing young men and women together in a social
environment that for the first time excluded their parents. Oddly
enough this mixing of the sexes drew scarcely a whisper of disapproval
from the community's old guard; having survived the tumultuous
1930s, the *farhud,* and the long and uncertain years of war, even they
seemed finally to have accepted that things change.

There were exceptions, however. Salha's brother once stormed into
her house, searching for his daughters and ranting about the way-
wardness of modern youth. The daughters were going to the club
with Solomon, and to avoid discovery they quickly slipped their coats
over their evening gowns, making sure to cover every buoyant frill,
leaving Salha to do the necessary smooth talking. Salha scolded her
brother with a gentle "Come now," and informed him that the club
was quite the fashion. Its membership was drawn almost entirely
from Baghdad's best families, while its activities—tennis, lectures, musical evenings, and theatrical productions—were nothing if not improving. "Who could object to that?" she said.

But the club's chief point of interest was that it served as a refuge.
Here was a space in which politics had no place, where issues of na-

tional loyalty were left at the door, and where young Jews could relax and pretend that their futures in Iraq were assured. Instead of discussing the troubled economy, the prevailing bread shortages, or the relative merits of Zionism and communism, the patrons of Solomon's club listened to chamber music, attended lectures on Balzac, and batted tennis balls across anglicized clay courts, upholding the civilized cultural values that the *Alliance* had inculcated in more than two generations of Iraqi Jews. Whenever I hear about this club and its legendary picnics and dances, recalled with rosy affection by all who attended them, I can't help thinking of the orchestra on the Titanic, which valiantly played on as the icy Atlantic claimed its hulking prize.

As for the sinking ship itself, in 1947 domestic affairs in Iraq were in a state of unprecedented crisis. Popular unrest was spreading to every quarter, expressing itself in mass demonstrations and general strikes that were bringing the country to a standstill. Much of the civil disobedience was directed against the government's continuing alliance with Britain—an alliance the prime minister and the regent planned to extend formally under the banner of a new agreement, the Portsmouth Treaty, steadfastly ignoring the depth of anti-British feeling among the people at large.

When the Portsmouth Treaty was signed in December 1947, the people of Iraq exploded onto the streets in protest. Every major city witnessed violent clashes between protesters and police, and a string of attacks on British premises was launched. In Baghdad, the mob overran the offices of the *Iraq Times,* the British Embassy, and the British Information Agency. In Kirkuk the British consulate was attacked; and in Sulaimaniyah a rowdy group of protesters hounded an English teacher out of town and burned the British Institute to the ground.

Horrified by the extent of public anger and violence, the regent began backpedaling furiously, publicly disowning the treaty and leaving the prime minister to answer to the people's displeasure. The mob, meanwhile, had acquired its own momentum. Amid larger, more rampant demonstrations, noisy crowds stomped through the streets waving patriotic banners. They called for death to Iraq's

enemies and demanded free land for all. In one particularly ugly incident, the police opened fire on demonstrators, killing about fifty people and injuring some two hundred more. The dead became martyrs
to the *wathba,* or leap forward, as the period became known, and
more than a hundred thousand mourners attended their funerals.
With so much death on his hands, the prime minister resigned and
fled for his life.

The *Shurah* was on alert throughout the riotous month of January
in case the demonstrators began funneling their anger toward the
Jews. But its officers needn't have worried, because for perhaps the
only time in Iraq's short history as an independent nation Jews stood
shoulder to shoulder alongside their Arab compatriots in calling for
greater democratic freedoms and an end to British influence in Iraq. It
was a brief, wonderful interlude in which the Jews were welcomed by
the rest of Iraq's people as allies, and they felt a sense of real equality.

Even Chief Rabbi Sassoon Khedouri cast off his usual reserve and
marched down Rashid Street surrounded by a gaggle of rabbis and
Jewish dignitaries. Thousands more Jews swept behind them, brandishing antigovernment placards and lamenting the loss of the martyrs for whom Rabbi Khedouri had sat in mourning just days earlier,
accepting condolences from Muslim and Christian notables. Such was
the spirit of shared loss that even the right-wing nationalist press paid
homage to the Jewish martyrs who had laid down their lives for "the
Iraqi people in their fight for freedom."

The authorities were less impressed. Jewish participation in the
wathba uprisings surprised and infuriated them and led Nuri as-Said,
long regarded as a friend to the Jews, to vow that he would strip them
of all social standing and reduce them to paupers selling chickpeas in
the street. Nuri would not have long to wait before he was able to
make good on this promise.

Following the hasty departure of the prime minister, an interim government was led by Shia cleric Muhammed al-Sadr, the sixty-six-year-
old head of the Iraqi Senate, who became grandfather to
contemporary U.S. bogeyman Moqtada al-Sadr. Al-Sadr lost no time

appealing for unity and tranquillity, and as a sop to protesters he announced that the Portsmouth Treaty would not be ratified. But still the riots continued. Baghdad was uncontrollable, the scene of almost daily street fights between police and protesters, of roadblocks, curfews, burning buildings, gunfire, confusion, and general disorder. To complicate matters further, the people were now up in arms over developments in Palestine, specifically, the UN's decision, announced at the end of 1947, to divide the territory in two, establishing an independent Jewish state directly alongside an independent Palestinian state.

The proposed partition of Palestine shook the Arab world to its core, sparking public demonstrations from Morocco to Yemen. It was immediately rejected by the Palestinians, who had drawn the short straw in the deal: the proposed Jewish state was the larger of the two, though it was to serve as home for a smaller population, and it contained nearly all the citrus land and 80 percent of the cereal land. The Arab League was equally put out on the Palestinians' behalf. But while it was ostensibly the mouthpiece of the Arab world, the league could do little in response to the UN resolution without falling afoul of the international community—other than to encourage guerrilla infiltration of Palestine.

Iraq's beleaguered government hurriedly assembled an Iraqi volunteer force, consisting of several hundred *jihadis* with negligible soldiering skills, and dispatched it to Palestine in the vain hope that it would help strengthen the local resistance. Thanks to an aggressive campaign on the part of the Palestine Defense League to levy funds from Iraqi Jews for what was called "the rescue of Palestine," this pitiful force had both official approval and lavish financial backing. Yet nothing could prevent its demise, alongside the collapse of the Arab resistance in Palestine.

When Abd al-Qadir al-Husseini, the most prominent commander of the Arab fighters in Palestine and a cousin of the Mufti's, died on the battlefield in April 1948, there were huge demonstrations in Baghdad, led by pressure groups demanding that the government send regular troops into Palestine. By then public anger had reached such a pitch that it could not expend itself in protest alone, whether against weak government or against the hated British, who had spent nine long years reneging on promises made to Palestinians in 1939. And so the Jews got to bear the brunt of public fury. During the Baghdad demonstrations thousands of people began shouting, "Death to the Jews." In the general frenzy a synagogue was attacked and desecrated.

Once it was clear that the Zionists would proclaim the State of Israel the minute the UN mandate officially expired on May 14, the Arab League at last approved a policy of large-scale intervention. The Iraqi government felt it had no alternative but to send in troops. Under General Salih Saib, several battalions of ill-prepared and ill-equipped Iraqi troops with inadequate supplies and reserves moved from their home stations in mechanized or truck-borne units and took up positions on the western fringes of Transjordan. They crossed into their allotted sector of Palestine on May 15, 1948, and spent the next few months battling for their lives in the east Palestine triangle.

Meanwhile the Baghdadi Jews petitioned the government for protection. But it was too late. A pattern had been set. From now on their fate was linked to that of Palestine.

With the outbreak of the Arab-Israeli War, martial law was imposed throughout Iraq, restoring an outward appearance of peace. Yet the preternatural calm fooled no one. Regina spent her days pacing the house furiously and worrying about her business interests. She longed to head into the Old City and visit Albert at the bank; he would have a better sense of how the markets were being affected by the fighting. But for the first time in her life Regina felt self-conscious as a Jew on Baghdad's streets. It wasn't just that the papers were filled with breathless rants against what they called "the three evils: the Communists, the Zionists and the Jews," but Arab shopkeepers she once exchanged pleasantries with now looked at her as if she were a traitor.

Solomon had even greater reason to fear the current state of emergency, for if anyone could be classed a traitor it was he and his comrades in the *Shurah*. Now that the Iraqis and the Israelis were official

enemies, it seemed incumbent on him to take sides, and it pained him
to admit that his loyalties lay primarily with his coreligionists and not
his countrymen. In spite of Nessim's disapproval Solomon continued
to attend underground meetings, even as martial law meant that political meetings were banned along with trade unions and opposition
party activities. He told himself that the only life he was risking was
his own: unlike Nessim, he had no wife and no children, and there
would be plenty of years ahead for compromise.

Solomon understood the danger he was courting. After all, Jews
who had figured prominently in the *wathba* uprisings were already
being herded into a concentration camp in the southern desert, along
with other supposed enemies of the state, such as communists. However, at the end of June the government upped the ante and declared
Zionism to be a state crime under paragraph 51 of the Iraqi Criminal
Law. From then on Zionism would be an offence punishable by death.

Throughout the summer months of 1948, as war raged in Palestine, Jews in Iraq were rounded up by the hundreds and thrown into
jail without trial, accused of passing military secrets to Zionists in
Palestine. Many of the arrests were arbitrary. But it was no more reassuring when they were given the patina of legitimacy by police officers using door-to-door searches to seize people on the scantiest of
circumstantial evidence. All that was required to obtain a conviction
under paragraph 51 was the testimony of two witnesses. Thus anyone
with a grudge against a Jew or who owed money to a Jew could exact
a sure revenge.

Although the government repeatedly assured the Jews that they
had nothing to fear, provided they had no association with Zionism,
the most innocent activities were treated as suspect. Being overheard,
even in private conversation, expressing support for the Israeli state,
having any contact with a Palestinian Jew, even making a disparaging
remark about the Iraqi army—all were read as evidence of Zionist
leanings. It was as if simply being Jewish were a Zionist crime.

An absurd but not atypical case was that of Ibrahim Lawee,
co-owner of the Lawee Brothers car company, who was summoned
before the military tribunal for receiving a letter from Palestine.

Although nothing incriminating was found in the letter, Lawee was fined five hundred dinars because the president of the court judged that it had "a Zionist smell about it." A higher-profile casualty was Reuben Battat, a retired judge and former member of the Iraqi parliament, who was imprisoned on a charge of authorizing the transfer of £140,000 to a Zionist fund.

Marcelle remembers coming home from school one afternoon to find Regina and Salha busy boxing up prayer books and menorahs, Sabbath candles and the Haggadahs they kept for Passover. "What are you doing?" she'd asked her mother. "Getting rid of our contraband," Regina had said. Salha had chuckled drily, but Marcelle could tell that she was nervous. The Sehayeks were not alone. Seized with panic, many Jews began destroying anything that might incriminate them. They tossed letters and photographs into the fire and took scissors to prayer shawls embroidered with the Star of David. Jewels and trinkets bearing Jewish motifs that might have fetched a fair price at the pawnbroker's were thrown away without hesitation, while Jews who owned weapons of any kind, Solomon Sehayek included, now contrived to lose them.

Although the arbitrary nature of the arrests suggested that the police had no inkling of the existence of the underground, most activists erred on the side of caution. One acquaintance of Solomon's went to the elaborate lengths of taking a dip in the Tigris in order to dispose of a revolver he had tucked into his trunks, hoping that the bulge it created would not be too obvious. Another waited until he had the house to himself before clawing a hole in the wall into which he bundled his meager stock of weaponry. It was only after he had replaced the bricks and tidied away all evidence of tampering that he learned that the police had begun using metal detectors.

One of the underlying motives behind the wave of arrests was extortion: somebody, after all, had to pay for the country's military adventure in Palestine. That June, forty leading Jewish businessmen were arrested on charges of illegally trading with the Soviet Union. All forty were released after it was established that the transactions in question had been made years earlier as a direct result of a Soviet-Iraqi trade agreement, but only after they were fined ten thousand dinars apiece, payable to the Ministry of Defense.

In July there was a drive to arrest Jews who were guilty of "subversive activities." Once again fat files compiled simply as a matter of public record were raided for incriminating evidence, in this case for the names of people who had participated in antigovernment demonstrations during the *wathba* and who had been unlucky enough to be stopped by the police. These included onlookers who happened to be caught up in the crowds and mere passersby. These "subversives" faced the same procedures as suspected Zionists: they were arrested, brought to court, and summarily sentenced. Then they were given the option of being imprisoned or paying a hefty fine.

Finally, in August, came the arrest in Basra of Shafiq Ades, a wealthy businessman who owed the vast bulk of his fortune to his ownership of the much-coveted Ford concession. Ades was an assimilated Jew who boasted Arab business partners and close connections to the Iraqi elite, including, it was rumored, the regent himself. A political pragmatist, he had no time for ideologues of any stripe, least of all Zionists, and thus it was widely assumed even after his arrest that he was a victim of mistaken identity. Ades, however, had been chosen as the object of a show trial.

In court Ades was accused of selling surplus arms purchased from the British army during the war to agents in Italy whose job it was to divert the shipments to Zionist fighters in Palestine. Twenty witnesses for the prosecution described his lurid exploits with such conviction that the military court decided there was no need even to hear the defense. Without a shred of actual evidence being produced against the defendant, the court sentenced Ades to death by hanging. His estate, which included businesses and property estimated to be worth some five million dinars, was confiscated by the Ministry of Defense, and the lucrative Ford dealership passed to an Arab competitor.

Of the hundreds of Jews detained that summer, Shafiq Ades was the only one to receive a death sentence. Within weeks of his arrest, he was hanged outside his Basra mansion before a cheering crowd. None of his Muslim or British business partners were punished; some escaped trial altogether, while others were acquitted by the courts. Only Ades, who was the sole Jewish partner in the joint venture, paid for their supposed crime. His hanging delivered an unwelcome jolt to Iraq's Jewish community, because it proved that neither wealth nor high connections could save a Jewish skin.

The war in Palestine did not progress well for the Arab armies. They were hopelessly divided on every issue, from unified military command to armistice proposals to the Mufti's ludicrous exile "government of all Palestine." These weaknesses were exposed in June, during a UN-negotiated truce whose principal effect was to deprive the Arab invasion of all impetus. For while the Arabs fell to arguing among themselves, the Jews used the truce to amass huge reserves of equipment, thereby reversing the initial Arab advantage in heavy arms.

After fighting resumed the Iraqis attempted to take the city of Natanya, but the attack was rebuffed and the Jews swept on into Galilee, their deeper advance stopped only by a second UN truce. Realizing that the stop-start action was hurting Arabs, the Iraqis rejected the truce. However, it remained operative, and the war, for Iraq at least, was effectively over. Troops remained in eastern Palestine for the better part of a year nonetheless, dependent as ever on their long lines of communication through Jordan and receiving irregular pay from the near-bankrupt treasury at home.

Back in Baghdad, it proved extremely difficult to paint this failure as a victory, and so the press took to attacking the Jews instead. When Zionist forces advanced into Galilee, the nationalist paper *al-Yaqtha* called for a boycott of Jewish shops that would "liberate the people from the economic slavery and domination imposed by the Jewish minority." And when the Zionists drove the Arabs back across the partition lines, it began agitating for revenge. "An eye for an eye," wrote *al-Yaqtha*'s editor, invoking Hammurabi's ancient law: "He who took the first step is to blame."

Around this time the first waves of Palestinian refugees began arriving in Arab countries. Eight thousand refugees were allowed to stay in Iraq during the summer of 1948, and thousands more trickled into the country over the next eighteen months. The Palestinians fled for a variety of reasons: some because of the war, some succumbed to panic, while others left at the recommendation of Arab leaders who wanted to evacuate the region so that their armies could overrun the prospective Jewish state without having to distinguish between friend and foe. The Israeli government was unsympathetic to the plight of these refugees. Not content with their straightforward removal, it decided to freeze their assets and announced that it had no intention of funding programs that would ease the settlement of Palestinians in Iraq, Syria, Jordan, and elsewhere. In many cases the government offered the homes of Arab refugees to newly arrived Jewish immigrants.

These Israeli actions had immediate repercussions for Iraqi Jews, beginning with a determined campaign to eliminate them from the civil service, the army and the police. Between July 1948 and December 1949, roughly eight hundred Jews were dismissed from public service, without notice, severance pay, or pensions. The most senior of these was Elazar's cousin Ibrahim Elkabir, controller general at the Ministry of Finance, who lost his position just weeks after being sent to London to negotiate a new financial agreement between Iraq and Britain. Efforts were also made to boycott, restrict, penalize, and in every way hamper Jewish trade. Contracts and trading licenses were cancelled or revoked, Jewish banks were deprived of their licenses to deal in foreign exchange, and revenue inspectors were given free rein to tax Jewish businesses to the hilt.

This combination of blows was particularly damaging to Nessim Sehayek, who was dismissed from his job as a railroad official only to face an obstacle course of restrictions and prejudice when it came to starting a new business. His connections in the Muslim world served him well, however, with his friends in the banks and the souks easing his path from the tiled corridors of the civil service to the narrow and musty passageways that were the familiar realm of the fabric wholesaler. Much to his own surprise, Nessim discovered that he possessed a flair for the textile trade, and after just a few months of treading water and living off his savings, he found his business feet, developing a nice line of work trading in fine wools and silks with Tehran.

Solomon was not so lucky, though he managed to retain his job at the Ottoman Bank. His troubles began on a mild November morning in 1948 when he was summoned to the Ministry of Defense and asked to produce various documents to verify his identity. Solomon did as he was asked, eyeing the minor officials who passed his citizenship papers and driver's license back and forth between them, scrutinizing every detail. He was convinced that beneath the formalities it was his secret double life that was at issue. But the officials only grumbled their displeasure at him before handing back his papers and pushing him on up the chain of command.

After enduring yet more rubber-stamping of paper and several long waits in a variety of identical empty corridors, Solomon was led in to see Sayeed al-Rashid, the sole occupier of a smartly furnished office. Al-Rashid beckoned him to take a seat. "Coffee?" he offered. Solomon declined. And so al-Rashid began. Surely Solomon recognized that sacrifices needed to be made in times of war and that it was the patriotic duty of all Iraqis to do whatever was in their power to serve their country. "Isn't that so?" said al-Rashid, his voice as raspy as the whirring fan rotating overhead. Solomon mumbled his agreement, and al-Rashid hurried on. "Our brothers from Palestine are our guests in Iraq and it is the duty of every Iraqi to help them as best they can. Many members of your venerable community have come to their aid, offering our Palestinian guests money, clothing, food, and accommodations. I believe that you, too, have something to offer. Isn't that so?" said al-Rashid. Solomon nodded, about to reply, but then he thought better of it. Instead he reached inside his jacket pocket and extracted a set of keys. Placing the keys on al-Rashid's desk, he said: "I think you'll find that the club's facilities will meet your needs."

After going over the details involved in making over to government the deeds of the club and maintaining its supply of basic utilities, the two men shook hands and exchanged feeble smiles, relieved that their potentially thorny transaction had taken place with a minimum of fuss. However, Solomon grieved deeply for the loss of his club, his safe haven, his last stand against what had fast become an oppressive regime. To this day Solomon is able to work himself into a lather when he recalls how his pristine tennis courts were turned into makeshift transit camps and covered with white tents housing dozens of families teeming with children and ragged dogs.

When the Arab-Israeli War ended in January 1949, the Zionists, who had been allotted 57 percent of the country under the UN partition resolution, occupied 77 percent of it. Of Palestine's 1.3 million Arab inhabitants, nearly eight hundred thousand had been displaced, and Israel was in possession of entire cities and hundreds of villages that had not been planned as part of the Jewish state. But if the war cost the Arabs dearly, it was no less disastrous for the Jews of Arab lands. In Libya, Aden, Egypt, Bahrain, Morocco, and Syria, as well as in Iraq, the Jews paid for the Israeli victory with their freedom, their jobs, their health, and their peace of mind. Many of them now began to fear that a higher price might yet be exacted from them.

The year 1949 began more promisingly. With the Arab-Israeli conflict at an end, martial law was relaxed, and with the return to power of a strong government led by Nuri as-Said (in an unlikely but workable coalition with the pan-Arab nationalist party) all that was needed was a face-saving exit from Palestine that would allow defeated Iraqi troops to withdraw without disgrace. This was easily achieved by snubbing the UN-sponsored Palestine Conciliation Commission at Lausanne, insisting on the renewed validity of the 1947 partition resolution and hoping for an internationally imposed peace settlement that was more tolerable than the present one. Under those conditions the victimization of the Jews was somewhat eased.

But no sooner had Nuri Pasha succeeded in stabilizing the country to outward effect than he lashed out against the Communists—still considered the number one internal enemy of state. Five party leaders were hanged, among them the Iraqi Communist Party's chief ideologue, Yusuf Salman, universally known as Fahd, and a fresh round of persecution was launched, aimed at wiping out Communist activities once and for all. In the hunt for Communists that took place that summer the authorities made an unexpected discovery. They arrested a young Jew by the name of Sayeed Khlastchi, who, until 1946, when he'd defected to the ICP, had been a member of the *Halutz* movement. Terrified of what his captors might do to him, he informed on his former comrades in the Zionist underground and supplied the Criminal Investigation Department with a comprehensive list of names and addresses. In so doing he alerted the government for the first time to a new and potentially dangerous enemy.

Khlastchi's confession sparked a string of dramatic arrests in which the named activists were rounded up and thrown into jail. There they were beaten and starved and tricked into coughing up more names, thus giving the police a pretext to run riot in the community. Swarming into Jewish areas, fueled by the adrenaline of vengeance, the raiding officers kicked down doors, terrorized families, and dragged young men and women from their homes as their mothers wailed in terror. If the police failed to find the person they were looking for, they arrested a brother or sister or, in some cases, an entire family. Night after night, to the horror of the Sehayeks, who were fortunate enough to be spared, chilling shrieks rose up through the city's Jewish areas. This, Nuri seemed to be saying, to the satisfaction of his pan-Arab coalition partners who had begun baying for Jewish blood, was what happened when a seditious movement had the gall to operate under the nose of an unsuspecting government for the better part of a decade.

With nothing to lose now that its cover had been blown, the Zionist underground emerged from the shadows of anonymity and into the light of righteous conviction, there to accuse the chief rabbi of cowardice and inaction. In a bid to show community leaders just how much sway it now had over rank-and-file Jews, the underground arranged for a group of Jewish mothers whose sons and daughters languished in captivity to stage a demonstration outside the chief rabbi's house. They followed up this bravado by organizing a general strike on October 22, boycotting kosher butchers, and distributing leaflets that called on Rabbi Khedouri to resign.

Three days after the general strike began, a Jewish delegation led by Rabbi Khedouri went to see Deputy Prime Minister Umar Nadhimi to protest the latest round of arrests. They expected real concessions, such as the reinstatement of Jews in public service and the removal of barriers to trade, travel, and education. When they didn't get them they felt obliged to concede the leadership of the community. Without further ado Rabbi Khedouri was replaced by Heskel Shemtob, president of the lay council, a man known to be broadly sympathetic to the Zionist cause.

Regina was certain that the chief rabbi would have never deserted his post had he not sensed that some sea change had taken place within the community at large. Everyone else, after all, could sense it. Unable to pinpoint exactly how and why, Regina felt the community's centre of gravity shift as its stance toward Zionism gradually softened. She knew that, if pressed, most Baghdadi Jews would confess to taking secret pride in the Israeli state. They wouldn't want to live there necessarily, nor did they feel any less Iraqi, but the simple fact that Israel existed stirred something deep inside them. It was as if an identity of old, an ancient sense of being and place had been reawakened, causing the Jews to experience what Moroccan writer Albert Memmi would soon after term a *"retour a soi"*: a return to self.

When so many Arab countries had pounced on the new state and attempted to destroy it, the Iraqi Jews found themselves in a quandary because, for once, their loyalties were genuinely divided. Whom should they cheer, their Iraqi compatriots or their Israeli coreligionists? And whose deaths should they mourn? Oblivious to the community's hidden anguish, Rabbi Khedouri chose this time to make a number of ill-judged statements. Commenting on the treatment of the Jews during the Arab-Israeli War, he declared that compared with the way that Washington had treated America's Japanese citizens during World War II, the Iraqi government had shown leniency. He also reiterated his belief that being Jewish was a matter of religion alone. Being Jewish, in other words, was not an identity—and the Jews were certainly not a race.

None of this played well with the Jews anymore. It didn't solve the problem of their dual allegiance, and it didn't make life in Iraq any easier to bear. When martial law was finally lifted in December 1949, the Jews began to pour out of Iraq.

Eleven

A FAIR EXCHANGE

One by one people began to disappear. Without confiding their plans to anyone, they rubbed out their identities and simply vanished. Men and women from the *Alliance* who had joined the underground after the *farhud* were the first to go, hustled out of the country by Zionists who supplied them with false papers and disguises. Then businessmen with connections began to absent themselves from the souks and *khans*: entrusting thriving concerns to their cousins and pending contracts to their Muslim partners, they made their excuses and quietly slipped away. Whole families managed to melt into thin air. One day they'd be exchanging news with the neighbors. The next their houses were empty.

Most émigrés didn't bother applying for travel documents, since these now cost a king's ransom in *baksheesh*. They just left, paying Kurdish guides to lead them across the mountains in the north or bribing boatmen to ferry them across the Shatt al-Arab in the south. Some even managed to find truck drivers willing to conceal them among supplies destined for Jordan, and from there they made their way to the Jewish state.

There were many surprising departures. Young bank workers and subordinate officials in the railways or the post office, whom one would never have suspected of having a personal conviction, packed their bags and went off to join the Zionist army, while well-known firebrands who'd spent the past few years espousing the Communist credo put down their protest placards and defected, leaving their comrades none the wiser as to whether they'd secretly been Zionists all along or had simply lost faith in the coming revolution. What began as a slow trickle soon became an unstoppable flow. Whole offices were emptied, political groups lost their leaders, fathers bade good-bye to their sons, while the younger generation lost brothers, sisters, classmates, and neighbors.

Regina noted the phenomenon early, before it had become the subject of endless speculation and concern within the community. First her favorite fabric supplier at the textile market closed up shop, followed by the spice merchant who owned the *khan* next door to Elazar's. Then the dentist, the blind rice seller on Taht al-Takia, and the friendly manager at Dellal's bookstore had in short order disappeared. The word on everyone's lips was that there was no hope for the Jews in Iraq, and yet people's willingness to cancel their existences and flee did not give Regina undue cause for alarm until her oldest and most cherished friend succumbed to the fever for departure.

Louise didn't need to confess her thoughts outright for Regina to know that she, Freddy, and the boys would soon be gone. Regina had guessed that something was afoot when she'd noticed a new lightness about her friend's being. When Regina pressed her on the subject, the two women were sitting in Louise's living room in the smart villa in Alwiya that Freddy had bought after the war, on the proceeds, it was rumored, of a string of successful speculations. The maid had just left them alone with cups of scented black coffee and a plateful of warm *sambouseks*.

"There isn't any future for us here," Louise said. "I know that now: actually, I knew it when they hanged Shafiq Ades, though I wouldn't admit it. And don't go thinking that I'm some dupe who's fallen for those Voice of Israel broadcasts that keep promising Iraqi Jews salvation, because I'm not."

A dupe was the last thing Regina took her best friend for. In any case Regina was ready to admit that she, too, was wavering in her commitment to a future in Iraq. She knew as well as anyone how untenable it was to be constantly worrying if your husband or brother or father would still have his job next week or next month; whether one sunny afternoon the police might suddenly decide to come for your children, or whether the government would reintroduce martial law and make the Jews suffer all over again for imaginary crimes against the state.

"I don't blame you for feeling as you do. I'll only miss you—all of you," she said. "Just don't go ending up like Ibrahim Hayim and Nafatali Yacoub."

"What, those two *malouneen?*" said Louise, referring to the two conspirators who had each been sentenced to ten years' hard labor for helping smuggle Jews to Palestine. "Not a chance. Anyway, now that martial law's been lifted, the penalty for crossing the border illegally is six months maximum, and you can wriggle out of that too if you've got a hundred dinars to spare. That's why so many people are leaving—though you can rest assured that getting caught is not in my plans."

"What will you do in Israel?" Regina asked.

"Well, Freddy can play the markets there as well as anywhere, but he's quite willing to attempt the agricultural life, buy some land, grow vegetables, keep chickens, the whole deal. It's funny, but once you commit yourself to change, the possibilities seem endless."

When it came to parting, Louise hugged Regina tightly and urged her to think about leaving herself. "I've never been a Zionist, and I'm not one now. But you have to admit that there's something to be said for living your life freely, without constantly looking over your shoulder. Besides," she giggled, imitating the self-important boom of the Voice of Israel radio announcer: "See how Jewish toil has made the desert bloom! See how our brave Jewish soldiers defeated the aggressive armies of five Arab nations! Israel beseeches you: seize the future, for it is impossible for Jews to live among Muslims."

Regina and Louise met for the last time in Baghdad in January 1950. Two months later the government decided that if the Jews wanted to leave, they could. Iraq would not miss them. On March 6, 1950, after what was described by Ramallah Radio as a "stormy debate and much opposition," the Iraqi parliament approved the Denaturalization Bill. This clinically named piece of fast-track legislation permitted Jews to leave the country for good, on penalty of forfeiting their Iraqi nationality. The window for legal departure was one year, and Jews wishing to avail themselves of the right to leave were invited to register their names forthwith with the authorities at the Ezra Daoud Synagogue.

The announcement of the Denaturalization Bill coincided with the Jewish celebration of Purim, the feast that commemorates Queen Esther's salvation of the Jewish people just as the evil Haman, the king's chief minister, planned to put them to the sword. Perhaps because of their geographical proximity to the stage on which this ancient drama unfolded, Iraqi Jews had always held Purim in special regard. They threw fancy-dress parties, played practical jokes on one another, and sent delicious home-baked sweets to family and friends. They also indulged in card games and other forms of gambling that symbolized "the casting of the lots," or the sudden turn of fate that the feast commemorated. And so it was on Purim that the lots were cast once more. As the Jews gathered in their synagogues to recall their deliverance at the hands of Esther, they learned that the new law was being drafted. Within days it was ratified.

Regina made up her mind to leave Iraq as soon as notices publicizing the new law started appearing in the papers. Wasn't she still young enough to start over? Wouldn't her children later thank her for giving them this shot at a future? What was there to keep her in Baghdad? Perhaps Bertha had been right when she'd nurtured dreams of emigrating: perhaps in Palestine, Jews like them could find fulfillment.

Her only quibble was with the concept itself: denaturalization. For in being invited to renounce their nationality before leaving, Jews were being turned into refugees in their own country. Regina felt that the bill placed government ministers in a far worse moral light that they had intended, for they clearly had no qualms about stripping Iraq's Jewish citizens of belonging, bundling them off to Israel, and bidding them good riddance. Still, she told herself, at least it permitted Jews to break the cycle of persecution to which they'd been subjected for more than a decade, and in her more optimistic moments she convinced herself that it gave them the right to determine their own future.

Regina was certain that Solomon, for one, would be proud of her resolve. But he reacted to the new law with suspicion, thinking that it had to be a ruse to trap Zionists.

"You'll see," he said, after Regina had called a family conference to announce her decision: "they'll use the registration lists to justify yet another round of arrests, and everyone who signed up will be accused of disloyalty and treason."

Nessim had other ideas. "You're misreading the Arab mind," he said to Solomon. "As far as I can tell, the government simply wants to wash its hands of a problem it doesn't know how to solve, and if it can unload that problem onto the Israeli state, then so much the better."

Salha, who was in no mood for empty theorizing, fell to weeping. She begged her daughter not to register, to stay. Nobody else, she told Regina, was rushing to the Ezra Daoud Synagogue to sign away their identity. Why was she in such a hurry? "You should see the place," she said. "It's deserted, and the police and other officials are sitting behind trestle tables in the synagogue's great hall, twiddling their thumbs and playing *towli*."

Salha was right. They could go on speculating about the government's motives, arguing themselves into knots, but the facts were that no one had registered for denaturalization. Large crowds milled around the synagogue compound to discuss the situation daily, but nobody ventured inside to sign away their nationality. Unable to give up the patriotic ideal, community leaders cautioned against denaturalization, while the Zionists waited for the Israeli government to formulate a suitable response. The Iraqi bill had taken the Israelis by surprise: although the government was eager to see an influx of immigrants that would stabilize the country after the Arab-Israeli War, it had not expected Iraq to act with unilateral decisiveness. As things stood, Israel's immigration quota for Iraq hovered unhelpfully around the five-person-per-month mark. The prospect of having to absorb what might amount to tens of thousands of Iraqi Jews would require a complete rethinking of the country's immigration policy.

In fact, Prime Minister Tawfiq al-Suwaidi had settled on the terms of the Denaturalization Bill in good faith, thinking mainly of the good of Iraq. The country's reputation had already been tarred by an international Zionist campaign that had used inflated accounts of torture and concentration camps to prompt Britain and the United States to pressure the Iraqi government into opening the door to Jewish emigration. Now the upsurge in illegal emigration threatened further embarrassment: since the beginning of the year Mossad had helped nearly four thousand Jews reach Iran, and almost half that number again had escaped on their own. From al-Suwaidi's perspective, a public demonstration of largesse was just what was needed to restore Iraq's good character before its critics. Thus the Jews would be allowed to go, freely, on a first-come, first-serve basis and without hindrance of any kind.

Behind the scenes al-Suwaidi had made a number of shrewd calculations. He knew that the majority of Jews were deeply invested in Iraq and would not want to leave, and he knew that these Jews were loyal citizens—despite the rhetoric of treachery that successive governments had mobilized against them during and after the Arab-Israeli War. Mentally totting up the number of Jews that he thought might leave—malcontents, troublemakers, Zionists, Communists—he managed to persuade himself that no more than seven to ten thousand would apply for denaturalization.

This figure suited al-Suwaidi just fine. Unlike the nationalists who complained that the Denaturalization Bill was too lenient and argued that Iraq should simply throw the Jews out, the prime minister did not wish to have a wholesale exodus on his hands. That would be disastrous for the economy and for the country's credibility. If 130,000 Jews simply packed up and left, then Iraq would indeed appear guilty of having mistreated them. As al-Suwaidi saw it, what counted was the gesture of openness made by the bill and some visible sign of Jewish uptake: not too much, but just enough to make a difference to world opinion.

In that sense Nessim had it about right. The Iraqi government did want to offload the Jewish problem elsewhere. However, even Nessim could not have guessed at the ease with which the major international players in the region considered the large-scale transfer of peoples from one country to another, moved by the idea that a racially based "sorting out" of ethnically mixed populations in the Middle East would lead "to the greater stability and contentment of all involved."

Long before Iraq seized on denaturalization as a means of stemming illegal Jewish emigration, the powers that be had been weighing the merits of various population exchange schemes. Like chess players moving pawns from one side of a giant game board to another, they bargained over which Arab countries might receive multitudes of Palestinian refugees in return for a prospective Israel agreeing to absorb a similar number of Jews from Arab lands. At different times the British government's Peel Commission of 1937, the Union of Zionist Workers, and the American Zionist Federation all favored such a plan, while in the summer of 1949 Nuri as-Said privately proposed a population-exchange scheme to Israeli intermediaries in Paris.

For a time Nuri had the British excited about his plan. In September, Britain's ambassador to Iraq, Sir Henry Mack, wrote to the Foreign Office in London, elaborating on "an arrangement whereby Iraqi Jews moved into Israel [and] received compensation for their property from the Israeli government, while the Arab refugees were installed with the property in Iraq." As he saw it, everyone would gain: "Iraq would be relieved of a minority whose position is always liable to add to the difficulties of maintaining public order in time of tension. For its part, the Israeli government would find it hard to resist an opportunity of bringing a substantial number of Jews to Israel."

At the peak of his mania for solving this problem, Sir Henry worked out a resettlement scheme that allowed for the absorption of a hundred thousand Palestinians in new developments in the mid-Euphrates area, which the Americans were expected to pay for, having recently become players on the Middle Eastern stage. However, none of the parties involved expressed any interest in his proposals: neither the Americans, who didn't want to foot the bill, nor the Iraqis, who resisted British manipulation, nor even the Palestinians. Indeed, all such schemes tended to overlook the simple fact that the Palestinian Arabs wished only to return to Palestine, while the Jews of Arab lands, for the most part, wanted nothing more than to stay put.

By 1950 Iraqi officials were decidedly cool about the idea of population exchange, since the Jews were leaving anyway and they had no intention of absorbing so many Palestinians: they wanted Israel to take them back. Meanwhile the Israelis rejected out of hand any idea of compensating Iraqi Jews for property abandoned in Iraq. According to Israeli Foreign Minister Moshe Sharett, Israel "could not in any circumstances agree to receive the Iraqi Jews as penniless displaced persons." With the key players displaying such antipathy, the idea of an exchange of populations eventually withered on the vine, to be replaced by denaturalization.

Denaturalization had its own problems. In theory the concept ought to have appealed to all parties concerned, since the attractions of permitting voluntary emigration were obvious. In practice, however, there was so much mistrust between the Iraqi Jews and the authorities on the one hand, and between the Iraqis and the Israelis on the other, that no sooner had the Denaturalization Bill been passed than a stalemate was reached. As Salha and many others observed, barely anyone registered to emigrate.

On April 8, 1950, everything changed irrevocably for the Jews of Iraq. It was the last day of Passover, and in Baghdad the Jews spent the day strolling along the banks of the Tigris in celebration of the "Song of the Sea," an ancient hymn marking the point when the Jews became a people with a common faith and a common fate. This was one of the oldest customs of the oldest Diaspora in the world.

Thousands of people thronged the esplanade, dressed in the clothes they reserved for the Sabbath and feast days. They dawdled under the hot sun, shading their eyes with their hands as they greeted friends and relatives, and gorged themselves on the rare sight of their community in fine spirits. It was a bittersweet moment, since no one knew how many Jews would celebrate Passover by the Tigris the following year.

By nine o'clock the crowds began to thin out. But along the winding length of Abu Nuwas Street, young Jewish intellectuals and office workers lingered on, chatting and smoking in and around the coffeehouses that looked out across the turbid river to the west bank of the city. Minutes later their idling was brought up short by a sharp crackling roar. A small bomb, hurled from a passing car, had exploded on the pavement outside the Dar al-Beida coffee shop, shattering its windows and obscuring its frontage with billowing smoke. There were no fatalities, but four Jews were seriously injured, and several more suffered bad cuts and bruises.

The bombing sent a tremor of fear through the entire community. For the first time in many years it brought back all the horror of the *farhud,* and forced the Jews to admit that for all the efforts of the underground, as a community they were no more able to defend themselves now than they had been a decade earlier. Having suffered almost two years of near-continual harassment, discrimination, and intimidation the community was understandably jittery. But the Abu Nuwas bombing tipped that nervousness into full-blown panic. It left the Jews without a shred of doubt that the Iraqis—at least the more militant among them—now intended to kill them.

The next day there was a rush on the Ezra Daoud Synagogue as thousands of Jews gathered to renounce their Iraqi citizenship. Jostling in huge crowds, people clamored for attention and waved their identification papers in the air. Many carried suitcases with them. Others had tight wads of money tucked inside their clothes, the better to bribe officials with. A pitiful few—illiterate, destitute, and disoriented—threw themselves on the mercy of the authorities and begged shamelessly for their *laissez-passers.*

The police officers and volunteer clerks brought in to supervise the registration process worked round the clock for a week to complete the task of registering the crowds for emigration. A special kitchen was set up to feed these workers, and a few enterprising Jews who hoped that some small act of kindness would help bump them up to the head of the line brought them additional gifts and tokens of thanks. Most of the would-be emigrants came from the poorer classes.

They had little to lose and few affairs to wind up: without too much trouble they could simply pack up and leave. But the middle classes were equally agitated by the bombing. There was a sense of urgency to their activities now, as they stepped up preparations for departure, egged on by Zionist pamphlets. "O Children of Zion," began one of these polemics: "You are the backbone of your people and its main support. Do not let the torch be extinguished in the darkness of exile. . . . Israel is calling you—Get out of Babylon!"

Even before the Abu Nuwas attack, Jews anxious to leave Iraq were selling their property in such large numbers that the housing market quickly became saturated. As the *Jewish Chronicle* noted in March 1950, "the price of houses and also rents, which until recently were excessively high, particularly in Baghdad, have dropped by about 80 per cent. Houses which formerly were sold for £10,000 can now be had for £2,000. The price of furniture has also dropped considerably, and the second-hand market is flooded with household goods hurriedly sold by auction."

It didn't help that anti-Jewish propagandists were giving market forces a helping hand. The Baghdad daily *al-Hossoun* alleged that "Jewish furniture, which is being sold daily by auction, is contaminated with a special poison sent to Iraqi Jews in small parcels by the Israeli Government," while one of the city's spiritual leaders issued a *fatwa* forbidding faithful Muslims to buy goods, furniture, or property from Jews.

Salha was outraged by the foul play. "These Arabs would like nothing better than to get us out of their hair and yet at every turn they put obstacles in our path. What's the word for that kind of knife-turning?" she asked Regina, "Sadism?"

By the end of April more than forty thousand people had registered for emigration, and Regina saw no reason to wait any longer before adding her name to the growing list. She insisted that Solomon accompany her to the Ezra Daoud Synagogue, where she intended to denaturalize both herself and her children. Although the American-based Near Eastern Air Transport Company (an Alaskan Airlines subsidiary, which, unknown to the Iraqis, was part owned by the Israeli

airline El Al) had won the lucrative government contract for trans-
porting Iraqi Jews to Israel, it had not yet begun flying emigrants to
their new home. Instead the first emigrants were being shipped to
Iran and were flown to Israel from there. Regina had set her heart on
being among them.

Long years of experience had taught Regina that when it came to
dealing with the authorities one needed to demonstrate just the right
mix of humility and self-respect. It was necessary to be polite but in-
sistent, deferential but resolute. On the day she planned to register she
took some care with her appearance. She wore a light wool suit that
she had made herself from a French pattern. It was wine colored, with
mother-of-pearl buttons and in spite of the heat, she pinned a match-
ing wool hat to her hair. The overall effect was smart but not intimidating. Solomon, too, was well turned out, and, after Regina had
double-checked to make sure she had all the necessary paperwork
with her, the two of them set off toward the Ezra Daoud feeling confident and decisive.

At the synagogue they joined one of several long lines leading to a
series of wide tables at each of which sat a representative of the Iraqi
Central Intelligence Department and a member of the Jewish community. The Jew was there to explain the regulations to those who had
trouble understanding them and to be a reassuring presence in the
face of officialdom.

While Regina and Solomon waited their turn, a number of alterca-
tions broke out between officials and registrants who had failed to
bring the relevant documents of identification—proof of citizenship,
birth certificates, and the like. Most of these did not end well: voices
were raised in frustration, threats were issued, curses flew, and in one
instance a rowdy young Jew was manhandled out of the synagogue by
a uniformed official. Regina watched him leave, wincing slightly as
she saw him try to shrug off his escorts. In that instant she was
reminded of the gravity of what she was about to do. She'd be
renouncing something of infinite value. Without nationality one
was consigned to a kind of limbo. No wonder there was such tension.

"Mrs. Regina Levy," the official read out as he began riffling through the bundle of papers Regina had placed on the desk before him.

"That's right," said my grandmother.

"You are an Iraqi citizen. Forty-five years of age, brown hair, brown eyes, five feet and one inch high?"

"Yes."

"Can you prove that you do not owe the Iraqi government any money in uncollected taxes, fines, or unpaid debts?"

"Yes, I can," said Regina, and she handed the official a second set of papers. As he perused these, the Jewish observer smiled at her and told her that the regulations had been relaxed and that the government no longer required her to pay her own way to the Persian border.

"Mrs. Levy?" the Iraqi official said. "I see that you wish to emigrate with your three children."

"That is correct," said Regina, "I have given you each of their birth certificates."

"Yes you have. But they are all under twenty-one".

"My eldest daughter is almost twenty-one, my other daughter is eighteen, and my son is twelve."

"But you are a widow, Mrs Levy?" said the official, raising a quizzi-cal eyebrow, as if reproaching my grandmother for some unwitting act of stupidity.

"That's right," said Regina. "My husband passed away in 1942."

The official scratched his chin, exchanged a few inaudible words with the Jewish observer, and then addressed Regina in the tone of someone whose goodwill was in short supply.

"Mrs. Levy," he sighed. "There is no problem with your registering for denaturalization yourself, but you cannot register your children because they are not yet adults in the eyes of the law."

"But they are my children."

"That may be so, but only the children's father, as head of the household, has the authority to denaturalize your children, and since your husband is no more, they cannot be denaturalized. I'm sorry, Mrs. Levy, but your children cannot leave the country."

"That's impossible," said Regina, ignoring Solomon gently tugging at her arm. "I cannot leave without my children, and the State of Iraq has no right to detain them."

The official stared at Regina—or was it through her?—in silence. Their conversation was over. "Next," he said.

Outside the synagogue Regina needed to sit down and collect her thoughts, while Solomon ran off to get her a cold drink. She was hot, and her head felt a little light. All she could think of was the gall of it: how dare they undermine her authority as a mother and presume to tell her who or what her children might be or become. By the time Solomon returned, feeling was coming back to her, like blood rushing back to a sleeping limb, and Regina was all fire. She and the children, she told Solomon, would remove themselves from the country re-gardless, slip past the red tape, and vanish. They would become ghosts, just like others before them.

Twelve

LAST TRAIN TO BASRA

My mother's memories of the family's "Baghdad years" are preserved in two fat albums whose spines are so strong that when you open the covers the thick paper pages start fanning out stiffly and creakily. Most of the black-and-white photographs have yellowed with age, and some of the stick-on plastic corners that once secured them in place have been lost. But the albums are richer for the weathering, and I've thumbed through them frequently, mostly looking for pictures of Regina.

She almost never appears alone. She's either with her siblings or else with Elazar, the children, or the larger extended family, and she's invariably smiling and posed. Many of the photographs are formal portraits, shot in photographers' studios, labored pictures that hide more than they reveal. There's a wealth of detail in them—a characteristic expression, a specific setting, a special dress, a new hairstyle. But it is only in a series of imaginary snapshots that I'm able to chart the landmark events of Regina's life. In these I see her nervous features freeze-framed in the mirror on the morning of her wedding day, and the mixture of pride and contentment she beamed to the world as she cradled one of her newborns. I see the desolation in her eyes after she and Elazar were forced to sell the big house on Taht al-Takia and the mischief that danced in them as she reveled in her newfound career as a commodities trader. And I have a clear mental image of Regina's weary form resting outside the Ezra Daoud Synagogue after all her hopes to emigrate turned to dust. Exhausted and deflated, she stares into the middle distance.

But there is another picture—one of the last in the Baghdad series that exists only in my mind. In it Regina is standing behind the passenger rail of a gleaming white ocean liner. She's wearing white, and she's holding onto the rail and pushing away from it, as if drawn by the movement of the ship. The sea breeze is messing up her hair, and she's smiling broadly as the sun shines down on her and bounces dazzlingly off the white. The picture is carefree and full of motion, and it represents the way I see my grandmother, looking younger than her actual years, on the day she finally left Iraq in September 1950.

Regina did not end up joining the disappeared. The family judged that a risky and clandestine escape to Iran, abetted by Arab smugglers and Jewish operatives running secret halfway houses near the border, was too dangerous an undertaking for a widow traveling alone with her three children. After all, one still heard of people being detained at the border for weeks at a time, cut off from civilization and with access to only the most primitive of amenities, because they were suspected of smuggling money out of the country. For all their fighting spirit, the Levys were hardly fit to endure such privations. How would they survive on scant rations of bread and water? And what if some coarse and filthy prison guard took a shine to one of the girls? With such evils all too easy to envision, it was decided that an attempt would be made to secure Regina the necessary papers that would allow her to leave Iraq in a calm and organized fashion, and with most of her assets intact.

The question of what to do with one's assets was problematic, since the government imposed severe restrictions on what registering emigrants were allowed to take out of Iraq. Gold and silver were both prohibited and luggage was limited to sixty-seven pounds for adults traveling alone, and four-hundred pounds for families. According to strict regulations issued by the authorities, what the Jews *were* permitted to take was this: three summer outfits; three winter outfits; one pair of shoes; one blanket; six pairs of underwear, socks, and sheets;

one wedding ring, one wristwatch, one narrow bracelet, and no more than fifty dinars—that is, four hundred dollars. No wonder so many of them resorted to smuggling their life savings out of the country.

Regina had other reasons to be grateful for the twist of fate that excluded her from what had come to be known colloquially as "Operation Ali Baba." She would be spared a herding process in which emigrating Jews were stigmatized, branded as unpatriotic, and systematically degraded. As early as May 26, when the first flights began leaving for Cyprus—a disembarkation point the Iraqi authorities insisted on using to prevent planes flying directly from Iraqi airfields to a state the country refused to recognize—the business of emigration took on aspects of the mass-production process. Individuals became mere emigrants, reduced to the sum of the documents they carried. They were inspected and questioned, prodded and searched, and then bundled onto Skymasters for a one-way journey whose destination, though by now longed for, was utterly strange to them.

At customs, departing Jews faced more humiliation at the hands of uncouth customs officials out to grab whatever they could. The *Jewish Chronicle* reported that in addition to pilfering hidden trinkets, family silver, domestic ornaments, and anything else that took their fancy, "in many cases, officials have destroyed the meagre personal belongings of the passengers." The reporter went on to relate how, upon arriving at Baghdad Airport, "one family of three . . . were ordered by three officials to unpack their luggage. One of the officials picked up a small portable radio and hurled it to the ground, smashing it beyond repair; a box filled with china was kicked to fragments by another of the officials. The emigrants were then told that they could not take out additional clothes or blankets, while some cooking utensils were also withheld." In many cases luggage confiscated by customs officials in Iraq failed ever to appear in Israel.

Hardening themselves against the rumors of rough treatment that filtered back from departing Jews, would-be emigrants lined up to sign up for emigration in ever-increasing numbers, setting in motion a kind of chain reaction within the community. Sons and daughters refused to leave without their parents, who would not be parted from brothers and sisters, who refused to budge without friends. In every case the bonds of affection and loyalty to clan proved stronger than the ties to the land. By and by, people who had no obvious desire to leave Iraq and who'd never given Zionism the time of day found themselves packing up and moving to Israel. Elderly folk who wanted nothing more than to die in Baghdad with their families around them were uprooted, and children were plucked out of school midway through their studies.

Amid the commotion and disruption of a mass departure whose scale was starting to defy all predictions, Regina was compelled to pursue a different exit route. For some years her sister Josephine had lived in Calcutta as part of a large and thriving expatriate community of Iraqi Jews. The Jews had initially been attracted to India by possibilities for trade and, later, by the British presence there. But they quickly acclimated to the easygoing pace of Indian life and to the inherent tolerance of a society in which several religious groups coexisted, for the most part, in peace. In India, Jews had never known persecution, and they listened aghast to the stories of terror and intimidation that poured out of Baghdad.

When the family in Baghdad alerted Josephine to Regina's plight, she undertook to help. She located a Jewish school whose principal was happy to write to the Iraqi authorities confirming that the Levy children had places to study English at her establishment, and she engaged a cousin, Reuben Zeloof, to act as Regina's sponsor. With these two critical arrangements in place, Regina managed to acquire a three-month visa to India from the British Embassy in Baghdad. "Apply and ye shall receive," Solomon had joked. Now she faced the harder of her tasks: that of obtaining passports and exit visas from the Iraqis themselves.

Every day Regina took herself to the Ministry of the Interior, whose imposing building was located in a Muslim part of town. After a very public scandal involving one of the ministry's employees, who along with a handful of Jewish accomplices had been found guilty of forging the minister's signature and selling fake passports to desperate Jews, officials were running a tight ship: they were scrupulous to the point of being tiresome. But the sour-faced and thickly whiskered minion whom Regina had the bad luck always to encounter seemed merely sadistic. Staring at her as if he objected to her very existence, he would say: "It is a very serious process to grant travel documents to you and your children. It takes time, lots of time. Come back tomorrow." Then, when Regina appeared before him the next day, he would throw up his hands in annoyance and say: "Do you think I have nothing better to do than to work on your case? Come again tomorrow, and I'll see what I can do." So it went, day after day.

Around this time the Israeli government passed the Law of Return, a simple piece of utopian legislation that harked back to the dreams of Zionism's founders. It began, "Every Jew has the right to immigrate to this country." These were wonderful words, but they were of little help to Regina. For here she was applying daily for a passport that meant everything to her now, but that would be worthless the moment her three-month visa expired. Provided she ever got to India in the first place, she would soon find herself stranded there, stateless, for once she refused to return to Iraq with her children their citizenship would be revoked. The indignity of it tortured her all the more now that Israel had decided to embrace every Jew as a potential son or daughter.

When Regina felt her spirits flagging, such thoughts could send her spinning into a lightless place from which her whole life appeared to be marked for failure. At such times she felt as if she had merely tumbled from catastrophe to catastrophe, as if her life lacked the gentle structuring arc that gave other people's experiences some backbone. And yet, conscious of her maternal duties, she always managed to rally her strength. She'd focus her mind on practicalities and think how proud her late husband would have been to see her forge ahead. Having honed her survival skills through years of adversity, Regina had, without realizing it, become a formidable woman.

One day in August, Regina went to the ministry as usual, but when her old foe summoned her to his desk for what to him had become a game of ritual humiliation, a man she had never seen before stepped in and informed the official that from now on he would be handling Mrs. Levy's case. It turned out that this civil servant had recognized Regina as the sister of his coffeehouse acquaintance Nessim Sehayek, and out of respect for Nessim's family he took it upon himself to help her. Within a few days he had four pristine passports and four stamped exit visas ready to hand over to Regina. He was more than a little embarrassed by her fulsome thanks. *"Allah khalik,"* she told him, over and over—"God bless you."

With her precious papers safely in hand Regina became a dynamo. She conspired with Elazar's nephew Albert to have the bulk of her funds quietly transferred to Reuben Zeloof in Bombay. She sold off a dozen or so beautiful carpets that remained her prize assets after the big house was gone, and she steeled herself to dispose of her linens and lace and silver and china—many of them wedding gifts—as well as the few tokens she had left of Elazar and his family. One of the heirlooms that proved hardest to part with was the boxed set of strange-looking, polished-brass dental instruments that had once belonged to Elazar's father, which Regina had kept as a kind of talisman after they'd left the house on Taht al-Takia. It was several weeks before she let the metal merchant set his greedy eyes on them.

This torturous process of divestment pained my mother, too. A hoarder by nature, Marcelle was attached to her possessions, especially to her books, which were dog-eared and tattered with use and which Regina implored her at least to give away if she could not bear to discard them. "What, even my Balzac?" she had cried, as if this literary giant were her own child. In fact, Balzac and Hugo and Molière had been her stoic companions, friends who'd stuck with her through thick and thin, and who shone the light on bigger things than existed within the four walls of her Baghdad home.

At eighteen Marcelle had the reedy figure and gamine looks of a young Audrey Hepburn; a shy smile, a fashionable feathery bob, a limber-limbed walk. She was the kind of girl who turned heads. But whereas most girls her age dreamed of love and romance, she had set her heart on a college career. Whenever she got top grades in class, she could practically see the shining path that as a successful young lawyer she would one day beat to the hallowed halls of justice. Years later that lost vision still moved Marcelle to tears, not least because she understood that giving away her books before leaving Baghdad was the first step in its dismantlement.

But there were difficult moments all around. For Regina the most bittersweet of them came with the rushed bar mitzvah of her son, Haron, at the newly built Meir Tweg Synagogue in Betaween. A bar mitzvah is usually a joyous event celebrating a boy's passage into adulthood and maturity—a journey that most Iraqi Jews had, until meantly, viewed as a gateway to a brilliant future. But Haron's bar mitzvah was a different order of celebration, one in which the central theme of life's progress was twisted into something that more closely resembled the experience of a young girl who, on the threshold of marriage, would be forced to sever her links with the past and step boldly into the dark unknown.

When Haron read his portion of the Torah, rocking back and forth on his heels the way he'd seen grown men do it, Regina felt a terrible sense of loss wash over her. She thought of everything they would soon be giving up: a language, a way of life, a community, a complete world. And she thought of Elazar and of how much he would have wanted to witness this day alongside Salha, who was quietly shedding tears of joy behind her handkerchief, and Ezra, who had personally coached the boy in Hebrew, and was now craning his neck in order to catch his pupil's every word. Only Haron was oblivious to his mother's grief. In his child's innocence he read his lines with the confidence of one who still believed that his future was assured.

With the last of their possessions packed and the final ritual faithfully observed, all that was left was for Regina to secure the family's passage to India aboard a British steam liner and then take the train down to Basra to board it.

Neither Bertha nor Marcelle can recall those last late-summer days in Baghdad in any appreciable detail—perhaps because it's in the detail that the intrinsic pain of departure resides. There would have been last visits to favorite haunts, last meetings with dear friends, last rites, last words, and several rounds of tearful farewells. But all these things have faded from view, buried beneath the better memories that supplanted them.

For Bertha and Marcelle, the final chapter of their Baghdad experience begins with the family's hasty departure for Basra. Each of them had just one large suitcase, and there were two carpets that Regina could not bear to part with. One she would keep, the other she planned to give Reuben Zeloof in thanks for his sponsorship. Leaving Baghdad station shortly after lunch, their train powered southward along the line built by the British after World War I, trailing a plume of black smoke through the towns of al-Hillah, Diwaniya, Samara, and Nasiriya. By evening the family was sipping tea with their hosts, Victor and Violet Battat, and looking out over the palm and date trees that dotted the Battats' lush, landscaped garden. Basra's Jews, unlike Baghdad's, seemed unruffled by the business of denaturalization. But according to Victor, appearances were deceptive. "I don't think a single Jew will remain here once registration closes," he said. "On the surface, life continues as before. But mark my words, everyone will leave."

According to Salha, their cousin Victor was "something big," at the Port of Basra Authority, and he certainly seemed to Regina to lack nothing in stature. His modern villa was spacious and tastefully furnished and its grounds were the same size as some of Baghdad's smaller public parks. The arrangement was that Victor and Violet would shelter Regina and her children for the night until it was time to board the ship the next morning, and that, conditions permitting, Victor would pull a few strings on their behalf when it came to dealing with officialdom. For now, all Regina needed to do was relax, eat well, bathe, and sleep. This was one of the rare times in her life that she was someone's else's guest, and she tried to allow herself the luxury of an evening off.

The family's last day in Iraq was destined to be a long one. It began at dawn, when Victor drove them to the Gulf port, pulling up in front of a series of low brick buildings that were set back from the quay, blocking any decent view of the docks. The buildings were home to customs and passport control, the last barriers between the family and their new life. Regina braced herself for trouble. She knew as well as anyone that Iraqi customs officials enjoyed baiting Jews; detaining them unnecessarily, questioning the validity of their travel documents, roughing up their luggage, and helping themselves to whatever pickings they could find. But she had Victor with her.

As if able to read her mind, Victor exuded calm confidence. This was his territory, a place where he was seen not as a Jew but as the boss: it was his ship, his charge. With a terse clap of the hands, Victor summoned a couple of porters, who began loading Regina's luggage onto a large wheeled cart. Regina's instinct was to watch over them, monitoring each item's journey from car trunk to cart, but Victor gestured her into the building. "Don't worry about them, they're good men," he said.

The next half hour was nothing like Regina anticipated. With Victor at their side, the customs officials couldn't have been nicer. It was "Sayeeda" this and "Sayeeda" that, and there was much bowing and genuflection. One young official was even dispatched to fetch them all cold lemonade. Thanks to Victor, Regina and her children were waved through customs without having their bags searched at all. They were issued certificates that cleared them for departure and waved on to passport control with a nod and a smile.

There Victor bade them a fond farewell. "The worst is over," he said.

Marcelle recalls that each member of the family party was then interviewed individually at passport control. "You're leaving for good, aren't you?" an official asked her, as he leafed quickly through the unblemished pages of her brand-new passport: "You're not coming back."

"No, we're only going for three months," she told him, repeating what her mother had instructed her to say. She was certain that she had given the game away. Her heart was thumping loudly as she voiced the words, pounding in her rib cage, her head, and her ears.

Marcelle was, and still is, a terrible liar and she must have looked incredibly unconvincing with her face flushed red and her eyes darting everywhere with evasiveness. But who knows what motivated

this official? Perhaps he took pity on her, a shy Jewish girl, clearly innocent, clearly unused to dealing with authorities: what could she
have to hide? Or perhaps the rest of the family's confident assurances
convinced him where Marcelle did not. Then again, maybe he had
no ax to grind against Jews. It wasn't impossible. Whatever the reason, he let Regina and her children through, and they proceeded to
board the British India Steam Navigation Company's finest liner, the
multi-storied *Dumra,* a fleet, sturdy vessel that sailed back and forth
along the Basra–Bombay route under the watchful eye of her British
captain.

Then the family's luck ran out. Barely had they settled in to their
cabin when a trio of customs officers came looking for them. Regina
had spotted them talking with the captain outside on the deck and felt
sick with dread. Later she would discover that the officials had been
demanding that the captain offload them but that the captain had refused to comply. His passengers were on British property, he'd said,
and no longer subject to Iraqi law: if the officials wanted to search the
family, then they'd have to do so on board.

Barging into Regina's cabin, the customs officials pounced on her
suitcases like wolves, and in minutes the place was an unholy mess.
Pages from torn books lay scattered over clothes tossed willy-nilly
onto the bunks and the floor. Private things—toiletries, hairbrushes,
stockings, and underwear—were on display for all to see. The suitcases themselves had been ripped to make sure that nothing was hidden in their frames. Over everything lay a fine coating of face powder,
spilled when the officials ransacked Regina's makeup case and flung its
contents across the cabin. The officials had left nothing undamaged
and nothing undisturbed. They had even taken knives to the shoulder
pads of Regina's suits.

Early in this process Regina had gone out on deck, complaining
that she needed some air. In truth she had smuggled out of the cabin a
cloth bundle containing her jewelry, which she planned to cast into
the sea. If she couldn't keep her gold and her pearls then the waves
could have them, she thought. Anything would be better than giving
them up to Iraqi customs officers. Watching Regina deliberate thus as

she held her precious bundle over the railing was an Indian boy, a rag-covered, greasy-haired, shoeless creature, no more than eighteen years old, who to judge by his whites worked in the ship's galley.

"Madam," he called up to her from the quayside below, "you look troubled. Can I help you?" Regina was taken aback by the boy's appearance, since she had thought she was alone. Yet in one of those straightforward exchanges that a crisis can sometimes produce, she cut to the chase and replied: "These are my jewels. I don't want the customs officers to find them."

"Then throw them to me," said the boy. "I'll look after them for you."

Without hesitating, Regina threw the boy her jewelry and off he ran, disappearing from view before she could say another word to him. Well, that's that, she thought. Better that this ragamuffin should have her gold than the Iraqi authorities.

When she returned to the cabin, a uniformed woman with thick features set in grim determination was there waiting for her, ready to conduct a body search. The children, too, had to undergo body searches, even Haron, on whose small frame Regina had for a brief moment considered hiding her jewelry.

The relief the family felt when the customs officials finally left them alone, having turned up nothing illegal or suspect in their search, was fleeting. Within minutes a couple of passport control officers came on board, making noises about the irregularity of Regina's travel documents. It would be necessary to contact head office in Baghdad, they said, and without further ado they confiscated the family's passports and marched off the ship. They were assuming that since the *Dumra* was due to leave that morning, the captain would simply sail without them. What they didn't factor in was that, unlike themselves, the captain was a man of principle, and he refused point-bank to abandon his passengers to the whims of the authorities. The *Dumra* would stay put until the family's passports were returned.

When it became clear that the captain meant every word, the authorities relented. That evening the two officials who had seized the passports returned with the documents. They were the worse for drink, and, finding themselves among a group of women traveling on their own, they decided they could use a little female company. The officers plunked themselves down in Regina's cabin and started berating her. Why are you taking such pretty young women out of the country? they asked, pointing to Bertha and Marcelle. And what about your son? He would make a fine soldier in the Iraqi army. Pulling out a bottle of cheap liquor, they each took a slug and then invited a reluctant Regina to join them. She was terrified—too terrified even to consider sounding the alarm.

Thankfully one of the ship's officers had seen the passport officials stagger on board and had grown concerned when he didn't see them leave again. The officer knocked on Regina's door to find out if company was something she desired, and when she indicated not, he booted the drunken Iraqi officials off the ship and promised Regina that for the remainder of the night she would be bothered by no one. Despite his assurances Regina maintained a sleepless vigil, not trusting the Iraqi authorities not to cook up yet another pretext to disembark them. She knew the Iraqi mentality, that the officials would look upon preventing her departure as a challenge or game. They'd probably already taken bets on the matter. Where was Victor now? she wondered.

Calm returned to her at first light. Preparations were getting under way for the ship's departure, and there were no Iraqi officials in sight. Regina went out on deck, from where she could survey the quay, to make sure that no one was coming for them, and there she grew fascinated by the myriad tasks involved in setting sail. She saw supply trucks pull right up to the ship, where a dozen or so men were loading goods into the cargo hold, and she watched white-shirted crewmen pace the quayside, uncoiling the thick ropes that prevented the *Dumra* from drifting. Soon after, the gangplank was noisily yanked back into the ship, and Regina felt the engines come to life beneath her feet, thrumming with a gentle purr.

"Madam! Madam!" she heard, a shrill voice interrupting her reverie, and then, *thunk!* she was suddenly clasping a package to her chest. It was the Indian boy from the day before, who'd come running up along the quayside and simply thrown her jewelry at her. She called after him: "Wait, let me give you something." But the boy had already run off.

When she examined her parcel, Regina saw that her jewelry was untouched. She marveled at the unlikelihood of it all. Like some benevolent genie, the boy had done her bidding in her hour of need and then vanished into thin air. If he'd lingered for just a moment before evaporating, she would have gladly given him a handsome reward, a gold coin, a jeweled hatpin, or perhaps a brooch. But she'd been stunned by the sheer surprise of him. It occurred to her that the boy was somehow incorporeal, somehow above the banality and grime of material transaction. And she didn't even know his name.

Regina thought about this boy many times after that day. She would always wonder what had moved him to help her. All she knew was that at the moment she had given up hope he had come to her, like a heavenly sign, and restored her faith in humanity.

"I declare willingly and voluntarily that I have decided to leave Iraq permanently and that I am aware this statement of mine will have the effect of depriving me of Iraqi nationality and of causing my deportation from Iraq and of preventing me forever afterward from returning." Solomon read the words out aloud to Nessim before he took his pen to the declaration and signed it. "There, it's done," he said. Ezra and Salha took turns signing next, followed by their youngest daughter, Marcelle. Only Nessim, who had accompanied the rest of the family to the registration center on a mild spring morning in 1951, did not sign up to emigrate. He and his wife were determined to continue their lives in Baghdad, throwing in their lot with the wait-and-see crowd, whose number was daily diminishing.

"I cannot for the life of me understand the mass hysteria," Nessim had exclaimed a few weeks back when Solomon informed him that official figures for the year 1950 stated that more than eighty-five thousand Jews had registered to leave Iraq.

"The entire community in Mosul has effectively liquidated itself," Solomon had said at the time, "and Basra is following suit. The rich are helping the poor to leave, communal property has been put up for sale, and all three of Basra's Jewish schools have closed down. In six months' time the only Jews left in this country will be in Baghdad—and what a miserable lot they will make."

"And I suppose you think you'll be better off in the transit camps in Israel?"

"That, Nessim, is a temporary state of affairs. As soon as the government allocates us to the towns, we'll be able to start building normal lives. Do you think I'd be taking our parents with me if I thought for a minute that they'd be better off here?"

"All I'm saying is that you are gambling with your future every bit as much as I am. Write to me after those six months of yours are up, and we'll see which one of us has made the right decision."

Like thousands of undecided Jews up and down the country, Solomon had his mind made up for him on January 14, 1951, after a hand grenade was thrown into a group of Jews gathered in the courtyard of the Massouda Shemtob Synagogue, an assembly point for emigrants on their way to Baghdad Airport. That day the synagogue was full of Kurdish Jews from Sulaimaniyah. Outside a Jewish boy was distributing candy among the crowd. The explosion killed him instantly and an old man standing near him was blinded. Eight more people later died from their injuries, including two Muslims who happened to be passing by when the explosion occurred.

Until January 13, 85,893 people had registered for emigration. After the bombing another twenty thousand rushed forward to add their names to the list, including the Sehayeks. Rumors gained ground that an Arab terrorist organization was plotting against the Jews and that further targets had already been marked for attack. It was no longer a question of if, but when, the culprits would strike again. Better to leave while there was still time. Such was the panic among departing Jews that on the night before the yearlong registration window expired, on March 8, people were paying as much as two hundred dinars (or eight hundred dollars) to ensure their names were on the list.

The Jews were not the only people actively hustling that night. Prime Minister Nuri as-Said was convening parliament in secret session in order to push through Law No. 5 of 1951. The new law, which was ratified on March 10, decreed that the possessions of Jews who had relinquished their Iraqi nationality were to be confiscated by the government and that their liquid assets were to be frozen with immediate effect. Overnight, virtually the entire Jewish community was transformed into paupers. Community leaders petitioned the British for help, but the British were reluctant to intercede with the Iraqi government in so delicate a matter when Israel was displaying the same intransigence toward the Palestinians.

The six Jewish deputies who had been excluded from Nuri's secret session complained loudly about being sidelined, and one of them resigned. But their power had already faded: even now their parliamentary colleagues were muttering behind their backs, asking what need the small number of loyalist Jews remaining in Iraq would have for six deputies once their coreligionists had departed.

Israel retaliated immediately, with Foreign Secretary Moshe Sharett announcing that twenty million pounds would be deducted from any compensation that Israel considered paying to the Arabs. What Sharett neglected to mention was that the Iraqi Jews wouldn't see any of that money either, even though one could contend—as did the British—that it was up to the Israeli government to compensate them. Meanwhile the U.S. State Department issued a public statement condemning Law No. 5 as "clearly a racist law, conforming to the spirit and letter of the Nazi Nuremberg laws."

The eleventh-hour theft of Jewish property and the subsequent failure of any government, principally an Iraqi one, to assume responsibility for compensating the Jews has been a running sore among members of the dispersed community. But at the time Law No. 5 was passed, the Jews were barely able to organize their personal affairs, let alone lobby for their collective rights. As the *Jewish Chronicle* reported on March 30, "The position of the Jews in Iraq is deteriorating rapidly. Shops, restaurants, and other establishments belonging to Jews awaiting emigration are closed, and communal life has come to a standstill."

Many Jews found themselves jobless as soon as they'd registered for emigration. Doctors and pharmacists who'd signed away their nation-

ality had their right to practice revoked; Arab banks fired all denaturalized Jews; and the government penalized Muslims who had business dealings with them. Already a class system was in operation in
Iraq, with Sunni Muslims at the top of the pile, ahead of the Shias, and
with minorities ranged beneath them. Now the denaturalized constituted a new underclass, akin to the Indian Untouchables: it was as if
everything they touched were contaminated.

Meanwhile the Near East Air Transport operation was unable to
move Jews to Israel fast enough. At the time Law No. 5 was passed,
only forty thousands denaturalized Jews had been flown to Israel out
of the 105,000 who had registered for emigration, and it was not unusual for emigrants to have to wait up to six months to leave the country. Stateless, often homeless, and for the most part jobless,
denaturalized Jews were forced to throw themselves on the generosity
of family members who had not renounced their nationality, and on
the charity of the wider community. With little else to do other than
await the call that would give them only twenty-four hours to ready
themselves for departure, they sat around bemoaning their fate and
wondering how it had come to this.

Reporting at the end of March, the *Jewish Chronicle* claimed that
under the custodian general who was appointed to oversee the se-
questration and disposal of all property belonging to denaturalized
persons, "forty 'liquidation committees' have been set up and these
have seized hundreds of business premises, cars, and large quantities
of merchandise." Everything that the Jews possessed was confiscated.
And what didn't go straight into the Iraqi treasury began stacking up
in warehouses around Baghdad. Confiscated gold and jewelry were
stored at the National Bank. Perishable foodstuffs and livestock were
sold on the open market.

The paper went on to report that Baghdadi Jews were subject to a
"reign of terror" in which gangs of hooligans cruised Jewish neighborhoods, burgling and vandalizing Jewish property, and that the police
were arresting Jews simply in order to extort money from them. The
Jews felt victimized on every level. Once the Iraqi government had
placed them beyond the law, they became easy prey for anyone wish-

ing to maltreat them, from Muslim business rivals fed up with Jewish domination of the markets and pan-Arab nationalists who'd felt all along that the Jews were a kind of cancer on Arab society, right down to ordinary thugs who wielded cudgels in place of ideology.

In response to the rapid deterioration of conditions in Baghdad, which saw two more bombs detonated in Jewish buildings in the spring of 1951, Zionists in America began making a great deal of noise about Jewish persecution in Iraq in an attempt to embarrass the Iraqi government. They also drummed up funds to help speed up the emigration process so that denaturalized Jews would not have to wait so long before leaving. At the back of their minds was the fear, shared to some extent by the Iraqi elite, that if nothing was done, the country risked another *farhud*-like uprising against the Jews.

The Israeli government also took action. After three thousand people marched in Tel Aviv, calling on the government to save the Iraqi Jews, it lifted all immigration restrictions on so-called "Oriental" Jews and allocated extra funds to the Jewish Agency for emergency housing. Every effort was made to absorb arriving immigrants as quickly and smoothly as possible. Not least, the number of flights leaving Baghdad—now directly—for Lydda Airport was doubled. Solomon, Ezra, Salha, and the remaining sixty-five thousand denaturalized Jews were shipped out of the country by the end of June.

And then it was all over. Twenty-five hundred years of Jewish history in the oldest Diaspora community were effectively at an end. Looking back, Iraqi Jews were never quite sure how and why it happened so quickly. They discussed it endlessly. They told their children about it. Then they did their best to build new lives for themselves elsewhere.

A deathly quiet hung over Baghdad that summer. Across the city thousands of buildings that had belonged to Jews were boarded up, while thousands of confiscated villas that had yet to fall under the auctioneer's hammer had nothing but the warm desert breeze blowing through them. Not even forty liquidation committees could dispose of Jewish homes and businesses fast enough to cover up the chasm left in city life after one-third of the population had disappeared. The economy was devastated. The markets were depressed, the souks deserted, and Rashid Street was a shadow of its former self. If one stood at one end and looked down the street, it was as if the color had somehow been drained from the scene.

By June 1952 it was estimated that no more than six thousand Jews remained in Baghdad, most of them mourning the departure of beloved friends and relatives, while every single provincial community had been liquidated. The Iraqis called it the *taskeet*—the denaturalization. Back then there was no urgent moral language to describe the political engineering of such wholesale shifts in a country's demographic makeup: today it would be called ethnic cleansing.

Part Three

FULL CIRCLE

Thirteen

THE ANNIVERSARY

On the crisp mid-March morning my plane pulled out of the clouds over Heathrow Airport and began speeding eastward toward Amman—from where Baghdad still lay a grueling nine hours' drive away—it occurred to me that I had to be one of only a handful of Iraqi Jews who had schemed to get into the country, rather than out of it, in many decades. No one from the dispersed community had ventured into Iraq during the long years of Saddam Hussein's reign for fear of not being able to get out again. And in the ten months since Saddam had been overthrown, I was aware of only two Iraqi Jews who had braved the journey: one an Iraqi-born British national determined to revisit his roots, the other an American-born lawyer from solid Iraqi stock, who was working with the Baghdad-based American administration, a body known as the Coalition Provisional Authority.

By spring 2004, when I made my trip, conditions inside Iraq were worsening and few pundits bothered anymore with optimistic predictions. Instead, debate in both diplomatic and military circles focused on what the best "exit strategy" might be, since there were 115,000 American troops deployed in the country at the time, and, even then, they were subject to almost daily attack. Most of my friends thought I was mad even to contemplate visiting Baghdad in such circumstances, and yet here I was turning my back on everything I held most dear—not least my husband and daughter—in order to chase after specters and shadows.

I was under no illusions about my trip. I knew that there would be few, if any, concrete traces of Regina's life left for me to uncover, assuming I was able to get anywhere near them. But the need to see Baghdad with my own eyes had taken on a near-obsessive quality. What began as a simple desire to return to the homeland of my ancestors had become a mission to mend a small tear in the fabric of time.

If I'd been faster on my feet, I might have taken advantage of the chaos into which Iraq was plunged in the immediate aftermath of Saddam's overthrow, slipped quietly into Baghdad, seen to my affairs, and then left again before anyone noted my presence there. In that scenario I would have had to contend with water shortages and electricity blackouts, but not the car bombings, kidnappings, marauding gangs of youths armed with knives, sniper fire, and mortar bombings that had since become part of daily life in the capital. As it was, my visit took place exactly a year after American and British forces unleashed a blanket-bombing campaign designed to "shock and awe" the city into submission, and on top of the violent disaffection already flaring, everyone anticipated fireworks of one sort or another.

Conditions for Westerners in Iraq had deteriorated appreciably in the weeks immediately preceding my trip. Just days before I left London, two journalists were carjacked and ruthlessly murdered on the road to al-Hillah. Word on the ground was that the then-nascent insurgency was growing stronger and bolder by the day and that the rising tide of enmity toward Westerners signaled that any non-Iraqi was now being held to account for the American invasion.

In terms of general security the Americans seemed to have lost the plot. After giving a tacit go-ahead to the widespread rioting and looting that attended the so-called liberation of Baghdad the occupying army looked as if it had no teeth. Indeed, after making one particularly memorable appearance, in which they formed a caravan circle around the Oil Ministry, American tanks practically disappeared from Baghdad's streets, leaving to the whims of the mob even those

Baathist strongholds that contained ample records of Saddam's extensive crimes against the Iraqi people.

This sense of American disengagement was confirmed by an intrepid Briton who ventured into Iraq a few months before me, and
who gave me the no-nonsense lowdown on his return. "The U.S.
forces have nothing on the ground, no people, no intelligence," he
said. "They just travel about in armored convoys and it's a joke. They
can't even follow a kid who throws a rock at their Humvees."

Naturally I was anxious about safety. The Foreign Office in London
had a single representative in Baghdad to deal with civilian emergen-
cies. But he was based in the Green Zone—the palm-lined territory in
the west of the city that included Saddam's former palace and a host
of other buildings then co-opted as the Coalition Provisional Authority's headquarters—and he was as out of touch with the reality on the
ground as his American counterparts.

A more proximate reason for my anxiety concerned some several
pounds of vacuum-sealed cooked meat that occupied more than half
my suitcase. I had no idea what customs officers would make of this
strange cargo. If questioned, I planned to claim that I'd be spending a
good deal of time in rural Iraq, far from villages and towns where I
could shop for provisions. Even so, it was more the type of meat I was
carrying that concerned me. Classic fare of its kind—salt beef, Wiener
schnitzel, Vienna sausages, and roast chicken—it was, to use a favorite
phrase of one of Baghdad's former chief rabbis, "kosher of the
kosher," and it bore the London Beit Din's stamp of approval to prove
it. I'd removed the Hebrew labels from the food beforehand and arranged to pay a "fixer" to express-track me through customs without
being searched. But until I was safely out of the airport and in the car
I'd hired to drive me to Baghdad I was unable to relax.

The meat was intended to be a novel kind of calling card that
would introduce and, I hoped, endear me to the handful of Jews who
still lived in Iraq after all these years—the last representatives of a lost
civilization. According to a cousin of my mother's, who only a couple
of years earlier had herself fled the country illegally, surprising us all
with her very existence, the last Jews were a fast-dwindling group.

Most were elderly and frail, some had more or less assimilated, while a few ailing souls were being plucked out of Iraq by well-meaning aid agencies.

By the time I arrived there were just twenty-two Jews left, all of them living in Baghdad. Since the war began they had been too afraid to come together as a community, either for prayer or solace, and when one of their elders died, they shied away from properly observing communal funeral rites. Fearing the kind of terrorist attack that destroyed a synagogue in Istanbul in 2003, the Jews had barricaded up the one remaining synagogue in the city, the Meir Tweg Synagogue in Betaween, where my uncle had been bar mitzvahed. No services had been held there in almost a year, and no meat had been koshered. Given this state of paralysis, it wasn't at all clear if they would open their doors to me. Still, I banished the nagging thought that I might have come all this way for nothing by imagining the long hours I hoped to spend talking to those among them who were about my age: those whose lives might, but for the workings of fate, so easily have been my own.

The idea that there were any Jews left in Iraq at all had at first struck me as extraordinary. After the mass exodus of 1950–51, Jews such as Nessim and his family had left Iraq in a succession of waves, following periodic routings of so called Zionist "spy rings," and, later, a constant slow trickle of broken-spirited emigrants succeeded in reaching Iran or Syria or Jordan, evading detection by Saddam's secret police. That a stubborn few had stayed behind and managed to resist the continual low-level pressure to convert to Islam seemed incredible. Perhaps they'd been trapped? Indeed, I remember hearing about an isolated group of Jewish families in the town of Hit that converted en masse roughly thirty years ago, and I remember thinking that was that: those forgotten apostates were the last members of their race in Iraq.

As I winged my way toward Baghdad, I could still scarcely believe that a handful of Jews remained in Iraq. In the aftermath of the war it proved extremely difficult to contact them, if only to verify their existence, much less alert them to my own. Telephone lines were down, the postal service had been suspended, and emails and faxes were still rare luxuries. Conceptually and even materially, the last Jews seemed unreal to me. Had they not ended up time-warped in a strange no-man's land where they could neither openly declare their true colors, nor cherish their identity as a shared secret, I might have been tempted to view them in an almost romantic light as quasimagical creatures who had somehow given history the slip. The only problem with this fantasy was that history had in no uncertain terms come back to claim them.

Everybody wanted a piece of the last Jews of Baghdad. The Hebrew Immigrant Aid Society (HIAS) had dispatched a representative to Iraq to entice them to emigrate to Israel. Relatives they had not seen in more than fifty years had begun petitioning the American military to protect them, and Western journalists, attracted by the mysterious survival of a meager band of representatives from a once-great community, had attempted to track them down, one by one.

Back in the flow of historical events, the last Jews of Baghdad were somewhat startled by the sudden attention and not a little ashamed of the condition in which the outside world found them. They had existed in straitened conditions for so long it was as if time itself had forgotten them; their clothes were shabby, their homes neglected, and in the aftermath of war, their confidence was battered. Fear now dominated their lives. One of the older women among their number, it was rumored, had not stepped outside her front door since the bombing of Baghdad commenced in March 2003. Another refused to go anywhere after dark unless accompanied by a Muslim colleague.

The six thousand Jews who'd elected to remain in Baghdad after the *taskeet* cannot have imagined that it would ever have come to this: that a community that had dominated both trade and finance, that had friends in the highest places in Iraqi society, and that, even in 1951 and beyond, had envisaged a future for itself that was as bright as its past, would be all but obliterated, its last members struggling on amid every conceivable disadvantage: persecution, war, sanctions, and now the uncertainty of what Iraq might become.

★ ★ ★

As Operation Ali Baba drew to a close, just one thing stood between those six thousand Jews and the return to normality they craved: the matter of figuring out who was behind the bombing campaign that devastated the community in 1950 and 1951. In the absence of any concrete evidence, speculation flourished. The Jews believed that agents of the Iraqi government had masterminded the bombings. The Communists were convinced that anti-Semitic ultranationalists were behind the campaign, while the nationalists, in turn, fingered the Communists, for no better reason than that they couldn't conceive that Communists stood for anything but trouble.

The Iraqi government was meanwhile determined to pin the bombings on the Zionist underground. The apparent motive (logical, if a little twisted) was that by sowing panic in the community, the underground could stampede the Jews into registration centers for a speedy dispatch to Israel. Without a shred of proof to support its case, however, the government was hog-tied: it had motives aplenty but no indication of means.

Then, on May 22, 1951, with the chance arrest in Baghdad of a Mossad agent called Yudke Tajer, the plot began to unravel. Tajer's address book yielded a host of underground contacts whom the police promptly arrested and then tortured to obtain further leads. Again! Baghdad's police cells began rapidly filling with suspects. But it was not until the capture of a young carpenter called Shalom Saleh Shalom that the fate of the detainees was sealed.

Shalom was in charge of building the underground's secret arms caches, consolidating stores of weapons left behind by departing Jews and transferring them to safe houses, where they'd be readily available in time of need. He built most of the new caches in synagogues, on the assumption that these buildings would serve the community until the emigration process was at an end. Though brave and venturesome, Shalom was not invincible, and after breaking down under an interrogation that involved his being suspended upside down by an iron chain from the ceiling of a room for several hours at a time, and having his eyelashes plucked out one by one, he led police from synagogue to synagogue, revealing where over the course of a decade the underground had stockpiled weapons and ammunition intended for the community's self defense. That the Jews had had no need to use the firepower they'd so diligently amassed was neither here nor there, because the authorities were now convinced they had discovered the means that for so many months had eluded them.

Before the end of the year nearly a hundred people had been brought to court in three separate trials and accused of detonating explosives in buildings where Jews congregated. The main evidence for the prosecution was that the police now had in their possession 425 grenades, 33 machine guns, 186 revolvers, 24,647 bullets, 79 cartridges, 32 daggers, as well as Yudke Tajer's address book. The evidence was, of course, circumstantial, but the Iraqi courts were not interested in due legal process. They had their men, so to speak, for there were at least a dozen women and girls among the accused, and they were going to nail them.

In the event, most of those accused of Zionist crimes merely got sentenced to terms of hard labor, except Yudke Tajer, who was imprisoned for life. However, Shalom Saleh Shalom and Yusuf Basri, a hapless underground member guilty of no more than intelligence gathering, were summarily sentenced to death. On January 20, 1952, the two men were publicly executed in a square in central Baghdad, after petitions for clemency by the Israeli government and the UN failed to secure an eleventh-hour stay. As was always the case in a country where the machinery of justice co-opted the stage of public theater, huge crowds turned out to celebrate their deaths.

The men were almost certainly innocent. Even if Zionists had been capable of bombing fellow Jews into fearful desperation, they would have deployed professionals more accomplished and certainly more ruthless than Shalom the carpenter and Basri the lawyer. Then, the deed done, those agents of death would have quit Iraq in a flash. But were Zionists actually capable of such violent recourse?

Shlomo Hillel, the Mossad agent who, posing as an American businessman, managed to close the airlift deal between Near East Air Transport and the Iraqi government, strenuously denies that Zionists would ever resort to such base tactics in pursuit of their goals. But other commentators claim that the "cruel Zionism" made infamous in the Lavon Affair argues otherwise. The Lavon Affair is the name given to the scandal that followed a spate of bombings of British and American buildings in Cairo in 1954. The bombings were initially thought to be the work of the Muslim Brotherhood, a cadre of Egyptian Islamists that, at the time, had an interest in stalling an impending rapprochement between Egypt's new head of state, Gamal Abdel Nasser, and the British. But after an Israeli mercenary was caught red-handed (his grenade exploded in his pocket as he was entering a British-owned movie theater in Cairo), the embarrassing truth emerged: Zionists were responsible.

In the case of Iraq it's impossible to say what really happened, not least because the Lavon Affair argues for Zionist guilt only by analogy and not by solid precedent. All that is certain is that by hanging Yusuf Basri and Shalom Shalom the Iraqis got what they wanted, which was to destroy every last vestige of Zionist activity in Iraq. Only then could Jews and Arabs revert to living together side by side in peace. Or so went the official line.

In 1955 an American rabbi and passionate anti-Zionist by the name of Elmer Berger stopped off in Baghdad during a whirlwind tour of the Middle East. His purpose in traveling through Egypt, Syria, Lebanon, and Iraq was to report back on the condition of Jews in Arab countries to members of the American Council for Judaism, an organization of which he was executive director and whose purpose was to promote Judaism as a "religion of universal and prophetic values."

Berger's chief quarrel with Israel was with the "State's Messianic pretensions toward all Jews": in other words, Israel's thinly disguised sense of itself as the means of Jewish salvation. This attitude was doubly misplaced with regard to Mizrahi, or Eastern Jews and, as often as not, hypocritical. As Berger saw it, Mizrahi Jews had legitimate claims to indigenous standing in their own homelands. Referring to the Egyptian Jews, he said: "The Jews here are Arabs. They speak Arabic. They dress like Arabs. They sell to Arabs. They buy from Arabs." And yet, Berger continued, "fund-raisers and Israeli MPs talk of these

Arab countries as if they were sub-human." Berger could just as easily have been writing about Iraq as Egypt. And when he did visit Baghdad, he found a kindred spirit in Sassoon Khedouri, who had been reinstated as chief rabbi in 1953. By this time, the remaining Jews had more or less resumed their place in society and Rabbi Khedouri was at pains to explain to Berger that conditions for Jews in Iraq had never been better.

One could argue that conditions in Iraq, period, had never been better. As Berger reported, the building of a modern nation-state was well under way. The country was "lusty and bustling." It was spending $150 million a year of its oil royalties on economic and social development. There was a school on almost every corner, and new housing, mostly low cost, was springing up everywhere. From this position of relative luxury, Rabbi Khedouri was able to look back on the unfortunate business of 1950–51 with regret and, truth to tell, not a little pique. "We did not lose our heads, but we failed to prevent others from losing theirs. . . . It was no little thing for us to stay and to see our friends and families going mad and being encouraged in their madness by American Jews and agents of Israel," he told Berger.

Rabbi Khedouri went on to complain that he and other community leaders were ignored in the months leading up to the airlift. "Why didn't someone come to see us instead of negotiating with Israel to take in Iraqi Jews? Why didn't someone point out that the solid, responsible leadership of Iraqi Jews believed this to be their country—in good times or bad—and we were convinced the trouble would pass."

Berger's account of this meeting is fascinating on all sorts of levels, but not least because it confirms that the Zionists had managed to capture the machinery of emigration in advance of the *taskeet*. The problem lies with extending this line of thinking, because, at the end of the day, the Zionists did not create the situation the Iraqi Jews found themselves in after the Arab-Israeli War, however much they may have used it to manipulate people into emigrating.

The anti-Jewish climate in Iraq in the late 1940s and early 1950s was entirely of the Iraqis' own making. In spite of having almost two decades in which to build a modern and inclusive sense of nationhood that might have given political minorities, such as the Shias, as well as religious minorities like the Jews, a participatory role in the formation of a national culture, the country remained dominated by a tribal elite that was intent on imposing a monolithic nationalism on everyone else. The irony is that under Saddam that tribal dominance became even more narrowly focused, so that defining nationalism became the prerogative of particular clans and families, and politics became a vehicle for maintaining loyalty to the new slimmed-down elite. It's as if Iraq set itself on the wrong course in 1932 and then, instead of turning back, kept compounding the original navigational error.

With hindsight, the Ottoman *Millet* system seems remarkably civilized. Then, each minority group was not only tolerated but given autonomy to manage its internal affairs. Although the ideal of diversity within unity was upheld during the mandate years, and also by King Faisal in his final years, in the Sunni-dominated, independent Iraq of the 1940s and 1950s, the nation's sense of self had become too fragile to accommodate minor differences. Separate ethnic groups such as the Jews began to constitute a threat to national unity. They were seen as a destabilizing influence in the country. And with the advent of Zionism, which gave rise to Jewish dual allegiance, there seemed to be no alternative but for the Jews to go. Rabbi Khedouri's view that the loyalist stance of the community's leadership could have settled the argument over the position of Jews in Iraqi society is thus fundamentally flawed. As long as Jews remained in Iraq, they ran the risk of being trampled and having their rights traduced in pursuit of the so-called national cause. They could never win the argument, no matter how sincerely they pledged their loyalty to the state. Nor could they know, in 1955, that the national cause would become the subject of endless infighting in the decades to come: the spur to revolutions, assassinations, and military coups, and the source of permanent civil strife.

A snapshot of my family's life at the time of Berger's visit to Baghdad is disorienting to say the least. It shows how far removed from Iraq and its problems the small Levy clan had become in just a few short years. If the old truism about being out of sight holds, I can think of no better example than my family's holiday in the hillside resort of Kalimpong, where they celebrated New Year's 1955.

At the time my mother was working in Calcutta as a ground hostess for Air France and spending a good deal of her energy smilingly chaperoning VIPs around town after their flights were delayed—a common predicament in the early days of mass travel. Whenever her patience was frayed, she took an impish delight in showing the airline's guests the wooden funeral pyres on the banks of the Hoogli, where bodies burned in the open. If the VIPs were particularly demanding, she'd take them to see the tall stone pillars known as the Silent Towers, where the Parsies left their dead to be picked over by vultures. Bertha, meanwhile, was working for the American Embassy, using her gregarious charm—not to mention her English—to acquaint herself with a new circle of fun-loving friends.

The holiday in Kalimpong was a well-earned rest from the arduous task of building a new life far from home, and the pictures that survive from the trip are rare mementos of carefree times. There's one of Bertha looking glamorous in a silk sari and singing into a big 1950s microphone at a smart New Year's Eve bash, and another of Bertha, Marcelle, and Haron trekking in the hills on donkeys. Best of all are shots of Regina enjoying the idling days and looking happy and rested, as if a burden had been lifted from her shoulders. Scarcely five years earlier the family had arrived in Calcutta feeling lost and homesick. Like most newcomers to the vibrant and teeming city, they goggled at people washing their clothes in the filthy waters of the Hoogli and at men shaving outdoors, squinting into bits of broken mirror. They shrank from grinning youths with paan-stained mouths. When they saw cows walking in the streets like Indian citizens, while men sweated like beasts of burden as they lugged heavy rickshaws, they shook their heads in wonderment. And they marveled at how many Indians managed to climb onto the local buses, some of them hanging off the roof racks, unable to get a footing at a window.

At first they'd stayed with Josephine and her husband in their large apartment on Chowringhee Lane, which Marcelle recalls as "Eastern-looking." It had large rooms with high ceilings, big windows, and tiled floors; and huge fans spun overhead, their blades cutting through the thick air like the oars of a boat breaking water. Marcelle remembers many a humid night when she and Bertha would lie awake under those fans, imagining they were back in Baghdad enjoying evenings filled with talk and laughter.

In India, life's exigencies demanded a break with Baghdadi tradition. Bertha and Marcelle had to adapt, to become independent, to work. They launched themselves into the working world almost immediately, finding it to be a harsh and pitiless place that drew heavily on their slim reserves of adult self-possession. Marcelle took a job with an Indian businessman, for whom she typed faultless letters. He was overweight and smarmy and he made her call him "Boss"; she quit after just a few weeks when he began suggesting after-hours assignations. Bertha's entrée into the working world was no less unnerving, her boss being a slave driver who daily threw a week's worth of work at her. After a succession of unsatisfactory and temporary jobs, Bertha leaped at the American Embassy position, while Marcelle clambered gratefully onto the life raft that was Air France.

Socially things were brighter from the start. Prompted by Josephine, Marcelle and Bertha joined the French cultural club, a youthful, forward-looking collective, as fresh and enticing as Solomon's club in Alwiya had been. It organized picnics and cocktail parties and brought together a wide assortment of young French expats and Calcutta Jews at gala dinners and movie screenings. Regina, meanwhile, took comfort from watching her children settle down. She found a place for Haron at the local Jesuit school and an apartment a flat for them all on Chowringhee Lane, not far from Josephine's. She also introduced herself to Lady Ezra Sassoon, a cousin of Elazar's, long established in India, who pulled Regina into an orbit of cultured Baghdadi women who watched cricket and took tea together.

One day, not long after the family's sojourn in Kalimpong, Regina returned home from a pleasant afternoon at Lady Ezra's to find a special delivery waiting for her: a brown paper package containing the Indian passports she had applied for after she and her children became Indian citizens. She could barely contain her excitement. When Bertha and Marcelle returned to Chowringhee Lane that evening, she told them the good news: "Now we can move to England," she said.

In Regina's mind Calcutta was just a stepping-stone, a necessary bridge to a better life elsewhere. She had no intention of settling in India permanently. Not when she could have Big Ben and Windsor Castle, proper seasons and main-street shopping, gas central heating, scones served with jam and cream, double-glazed windows, and English neighbors. The country whose culture she'd been absorbing since she was twelve would, she believed, be a home away from home. She had no inkling then of the distance that existed between her idea of England and the spit and grit of London's postwar reality. Nor could she anticipate how much she and her children would miss various members of the extended family who would remain in the East, in Israel, India, and Iran.

For years the Sehayeks had moved in and out of one another's lives, rubbing shoulders, sharing everyday intimacies, nurturing the same hopes and fears. It wasn't always harmonious. But now the family was atomized, its various elements scattered to the winds. Nessim was still in Iraq. Solomon, now married and the proud father of a baby girl, was happily settled in Israel, while Salha and Ezra did their best to acclimate themselves to their new home. Over in London, Regina and her children often rued the day they'd all gone their separate ways, bidding farewell to the Baghdadi Jewish life—the old life, the good life—now lost to them forever.

Half a century later my mother is filled with conflicting emotions at the prospect of my visiting Baghdad; she's excited, fearful, proud, nervous. If the country had been experiencing better days, I think she would like to have joined me. But I am glad she's not with me. I have lived with her nostalgia for so long now, appropriated it as my own, that I don't know what I would do if her rosy wistfulness about the wonderful city of her birth were to give way to disappointment.

As planned, a "fixer" met me at Amman's Queen Alia airport to escort me through customs. I don't think the officials even looked at my passport, other than to check that I had the regulatory entry visa for Jordan, and they expressed not the slightest interest in my suitcase: I could have been bringing anything into the country, never mind a mountain of cooked meat. As the fixer handed me over to Mohammed, who would drive me to the Four Seasons Hotel, one of several rendezvous points from where GMC Suburbans left the city for Baghdad, I pulled out the first of several envelopes stuffed with dollars in small denominations and gave it to him, and then I watched him slip into the shadows from where he seemed to have come.

Mohammed's car smelled of oranges. It was not an unpleasant aroma to live with for the short drive to the hotel, and Mohammed himself was agreeably chatty. At one point, when we were overtaken by an eight-wheeled Toyota truck carrying half a dozen camels, he told me that the camels came from Wadi Rum, where T. E. Lawrence had gone to round up Bedouin fighters who would serve under Faisal in the Arab Revolt.

The Four Seasons Hotel is a multitowered, modernist edifice that rises out of the earth like a stick of quartz. It is Amman's smartest hotel, and the two American journalists I'd be traveling with, in convoy, were staying there—one a veteran reporter from Dallas who'd been embedded with a company of marines during the war, the other his photographer. I was glad of their company, even though we set off in different cars, both of them white with blacked-out windows and green interior lighting, which gave everything a strange underwater glow. As for which party got the better drivers, it's hard to say. I had two, one fat and one thin, one who slept and one who smoked, and as we began our long journey, I attuned my ear to the Arabic they spoke between them, trying to pick out bits I understood, and accustomed myself to the bumpiness of the drive.

Before reaching the border we stopped off at a roadside café and supermarket. It was past two in the morning, but the place was thronged with men, leering, smiling, and smoking. This was my first taste of being a Western woman alone in an Arab world—a world of men, for the most part, at least in its visible aspects—and I didn't relish the experience, especially since the head scarf I was wearing did nothing to prevent me from being stared at. At the border it was the same. Though I stayed in the car while the drivers took care of the paperwork, I felt like a caged bird peeking back uncertainly at the various men peering in—Bedouin men so thoroughly wrapped in their head scarves that only their kohl-lined eyes showed.

I learned later why the border was so busy: the illegal trafficking of petrol from Iraq to Jordan is big business, and many of the cars waiting in line at the border were used in the trade. The border guards turned a blind eye to the goings-on in exchange for a little *baksheesh,* but it was the cars themselves that caught my interest: their gas tanks had been enlarged to hold more fuel, and when the cars were in motion, the tanks dragged only centimeters above the ground. Something about their misshapen, distended appearance reminded me of pregnant fish.

Once inside Iraq, and with a long drive ahead of me, I dozed fitfully in the back of the GMC for several hours, only to be woken just before dawn by the thin driver who'd been asleep earlier, asking me to hand over my money belt. He would hide it, he said, for safekeeping, as we approached Ramadi. I did as I was told. By now it was light enough to view something of the countryside. Northwest Iraq is incredibly flat and empty, and the desert is fawn colored. You can see for miles in every direction, straight to the pinkish horizon where the gravely sand meets the sky. The road, I noticed, was flawless, its tarmac smooth and unblemished, its highways immaculately ruled and laned. But other than white GMCs, the only other vehicles I spotted were trailers ferrying cheap cars from Eastern Europe into Iraq, taking advantage of the absence of trade controls.

Ramadi is a former Baathist stronghold, a place where top-ranking officials in Saddam's government liked to base themselves, away from the hubbub and grind of the city, and presumably, beyond the reach of sanctions. One heard a great deal about party privileges, and Ramadi was a place where Saddam's inner circle enjoyed them. The desert road seemed to bisect the town. On either side of us concrete compounds containing large neotraditional villas lined the road. Most of the buildings were two storied, with carports on the ground floor and ornately carved balconies on the upper floor. Most of them also looked empty—and most likely were, the officials who owned them having gotten wind of the CPA's de-Baathification program.

Next we skirted Fallujah, which is larger than Ramadi and less salubrious-looking. The buildings on the edge of town looked bombed out, deserted, and there was rubble everywhere. A few beat up cars were dotted among the buildings, the red, blue, and orange of their chassis providing the only color for miles. At this early hour the place was completely still. Even so, I could almost sense the tension that within a few weeks of my visit would vent itself in a torrent of violence.

Soon after passing Fallujah, my driver told me: "Finished. No more Ali Baba"—Ali Baba was the generic name the Baghdadis gave the bandits. We were both relieved. He put the radio on to celebrate, and jangly Arabic pop music blared out for the rest of the journey.

My first sense of Baghdad was a jumble of impressions. After the emptiness of the desert everything seemed to jump out at me; willowy date palms, electricity pylons, roadside stalls selling cigarettes and soda, people going to work on scooters, needle-thin modern minarets, shops selling bright plastic chairs, low-level buff-colored houses with interesting topiary outside, road signs reading "Presidential Truck Route," even other cars. The traffic was incredible: as early as six in the morning, we were periodically mired in it, to the accompaniment of honking horns. All in all, the place resembled a low-rent Las Vegas, minus the neon.

After passing a number of bombed-out ministries and former foreign embassies, we at last came upon the Tigris, a sludge-brown slick that wound its way from north to south through the center of Baghdad. As we crossed the Jumhariya Bridge, before heading south toward Karada, I had a rare 360-degree view of the broad river, so much wider than the river Thames in London that it ought to have felt majestic. But flanked on either side by vast factories belching black smoke, shorn of promenades, and empty of watercraft, it appeared neglected, sluggish, dull. I could see nothing in it of the light-reflecting, laughter-carrying Tigris my mother has so often described to me.

The only other impressions that lodged in my mind from that first drive through Baghdad came from glimpsing some of the monumental architecture associated with Saddam. The famous twenty-foot bronze statue of the dictator in Firdus Square was already gone. Ten months earlier the world's eyes watched as the Iraqi people threw a noose around its neck, tugged it to the ground, and set upon it greedily, beating it with their shoes and with sledgehammers in an ostentatious display of earthy irreverence. It looked like the kind of spontaneous act that often heralds a revolution. Except that it wasn't spontaneous, not according to the swirl of rumor citing American stage management. Nor was this a revolution. It was the opposite: an externally imposed change of regime that left a foreign power in the country's driving seat. In short, it was a repeat performance of what happened in 1917 when the British had invaded.

Among those monuments still in place was the blue-domed Martyr's Monument, which stands over 160 feet high on a vast circular platform, looking like an enormous, slightly pointy egg that has been sawed in two vertically and then pulled apart so that its ovoid halves face each other across space. Sheltering inside one dome is an eternal flame commemorating Iraqi soldiers killed in the Iran-Iraq war of the 1980s.

More phony nationalism was at hand in the victory arches commissioned to celebrate Saddam's Western-aided triumph over Iran. The arches are another colossus, built in duplicate, and towering 140 feet over the highway in the center of Baghdad. Each arch is formed by a pair of crossed swords held in place by giant forearms that rise out of the ground like something out of a horror movie. The forearms were modeled on Saddam's own, the German company that cast them having worked from photographs. At one time the helmets of captured Iranian soldiers dangled in a net between the two swords, while scattered around the base of the monument were another five thousand Iranian helmets gathered from the battlefield.

It seems a pity that nothing visible, nothing commemorative, remains from the brief and only era in which Iraq might be said to have enjoyed something approaching a genuine national identity. That era was ushered in with the revolution of July 14, 1958, which brought Iraq's "lackey" national sovereignty to an end and established Brig. Gen. Abd el-Karim Qasim as leader of the new Iraqi republic—the people's republic, no less.

The Free Officers movement that Qasim rose up to lead was inspired by the Egyptian original that had swept Nasser to power in 1952. But although it was equally anticolonialist—equally determined, that is, to get the foreigner out (and the same foreigner to boot)—it was less pan-Arab in orientation and more "Iraqist." Qasim encouraged the participation of all Iraqis in creating "national unity through revolutionary rebirth." Though it remained unclear precisely what "revolutionary rebirth" meant, for the four and a half years that Qasim ruled Iraq as "Sole Leader," he pursued a reformist agenda and tried to alleviate the plight of the poor.

The July revolution was not without its casualties. The royal family was shot dead in cold blood, and Nuri as-Said was run to ground trying to flee Baghdad dressed as a woman; when he realized there was no escape, he shot himself. Later, wild and exuberant crowds attacked the British Embassy, destroyed statues of General Maude and King Faisal, and hunted down people associated with the old regime. Then they disinterred the bodies of Nuri as-Said and Abd al-Ilah and dragged them through the streets, flinging them like rag dolls from one bloodthirsty group to another. The charred bodies were eventually hung as trophies outside the gates of the Ministry of Defense, in the same spot where, years earlier, after months of tireless pursuit by Nuri and the prince regent, the nationalists' favorite nationalist, Saleh al-din al-Sabbagh, had swung from the gallows after the failure of Rashid Ali's coup. If there was one abstract concept the Iraqi people understood, it was poetic justice.

The Qasim period was unique in Iraqi history. True, it was externally imposed on the country. But it came closer to addressing the people's needs than any regime that either followed or preceded it. A functioning health and education system, political freedom for different parties, workers' rights, the nationalization of the oil industry, land reform, and more: all these things were part of Qasim's legacy. For the Jews it was a hiatus of peace. Qasim looked kindly on minorities and believed that by building a society that embraced them as equals, eventually they would assimilate totally. For the Jews this meant that they were free to work, trade, study, and travel, and, as a gesture of good faith, Jewish prisoners detained on charges of communist or Zionist activity after 1948 were released. Even Yudke Tajer was freed.

When Nessim and his family finally left Iraq at the end of 1958, most people thought they were crazy. *"Habibi,"* they told him, "things have never been so good." But his wife was adamant. She had witnessed the barbaric scenes at Bab al-Shargi when the frenzied mob had pounced on Nuri's mutilated body, kicking it across the ground like a discarded toy. Before the year was out Nessim had resettled in Tehran, where he'd already established business links through his textile trade. With Nessim's departure, the last of my family had abandoned Iraq.

In retrospect, Nessim's wife made the right call. Political leaders in Iraq came and went with stunning frequency, and there was no reason to suppose that Qasim's tenure was any more secure than his predecessors'. Qasim himself understood the precariousness of his position, especially after 1959 when a botched attempt was made on his life by a young Baathist activist known then as Saddam al-Tikriti. But it was Qasim's estranged ally, Colonel Abd el-Salam Aref, who succeeded in ousting him in February 1963. Aref's Ramadan Revolution, enacted in the names of Arab union, socialism, and democracy, marked the beginning of the Baathist ascendancy in Iraq. Thereafter the Iraqi Jews knew no peace.

Fourteen

THE LAST JEWS
OF BAGHDAD

I waited for Emad Levy, self-appointed ambassador of the last Jews of Baghdad, in the marbled lobby of my hotel. The television was to one side of me, streaming news from around the Arab world, and a group of Iraqi drivers and interpreters, passing the time of day sipping sweet red-brown tea, was on the other. I felt the intensity of my secret keenly. I was a Jewish woman in the middle of Baghdad, waiting to hook up with another Jew who had lived here all his days and no one around me suspected a thing. Later Emad would say, "If anyone asks, just tell them you're a Christian." But no one asked: the obvious Jewishness of my name was a giveaway only to Western ears.

Anti-Semitism was on the rise in Iraq. Great symbolic waves of it were rolling down from the pulpits, from where clerics, newly released from long years of suppression, were lecturing and rousing the Iraqi people. Only that month Grand Ayatollah Ali al-Sistani had made a point of saying that returning Jews would be ineligible for citizenship under any government elected by the Iraqi people, and his eleven-point list of objections to the Americans' draft constitution (of which this was number four) was being circulated around the city on colorful flyers. In the press and on television the Jews were denounced almost daily, while out on the street anti-Jewish graffiti was popping up everywhere. "No USA. No Jews" was a common example. Across one of the walls of the antiquities museum in old Baghdad, someone had scrawled: "God is great against the Jews."

In the postwar atmosphere of hatred and suspicion, Jews were once again the bogeyman. Variously portrayed as friends of the foreign occupier, Zionist spies, or simply as individuals returning under cover of false identities to reclaim property stolen from them in 1951, the Jews were not to be trusted. They had become the very symbol of chaos: the Americans, I was told more than once, were all Jews.

This was an abstract and symbolic anti-Semitism that voiced itself in slogans and not a targeted campaign directed specifically against Baghdad's handful of indigenous Jews, who—let's face it—were too small in number and too insignificant culturally to bother with. Nevertheless, its presence was disconcerting. Jewish people will often remark that only in Israel does their feeling of Jewishness disappear, because only in Israel, where being Jewish is the pervasive norm is it inconsequential. Having visited Israel several times, I can vouch for having experienced this strange unburdening. What I had not experienced, until now, was a reaction of equal and opposite character: an amplifying of my Jewish identity that stemmed from being in a country where Jews are openly vilified. This was a new sensation to me, and it meant that when I finally met Emad Levy, I greeted him as one would greet a long-lost brother.

I recognized Emad instantly, as he pulled up outside my hotel in his battered white car and then climbed out and smiled, leaning backwards slightly and extending his hands in a demonstrative welcome. Like almost every other man I had seen in Baghdad, Emad had neatly cropped dark hair and a full mustache. He wore oversized, lightly tinted sunglasses and his Western dress sense was stuck somewhere in the polyester-loving mid-1970s. Although he looked every inch the modern, urban Arab, there was something about the set of his eyes, as well as a certain heaviness to the eyelids, which to my mind marked him as an Iraqi Jew. I told him that he reminded me of one of my cousins back in London, and we laughed about it, because in spite of the physical similarity, not to mention the coincidence of family name, we were related neither by blood nor by marriage.

At thirty-eight Emad was one of the younger Baghdadi Jews. He was also the friendliest and most forthcoming, the one who made it his business to get to know interested foreigners and then to vet them on behalf of the small community: if they failed to pass muster, he wouldn't introduce them to anyone else.

But I was more than just another inquisitive outsider. I shared a heritage and history with these Jews, not to mention a language and culture. In days not so distant, my ancestors and theirs would have been colleagues, neighbors, business partners, and friends. For weeks I'd been wondering whether on these grounds alone there would exist some kind of unspoken compact between us. But Emad warned me right at the outset that some of the older Baghdadi Jews were refusing to meet me. They were set in their ways and didn't like strangers, he said.

Fortunately there was no such hesitation on his part, and for the next few days, and much to my driver Mahmoud's annoyance, Emad offered to be my guide. He would introduce me to other Jews—Jews who, like himself, lived lives that were as close to normal as you could get in a war-torn city. He would show me the renovations he'd been overseeing at the Jewish cemetery in Sadr City, and he would accompany me to the tomb of Joshua the Priest, one of several Jewish shrines in and around Baghdad whose upkeep had been neglected by Saddam. But first the ground rules needed to be set. He would not arrange for me to meet seventy-nine-year-old Marcelle Daoud, who was the community's accountant and, by all reports, linchpin (he and she had apparently fallen out). And he would not take me to the synagogue or to the Jewish Committee Office in the Old City. It was simply too dangerous.

Emad talked a lot about caution: about the need for Jews to watch their step, to keep their heads down, to refrain from political engagement, because you never knew what the authorities might leap on as an excuse to arrest Jews. He told me that he'd been spied on for years during Saddam's reign, to the point where he'd been too terrified to visit his mother's grave. He also said that the intelligence service sent beautiful Muslim girls his way to trap him into working with them, a confession I put down to fanciful exaggeration until I learned that from the 1960s on the secret police liked to recruit Jewish informers so that they could keep tabs on the community and maintain a healthy level of paranoia among its already fearful members. He was glad that Saddam was gone, he said. Now he could begin planning the rest of his life.

I learned all this within the first ten minutes of meeting Emad. Over the coming days I would discover that he was a whirlwind of energy, always talking, always joking, always on the go, attending to one task or another. He was what my mother would call a happy-go-lucky soul, coasting through his days, trying to do some good in the world and tackle whatever life threw at him. Even the war and present occupation didn't seem to faze him much: he still went swimming, saw friends, and met his various obligations. Yet for all that, Emad seemed to sense that in the aftermath of Saddam's overthrow, he couldn't go on as before: "I have no future in Iraq," he said repeatedly.

Emad's concern about the future was in large part practical, because outside his duties in the community—duties that extended to caring for the elderly and distributing bimonthly care packages to the remaining Jews (a practice begun during the sanction era)—his life was in disarray. He had not worked in months. "I used to have a business buying and selling cars, but since the war began I stopped it," he said. He wanted me to believe that giving up his stock in trade was purely a matter of choice, but Iraq's newly opened borders meant that cheap cars like the ones I saw on the road from Amman were flooding into the country from all over the globe, making it impossible for Emad to compete. On a more personal level, any kind of family future or, at least a Jewish family future, was out of the question if Emad was to remain in Iraq. As it was there was only one Jewish woman of marriageable age in the community, and relations between her and Emad were decidedly cool.

Emad Levy was born in Baghdad in 1965. His father, Ezra, and mother, Sayeeda, owned a large, shady villa that sat across the street from the city's one remaining Jewish school. Many of their neighbors on the street were Jewish, and the family was on good terms with

those who weren't. Emad and his older brother, Saleh, were among
hundreds of Jewish children who attended the Frank Iny School, built
a decade earlier to educate the children of Jews who remained in Iraq
after the *taskeet*. Those were happy days, before the last major exodus
of Jews from Baghdad began, and Emad remembers them fondly.
When we stopped off at his childhood house one time—the same
rambling villa was now home just to him—Emad showed me a photograph dating from that era. It pictured him standing on the white
stone steps outside the school entrance, grinning amid a large huddle
of young classmates in short skirts or trousers. There were still
enough Jews in Baghdad to give an impression of normalcy. You
weren't different, weren't isolated, and the community still had some
substance to it.

"By the time I finished school," said Emad, "none of these kids was
still living in Baghdad."

The more Jews who left Baghdad, the more deeply Emad felt his
own Jewishness. It didn't matter that there were hardly any other Jews
around, that the community had no rabbi to guide it after Sassoon
Khedouri's long life finally came to an end in 1971, or that, as Emad
grew older, there was barely anyone left to celebrate his bar mitzvah.
What Emad cherished was his birthright. Because his father had
taught him some Hebrew as a child, he knew that he could always
turn to prayer as a source of solace and joy. That there was scarcely a
soul in town who understood the language well enough to read the
liturgy in synagogue was of no consequence.

Even now Emad identified himself primarily by his faith. That first
day we met, and in spite of the caution he urged on me, he had loudly
announced, "I am proud to be a Jew and I tell everyone that I am Jewish: I am not afraid of anything." This came practically by way of introduction. If we had been sitting in his car at the time, I would have
thought nothing of it. But we were the only customers at a plasticky
ice-cream parlor in Alwiya, where the wait staff, unaccustomed to
hearing English spoken in their establishment, eyed us suspiciously
across a deserted sea of press-molded white tables. Glaring directly
back at them, an unapologetic Emad boomed, "I love my religion."

The following day, when we visited the crumbling tomb of Joshua the Priest on the outskirts of the city and shuffled into the darkened stone chamber where people paid their respects to the prophet, Emad pulled a yarmulke out of his jacket pocket, placed it on his head, and began mumbling prayers in Hebrew, swaying back and forth on his feet. The two Muslim elders tending the shrine were clearly mortified. They exchanged quiet words, exiting the chamber for their consultation, but they did not ask us to leave. Later, as we accepted the offer of fresh dates from a peasant woman who'd set up a stand outside the building, and adjusted our eyes to the bright sunlight, Emad turned to me and said, "We're supposed to be free now, so why shouldn't I openly express my faith?" Then he spat his date pit to the ground.

After it crossed my mind that displays of bravado such as I'd witnessed at the shrine and the ice-cream parlor were staged largely for my benefit, I began dreading their recurrence. The last thing I wanted was to get him into trouble on my account. At the same time, I appreciated the point he was endeavoring to make, which was that Emad Levy was nobody's victim.

"We have a high tower in the desert. Each day this tower sinks— one inch by one inch. One day we will have nothing. This is how we are." According to Samir Shahrabani, this was the predicament of the Baghdadi Jews. Compared to Emad's Prince Charming, Samir was the poet-philosopher of the community. He often spoke as if he saw things through the long lens of centuries past and then translated back his vision of dour fatalism through a few well-chosen metaphors. As he saw it, the Baghdadi Jews had little alternative but to face up to the fact that the entire heritage of Babylonian Jewry, presently carried on their slender shoulders, would soon vanish beneath the quicksand of time.

When I suggested that the Baghdadi Jews might consider leaving Iraq before they were dragged down along with their history, he protested: "If we leave we will cut our roots. I am proud to be an Iraqi Jew and if anyone says, 'You're Jewish,' I tell him, 'I am the crown on your head.'" Should he stay or go? It was a classic case of being damned if you do and damned if you don't.

Samir and I talked behind closed shutters in the front room of the house he shared with his brother Jacob in Hindiyah. On a low table in front of me, he had served some fresh fruit and a can of 7-Up, while in the corner of the room the television buzzed inconsequentially. Thin shafts of light forcing their way through the slatted shutters revealed dark furnishings, Persian carpets, and a clutter of books and newspapers, but my impressions of Samir's house remain vague because within minutes of my arrival we were plunged into darkness. The electricity was out.

The rolling blackouts that Baghdad was still experiencing almost a year into the American occupation were as much a talking point as the sudden surge in city traffic or the ubiquitous presence of foreign contractors pinching Iraqi jobs. Everyone grumbled about them. "What kind of superpower is it that can't even get the electricity up and running?" they complained, even though they already knew the answer: one that doesn't care to.

Samir went outside to fiddle with the generator that he and Jacob shared with their neighbor next door. It had been acting up lately and he couldn't get it to work, so we resigned ourselves to talking in the dark. "What can you do?" he shrugged.

Like most people in Baghdad, Samir had learned to take the daily outages in stride. But for him, as for almost everyone else I talked to, their occurrence seemed to invite favorable comparisons with Saddam. When I asked what he could possibly miss about the man, Samir launched into a spirited defense of the former dictator.

"Under Saddam, Iraq was safe and secure," he said. "Now there's no security. A lot of people owe me money, and they are refusing to honor the payments because I am Jewish. In Saddam's time people were forced to pay, and if someone defaulted on an agreement he put them in prison for six months." Listening to Samir sing Saddam's praises was bizarre. But I soon realized that what was important was the subtext. Samir wasn't saying that things had been better before: he was saying that they had not improved since. While Emad was unable to compete in the radical free market that America's viceroy Paul Bremer had created in Iraq, he was falling afoul of the fact that, as yet, that market lacked all regulation. There were no checks and balances in place to encourage good practice, and no legal or judicial recourse for injured parties. Everything was up for grabs. In little over ten months, the business world had become cowboy territory.

Samir began working as a trader in the mid-1980s, after graduating from the University of Baghdad with a degree in economics. He began modestly, buying and selling iron, but then he expanded his operation to include factory and farming equipment. The business thrived, allowing him to acquire *khans* in Baghdad and Mosul and to purchase land near Baquba and property in Baghdad as investments. "When I was a student, I wanted to leave Iraq and take advantage of opportunities elsewhere. But my father had a stroke and I couldn't abandon him," he said. "And now, all these years later, I can't leave, because my wealth is tied up here." I took him to mean that he felt that his moment had passed, but before I could say anything, he raised an aggressive finger in the air and said: "And I would rather leave my house to dogs than to Muslims and throw all my money into the sea before I let the Iraqis have it."

Samir's talk was frequently peppered with caveats about how untrustworthy, two-faced, bad, miserable, and conniving the Muslims were. "Out of Iraq's population of twenty-six million, twenty-four million are bad," he told me. When we turned to the forthcoming prospect of Iraqi self-rule, he said: "How can you trust government, if government is in the hands of thieves?" Whenever Samir made such statements, inadvertently offending my unabashedly liberal, postcolonial, multiracial convictions, my first instinct was to raise an objection. But then I had never experienced persecution or discrimination at Muslim hands, whereas in all his forty-two years, Samir had known nothing else. Who was I to tell him what to think?

Samir Shahrabani was just one year old when the Baath Party helped propel Abd-el-Salem Aref into power in Iraq in 1963, bringing the precarious peace that the Jews had enjoyed under Qasim to an abrupt end. From as early as July 1964, Jews faced a whole range of new restrictions, the bulk of them economic. Most important, they were denied permission to leave the country. Some families escaped illegally at this time, but for the most part the Jews sat stewing in Baghdad, hoping to ride out their difficulties. Then, in June 1967, the Six-Day War broke out and any hopes for a brighter future were lost. At this time there were roughly thirty-five hundred Jews in Baghdad living in morbid fear of retaliation. Too frightened to leave their homes, they shut up their businesses, rationed provisions, and kept their children away from school, while out in the streets "the atmosphere was electric," as if the people couldn't wait for the bloodletting to begin.

When it did, dozens of Jews were jailed on trumped-up charges of raising funds for Israel or working as agents of imperialism. Many of them would spend years languishing in prison, being told each day that they would be hanged before nightfall, with their families never knowing whether they were alive or dead. Beyond the prison walls, the rest of the community was suffocating under senseless assaults on its freedom. Phone lines to Jewish households were cut, bank accounts frozen, and trading licenses revoked. On radio and television, ministers called on loyal Muslim citizens to sever their social ties with Jews and to cease trading with them. And the State Security Department recruited some three thousand secret police in civilian clothing to watch Baghdad's remaining Jews around the clock: one spy for every adult Jew.

In 1968 the noose was drawn tighter still. Economic restrictions were intensified to the point where Jews were forbidden from buying, selling, renting, or leasing property. The salaries of those who still had jobs were limited to one hundred dinars per month—well below what was needed to maintain an average-size family. As one firsthand account from the time records: "Families were left without anything, everything dwindled down until they reached their last crust of bread." But for Edwin Shuker, who was thirteen at the time, the worst aspects of Jewish suffering were psychological. "We couldn't travel more than ten kilometers without informing the police, we couldn't be in groups, and each police officer defined the size of a group his own way, and you couldn't talk in public because as soon as you opened your mouth, because of the Judeo-Arabic accent, someone might realize you were a Jew."

That July the Baathist Ahmad Hasan al-Bakr seized power, and his nephew Saddam Hussein returned from exile to become his second in command (after his failed attempt on Qasim's life in 1959, Saddam had fled the country). Radio and television broadcasts announced that there'd been a "white revolution": but, says one Iraqi Jew, "we could hear the tanks" in the streets.

The new regime immediately embarked on a series of purges aimed at crippling the opposition, and the Jews bore the brunt of the backlash. On December 14, 1968, it was announced that a major spy ring had been uncovered and that its American- and Israeli-backed operatives consisted of Jews, former military officers, and former senior diplomats. Twenty "spies" were arrested. In the televised show trial that followed, eleven Jews were charged with blowing up a bridge in Basra, allocating funds to Kurdish rebels, transmitting military information to Israel, and that old anti-Semitic canard—poisoning the water supply. Many of them issued false confessions under torture and were refused the right to be represented by counsel. Then, after the most perfunctory of hearings, the majority of the "spies" were sentenced to death.

The day of their execution in January 1969 was declared a national holiday, and the Iraqi people were invited to "come and enjoy the feast." They came in the thousands. Wave after wave of them poured into Liberation Square, cheering and chanting. They unpacked their picnics, clapped and danced, and hoisted their children onto their shoulders to give them a better view of the lifeless bodies that hung from the gallows, "just swaying in the wind." Afterward one group of ruffians hit the bodies with sticks, as if they were piñatas. Others stoned Jewish mourners who had come to collect the bodies of their loved ones for burial. Amid the wanton violence, President Bakr and Saddam Hussein drove around the square in an open-topped limousine, drinking in the euphoria of the crowds.

A misplaced rumor now popular in the West claims that Saddam always had a soft spot for Jews, because when his mother was destitute and pregnant with him a Jewish Tikriti family took her in and sheltered her. His human rights record argues otherwise. Until 1979, when he assumed leadership of the country, Saddam controlled the apparatus of state security in Iraq, and he used it to torment and crush the Jews on whim. Among Iraqi Jews, Saddam's infamous torture prison, Qasr al-Nihayyah (the Palace of the End), assumed gruesome familiarity. The only times Saddam eased up on the Jews was when the international community raised a protest, but as soon as the rest of the world turned its attention elsewhere, the intimidation resumed. During one of these brief hiatuses in 1970, many Jewish families took advantage of the relaxing of restrictions to make a speedy escape. The rest of the time, at least until the late 1970s, when Saddam was occupied first with purging antiloyalist elements within Iraq and then with gearing up for the long war with Iran, a low-key but sustained campaign of economic strangulation and psychological terror was waged against Baghdad's remaining Jews.

Brokenhearted, exhausted, and defeated, the Jews surrendered themselves to their miserable fate. Out of work and out of money, many families began to go hungry, and with bills and taxes going unpaid, basic utilities to Jewish houses were stopped. The men developed ulcers. The women turned sallow and gray. Thanks to the recruitment of Jewish informers, the threat of arbitrary arrest became more pervasive than ever. In words reminiscent of descriptions of the European ghettos during the Holocaust, one Iraqi confided that the Jews of Iraq were facing "a slow death or extinction."

The year 1973 was a particularly bad one. Dozens of Jews were arrested by the secret police, blindfolded, beaten, and then driven off to Qasr al-Nihayyah, from where many never returned. Samir Shahrabani remembers how in April of that year the entire Qashqoush family of six was killed at home, except for one daughter, Dora, who returned from school to find blood all over the house and no sign of her relatives. "She became half crazy after that," said Samir. After the prime minister of India and the president of the French Senate intervened on her behalf, Dora was given a passport and allowed to leave for Israel. By this time the Jews had had enough. Virtually every Jewish family that was able to abandoned everything and paid smugglers to get them out of Iraq as quickly as possible. Only a few hundred people remained behind. In 1990, on the eve of the Gulf War, a mere hundred and fifty Jews were living in Iraq.

While Samir was telling me about the Qashqoush murders, Jacob returned home from work. We shook hands in the dark. "Those Muslims are natural-born killers," he said. "The instinct of racial discrimination flows in their blood." When the electricity finally returned, I was struck by how dissimilar the Shahrabani brothers looked. Samir was thin, dark, and angular, while Jacob was larger and fairer. A pair of thin-rimmed rectangular spectacles completed his rounder features.

Jacob was the intellectual in the community. By day he worked as a jeweler, but by night he toiled at his Ph.D. dissertation: the rather grandly titled "A Discourse Analysis of Courtroom Interaction in English and Arabic." He was eager to have news from the outside world and to exchange views about the Americans' proposed constitution, the history of Jewish persecution in the West, and the underlying ideology behind Mel Gibson's newly released Christological epic *The Passion of the Christ,* which he had been reading about on the Internet. "Do you think that Mel Gibson is anti-Semitic?" he asked me.

Before I left the Shahrabani household, Jacob wanted to know if I could get in touch with his brother in London to see if he would send him books on discourse analysis and legal history. Then, chuckling, he shared with me his enjoyment at watching Saddam Hussein's recent capture on television: "The old fool surrendered like a sheep," he said.

The poor Shia neighborhood of Sadr City, with its dusty rubbish-strewn streets and its crumbling, sand-colored slums is as dismal a place as you're likely to find in all Baghdad. It is dirty, depressed, and neglected, slumped beneath an air of hopelessness; there's no electricity to speak of, and its residents are subject to periodic outbreaks of hepatitis B. All of which is profoundly ironic, given the origins of the place.

Sadr City was originally built by Abd el-Karim Qasim to provide modern housing for thousands of poor "hut dwellers" from southern Iraq. It was a signature build, designed to showcase the Sole Leader's magnanimity toward the most downtrodden and despised people in

Iraq, and it was named accordingly: Revolution City. Later on Saddam changed its name to Saddam City. Apparently he was convinced that the place was chock full of loyalists. But since I can't imagine Saddam ever mistaking slum-dwelling Shiites for his prime constituency, the name change seems more likely to have been a cruel joke. Not long after the war ended in 2003, the neighborhood was renamed for Moqtada al-Sadr, the rebel Shia cleric to whom the bulk of the militant population is devoted—a population which, at the time I was in Iraq, was paying the price in nightly firebombings for supporting a theocrat whose views were inimical to the occupying power.

Hidden away behind tall concrete walls in the heart of Sadr City's decaying midst is a two-acre plot to which the only access is a thick and forbidding metal door. This is the Jewish cemetery. The setting is incongruous, but when Qasim commissioned the building of Sadr City, he was simultaneously building a ring road around Baghdad that went right through the existing Jewish cemetery. His solution was to move the cemetery to Sadr City. The move had been a slapdash affair that either ignored or was ignorant of the Iraqi Jewish tradition of stacking bodies in vertical graves, and so only the topmost layer of skeletons was moved. To make matters worse, many of the gravestones were matched to the wrong graves. Yet the Jews chose not to complain. They knew that they were lucky to have a cemetery at all.

After making a great deal of fuss about safety, Emad eventually caved in and took me to Sadr City. One of his conditions was that I dress as conservatively as I could, and so I slipped a long dark jacket over dowdy clothes and covered my hair with a black head scarf, making sure to tuck away any straying strands. That done, we stole into the cemetery like thieves. The subterfuge was not without cause. Not long ago Emad had brought another visitor here, and the local street kids, seeing her Western dress, had started stoning her, lobbing small rocks over the cemetery walls and hoping for a hit. We weren't going to risk a repeat performance.

Once inside the cemetery, any sense of menace I'd been feeling melted to nothing. I found myself in surprisingly tranquil surroundings: bone-dry, silent, and, except for a handful of laborers busy at their work, completely deserted. The laborers were Christian and had been engaged via a hush-hush deal made the previous fall by an Israeli-born Iraqi whom the Jewish Agency had dispatched to Baghdad after the war. It looked as if Joshua trees had at one time broken up the uniform sandiness of the place with hints of green and shade; but the trees had been cut down, and only their ugly stumps remained. There were thirty-two hundred identical graves here, placed side by side under the burning sun in dozens of orderly rows. One by one each was being carefully remodeled in smooth concrete. Before, the rectangular blocks of brick that previously covered each grave were in a terrible state of repair, powdery and mightily eroded. After renovation the finished graves were much improved and looked like chunky gold ingots, minus the sheen.

In the four months since work began, roughly a quarter of the gravestones had been repaired at a cost of twenty million dinars (roughly fifteen thousand dollars) to the Jewish community. But there was a long way to go yet, and plenty of other work to take care of besides. "This place has been neglected for thirty years," said Emad, kicking up the dust beneath his feet. "In Saddam's time we were too frightened to come here in case we were spied on. So we only came to bury someone who died—and even then we would just make our prayers and go." Emad pointed me toward the guardhouse that sat to one side of the large plot. Its damaged septic tank had been leaking dirty water into the grounds. He had petitioned the American-appointed Iraqi Governing Council to do something about it and had managed to get two hoses attached to the tank to drain the water away beyond the cemetery walls, but he was impatient for the IGC to put proper pipes in.

That said, "The worst damage came during the war. A hundred and fifty *fedayeen* hid in here. They cut down all the trees for firewood, and the Americans kept shelling them. This went on for nearly two weeks." Emad showed me where bullets had skimmed the cemetery walls, leaving telltale pockmarks across their surface. Then he excused himself to offer a prayer at his mother's graveside.

I wandered among the rows of graves and noticed for the first time that affixed to the ends of many of them were pale marble tablets on which people's names and dates of death had been engraved in clear Hebrew lettering. I was immediately struck by two things: that these innocent stamps of personal identification must be the only Hebrew writing on display in modern Baghdad, and that had the local residents been aware of it, those visiting would have met with a good deal worse than stoning.

Like the gravestones themselves, the tablets showed signs of severe wear and tear. Some were just fragments, not much bigger than postage stamps. Some bore only half a name, others just a date, and some inscriptions had eroded away completely. As I bent down beside one of the graves and attempted to decipher the name of its occupant, it occurred to me that my grandfather Elazar Levy was most likely buried here. For a brief, excited moment I was gripped by the idea that if I spent long enough squinting at the gravestones I might find him. But the impulse was fleeting. Beyond it I felt myself saturated with an unexpected sense of contentment: it was enough just to know that he might be here. Indeed, the more I simply let that knowledge wash over me, the more proximate Elazar felt. This, I reflected, was the closest I would ever get to my grandfather.

Of all the places I visited in Baghdad, the cemetery was where I felt most at home. I was oddly comforted by the cumulative presence of so many dead. It was as if there, at last, I finally felt the pull of my Iraqi ancestry, because there, more than anywhere I had ever been, that ancestry was real. Stranger still, it was not Regina but Elazar—the grandfather I never knew as opposed to the grandmother I loved dearly—who seemed to be calling out to me.

My great-grandmother Salha Sehayek gave this portrait of herself to Regina on September 16, 1950, days before Regina left Iraq for good. On the back of the picture, she wrote: "A souvenir for my darling girl Regina." COURTESY OF MARCELLE BENJAMIN

My great-grandfather Ezra Sehayek was much loved by the family for his quiet wisdom and his sanguine outlook on life. COURTESY OF MARCELLE BENJAMIN

This picture was taken in 1918, less than a year after the British occupied Baghdad. The British soldiers on the roof terrace with Regina (on the left with the long plait) and her siblings had moved in next door to Salha and Ezra, pleasing my great-grandmother no end.
COURTESY OF MARCELLE BENJAMIN

Regina and Elazar (the couple on the left) as newlyweds, posing on the banks of the Tigris. The year is 1928. My grandmother routinely wore an *abaya* over her Western dress in public. My grandfather, meanwhile, wore a fez, even after it was no longer fashionable to do so.
COURTESY OF MARCELLE BENJAMIN

Solomon and Ezra snapped in the garden at the villa in Bataween in 1935.
COURTESY OF BERTHA TABIBZADEH

This picture dates from 1937 when Regina and Elazar were living in the big house on Taht al-Takia in the old Jewish quarter of Baghdad. My mother Marcelle is on the far right standing beside her father. Regina is holding one of her nephews.
COURTESY OF MARCELLE BENJAMIN

King Ghazi of Iraq in 1933, shortly after he ascended the throne. Within a couple of years he would be won over by pro-Nazi elements in the government and military, as the tide of public feeling began turning against Iraq's Jews. COURTESY OF POPPERFOTO

King Faisal I of Iraq, pictured in the 1920s, at the height of his struggles with the British. Faisal desperately wanted to lead Iraq to independence but was frustrated at every turn. COURTESY OF POPPERFOTO

A rare formal portrait of General Sir Frederick Stanley Maude taken after his arrival in Baghdad. Visitors to Baghdad still seek out his well-tended grave at the British cemetery. COURTESY OF IMPERIAL WAR MUSEUM, LONDON

The beautiful front façade and main entrance of the Laura Kadoorie School, where Regina, Bertha and Marcelle went to school. When the building was unveiled in 1913 it was considered to be the most ambitious modern construction in Baghdad, and admirers from across the city regularly gathered outside its gates to survey its elegant symmetry. COURTESY OF NAIM DANGOOR

This picture of older students at the Laura Kadoorie School was taken in 1931 and includes Regina's sister Josephine (back row, far left). Despite their obvious pretensions to sophistication, these middle class girls had few freedoms. COURTESY OF THE BABYLONIAN JEWRY HERITAGE CENTER COLLECTION

A group of Iraqi dignitaries pose on the steps of the Laure Kadoorie School. The year is 1924. King Faisal stands at the centre wearing a military jacket and a *keffiyah*. The white bearded sage to his left is Chief Rabbi Ezra Dangoor, and to *his* left stands the man who will in a few years time depose him, Rabbi Sassoon Khedouri. The man clasping his hands in front of him, to Faisal's right, is the Jewish Senator Menahem Daniel. COURTESY OF NAIM DANGOOR

Regina and Elazar enjoying a cup of coffee and a cigarette. This relaxed-looking picture, taken in the big house on Taht al-Taki in 1935, always makes me think of the calm before the storm. COURTESY OF MARCELLE BENJAMIN

Bertha and Marcelle in 1935. Even as small children their different characters were apparent: Bertha, the impetuous one, and Marcelle, who always held back. COURTESY OF MARCELLE BENJAMIN

1,600 pupils pose for their annual school photograph in the courtyard of the Laura Kadoorie School in 1924. Regina had already left by this time and had fallen prey to the designs of the local marriage broker. COURTESY OF NAIM DANGOOR

Chief Rabbi Sassoon Khedouri photographed in 1949 wearing his trademark turban and bottle-end glasses. Although he was much-loved by the Jewish community, he was viewed as a government yes-man. COURTESY OF EILEEN KHALASTCHY

This daredevil picture of Nuri as-Said is true to the character of the man. Taken in 1942, when he was prime minister, it shows him at the controls of the plane which he flew to Transjordan, accompanying Prince Regent Abdul Ilah. At this time, Nuri was still widely regarded as a friend to the Jews. COURTESY OF IMPERIAL WAR MUSEUM

Iraqi Jews on their way to Israel during Operation Ali Baba in 1950. The man sitting in the aisle seat in the second row wears a *sidara,* a uniquely Mesopotamian hat that was adopted by many Jews after Iraqi independence as a sign of their commitment to the new nation. COURTESY OF THE ZIONIST ARCHIVES IN JERUSALEM

My family's final days in their desert paradise. This photograph was taken outside the villa in Bataween in 1949. Regina stands in the center, with Bertha, Marcelle and Solomon to her right, and Nessim and his wife, Khatoun, on her left. Her son Haron is by her side, and Nessim's young sons complete the picture. Within eighteen months, the family would be broken apart. COURTESY OF MARCELLE BENJAMIN

Bertha and Marcelle on the street above Tollygunge market, Calcutta, in 1952. COURTESY OF BERTHA TABIBZADEH

My mother Marcelle. I've always loved this photograph of my mother, because there's hope in her eyes: her whole future lies before her. COURTESY OF MARCELLE BENJAMIN

Building a new life in a safe haven, Regina and her children adapt to Calcutta's noisy ways. This picture was snapped near their apartment in Chowringhee Lane.
COURTESY OF MARCELLE BENJAMIN

Regina relaxes on holiday in Kalimpong in 1995. She had sprained her ankle rather badly and was recouperating outdoors, when a bee landed on her big toe and stung her. COURTESY OF MARCELLE BENJAMIN

Inside the Meir Tweg Synagogue in Baghdad, 2004. This is the Jews' last surviving house of worship in the city. It is barricaded up behind towering concrete walls, though maintained in pristine condition by Muslim caretakers. The *bimah,* or platform, in the foreground is where Rabbi Khedouri would have read from the Torah. COURTESY OF MARINA BENJAMIN

Samir Shahrabani reveals the Meir Tweg's precious safer torahs . . . and some rather jazzy 1960s wallpaper. COURTESY OF MARINA BENJAMIN

In his nineties, Tawfiq Sofaer is one of the community oldest survivors. He used to be a merchant, but for the past thirty-five years he has lived in this tiny room in the synagogue compound. COURTESY OF MARINA BENJAMIN

Emad Levy offers prayers at his mother's graveside, 2004. For thirty years during Saddam's reign of terror, the Jewish cemetery in Sadr City was out of bounds to the Jews. Now it is being renovated by the community. COURTESY OF MARINA BENJAMIN

In its fundamentals, Rashid Street has barely changed in a century. Its crumbling buildings, Corinthian columns and cast iron balconies hark back to an era when the street was the haunt of Baghdad's smart set. Now, however, everything looks tired and shabby. COURTESY OF MARINA BENJAMIN

Precious few iconic images of Saddam Hussein were left when I visited Baghdad in 2004. This one, at the Jordanian border, had escaped destruction, even if the dictator had nonetheless been paint-balled. Its amazing how quickly the potency drains from imagery featuring formerly powerful figures: the old money I brought home with me, emblazoned with Saddam's portrait, looks utterly antiquated now. COURTESY OF MARINA BENJAMIN

Fifteen

GREAT EXPECTATIONS

Something Samir Shahrabani voiced about his hopes for Iraq's future has stayed with me. "I want democracy. I want freedom," he said. "I don't want to see any poor man and I don't want to see anyone struggle for his life. I don't see this happening, though, because you cannot rule the people of Iraq by democracy: you can only rule them with iron and fire."

One doesn't have to look far to confirm Samir's pessimism; to find eloquent pundits with long years of experience who will say that as individuals the Iraqis are remarkably nice people, educated, urbane, responsible; but that as a group they are unpredictable, and as a nation ungovernable. Most often the default position is to admit that what is needed after all is another strong leader.

The question of Iraq's future exercised every Iraqi I spoke to. Almost all those who expressed a desire for greater democracy also voiced grave doubts as to its workability. One influential Iraqi businessman I met with in London as I prepared for my trip told me that democracy would never work in Iraq because fiercely independent regional elements would never submit to majority Shia rule. What he envisaged instead was a Balkanization of the country along ethnic and religious lines, much as on the Eastern European model. This was exactly what he had told Paul Wolfowitz when the former U.S. deputy secretary of defense canvassed him for his views in Washington on the eve of the war.

Even those Iraqis who did foresee a role for democratic government in Iraq's future recognized that its incursions into Iraqi society
would be limited. Democracy would be unlikely to march hand in
hand with a broader building of civil society. It would not yield a
greater emancipation of women; it would not lead to the provision of
education for all classes; it would not generate feelings of ethnic harmony, and it would not put an end to government corruption. Much
more probable was a scenario in which a measure of democracy
would be introduced into society, but only in so far as it did not en-
croach on the practice, say, of sharia law, which many Shias are determined to reintroduce into the country, thus ending close to a half
century of secularization. Nor would it interfere with entrenched
tribal prerogatives.

But there are deeper, historical reasons why Iraqis are justifiably
suspicious of any foreign power that waltzes into the land singing the
tune of liberation and promising to deliver them self-rule. The lessons
of the twentieth century have taught Iraqis that such a power will first
and foremost seek to safeguard its own interests and that those interests, in turn, will limit what shape and form "self-rule" might take.

When Iraq rejected political liberalism in favor of state-
indoctrinated nationalism and militarism, first in 1941 and then again,
more decisively, in 1958, it was reacting against the lie of colonialism.
For decades Iraq had been independent in name alone. Politically, mil-
itarily, and financially, the country remained tied to the apron strings
of the British, who in spite of having imposed liberal institutions on
Iraq in 1921, attempted to govern from behind an Arab facade. All the
external trappings of a constitutional monarchy on the British model
were there—parliament, a senate, representational politics, even elections—but Britain remained the occupier. Its officers used illiberal
methods to maintain control of national affairs. They tampered with
elections, deported key figures in the political opposition, played competing factions off against one another, siphoned off oil revenues, fostered reactionary elements in Iraqi society, and bombed insurgent
minority groups into submission. The so-called liberal process was a
sham.

The Baathists were no better. When they began their ascent to power in 1963, they too promised democracy, only this time wedded to socialism and Arab union. But although the Baath Party was initially based on ideological politics and popular agitation, it never commanded wide public support. It came to power via conspiratorial politics and then proceeded to eliminate its rivals and all possible bases of opposition. Finally the party turned in on itself. Once Saddam Hussein had consolidated his position through a series of internal purges, there was nothing left but autocratic rule. Once again the promise of democracy turned out to be a lie.

Samir's words, and the punctured idealism they spoke to, have stayed with me because only in retrospect have I understood that I'd visited Iraq during a moment of transition. There had been great expectation in the country immediately after the war began. People were upbeat, hopeful, and the predominant mood was one of conciliation: the Iraqis, in other words, had been willing to give the Americans a chance. But one year later that expectation had soured. People had begun to ask who was benefiting from the free-market policies that had brought legions of cars into Baghdad only to cause mayhem on the city's already congested roads, or that had heaped shiny new refrigerators, rotisseries, irons, and electrical fans onto every market stand when ninety percent of households lacked the power to use them. Granted, there was now a Nokia outlet on Sa'adoon Street, and currency exchange centers on every major main street. But where was the economic investment that would rebuild the nation? And why were Iraqi companies barred from bidding for the lucrative reconstruction contracts that the CPA awarded to foreign firms?

While the talk was still of liberation, the United States was increasingly behaving as though its aim was domination. Samir had spoken of "iron and fire." Now America was using its brute force to counter opposition groups like Moqtada al-Sadr's Mehdi Army and to quash Sunni "resistance" in towns like Fallujah and Mosul. This was not playing well with the Iraqi people, whose loyalties Americans repeatedly misconstrued, failing to realize that however much Sunni, Shia, and Kurd disliked one another, they detested the foreign occupiers more. America also reneged on the promise of free elections after the Iraqis had endured every tangible wartime deprivation in order to cling to the intangible promise of eventual freedom and democracy. Instead they set up proxies like Iyad Allawi and his CIA-backed cohorts in positions of power, the better to rubber-stamp American policies.

Only in the face of threatened Shia uprisings on a scale that would make the Sunni-led insurgency seem paltry did America eventually agree to free elections. But even then U.S. spin doctors approached them as a public relations exercise to make the Bush administration look as if it were succeeding in Iraq ahead of the American elections in 2004. The timetable that mattered was America's, not Iraq's. Thus in rush-rush fashion, small teams of educators were dispatched into rural areas to build democratic caucuses in towns and villages that had no power or sanitation, and where the resident population was still being terrorized by Baathist loyalists.

The agenda that mattered was also American. On the eve of the Iraqi election in January 2005, it was widely reported that servants of the Bush administration had been whispering in the ears of the leading candidates. They told them that the United States would not countenance any government that attempted to edge American troops out of the country. Nor would they abide any move toward the building of an Islamic state—and that included developing closer ties with Iran.

America's great achievement was that in spite of all this meddling, few Westerners recall much about the actual election results. What they remember are the television pictures of jubilant Iraqis emerging from the voting booths proudly displaying their ink-stained purple index fingers.

In light of the violence that has continued to surge in its wake, the Iraqi election now looks like just one more artificial milestone imposed on a disintegrating Iraq by an American administration determined to portray conditions in the country as improving. The same may be said of the constitution hurriedly put forward for ratification in October 2005.

Until the United States—with the British government in tow—

proves that it is amenable to a gradual reforming process that will transfer back to the Iraqi people the basic right to govern themselves, Iraqis will continue to live under the shadow of violence. It has been estimated that as many as a hundred thousand Iraqi people have so far lost their lives to the promise of self-rule. But the ultimate human cost has yet to be tallied.

Next to the big picture of Iraq's ongoing and deepening crisis, my own tale of an identity lost and found continued—as did my hope that in its own small way it would find a happy conclusion.

In the end it was Samir who took me to the synagogue. He claimed he had errands to run nearby and that it would be easy to stop off there en route. In truth he was bursting with pride that the tiny community had been able to maintain this last house of worship built by Jews, in spite of the sanctions and the bombs and in the teeth of local hostility (it was not for nothing that the synagogue compound was encircled by twenty-foot walls). Since he clearly wanted to show it off, I didn't mention that Emad had judged such a visit too dangerous.

Once Betaween had been a Jewish neighborhood. Now its narrow streets were prowled by pimps, prostitutes, and idle youths who roamed the neighborhood in bands (the Arabs call them *hayateen*—"youths who lean against walls"). In such surroundings, Samir's high-seated and prim-looking 1960-model Ford Zodiac was riotously out of place. As we drove past one of the brothels, which were the only houses in the neighborhood whose front doors were wide open, a rough-looking prostitute, whose mouth appeared to be entirely devoid of teeth, gave its bonnet a naughty slap.

A thick metal door barred the entrance to the synagogue compound. Samir knocked at it and called out, while I craned my neck to survey the high-walled fortifications. I couldn't help feeling that if your intention is to deflect attention away from something, then the last thing you should do is surround it with towering walls. And yet the CPA had adopted the same tactic, erecting thick concrete blast walls around buildings in Baghdad that it wished to protect—mainly hotels—thus separating the defended from the undefended: foreigners from ordinary Iraqis. I seemed to spend most of my time in Baghdad behind such fortifications.

A moment later one of the synagogue's Muslim caretakers creaked the door open. He popped his head out into the street, looked sharply left and right, and then motioned us quickly in.

My first surprise was discovering how large the synagogue building was; my second, how austerely majestic its pale interior. Built in 1942, the synagogue is a generous two stories high. Its galleried upper level is supported by a dozen or more full-height pillars, while its ceiling is hung with two rows of plunging crystal chandeliers. When the chandeliers are lit, the whole place is bathed in a warm yellow glow. I found it easy to imagine the one-time congregation absorbed in the melodic incantations of an aging Sassoon Khedouri, reading from the Torah through his thick bottle-end lenses. More pointedly, I knew that my family had stepped inside this building, worshipped and celebrated here. Sadly the Meir Tweg had not seen a full house in many years. The last wedding to grace its aisles took place in 1982, and the last bar mitzvah was in 1978.

I sat down on one of the wooden divans that served as pews. Samir told me that when the community used to pray here, the divans were cushioned with colourful carpets. But now that even these last signs of habitation had gone the place felt bereft. After spending a few quiet minutes wrapped in our own thoughts, we strolled over to the ark at the back of the synagogue where the Torah scrolls, each encased in solid silver, were lined up like bowling pins. We recited the Shema Yisrael—or rather, Samir did, and I followed—and then we kissed the scrolls. I counted twenty-three. Thirteen more had been stolen without a word of explanation by the Ministry of Information in 1980.

Before leaving the compound, Samir took me to meet Tawfiq Sofaer, the synagogue's ninety-year-old former caretaker. For the last thirty-five years, Sofaer has lived in a cupboard-sized room under the stairs of a shabby office building adjacent to the synagogue. He relies on his manservant, Mohammed, a pleasant-looking and gentle-mannered Shia youth, to look after him, and on the community's charity. Although he is now old and frail, Sofaer remembers a time when Jews lived among the cream of Baghdad society. "I used to be a merchant," he told me. "But now I am all alone. I am too tired to go on. What can I do?" I tried to concentrate on what Sofaer was saying and not on the bareness of his room, the peeling plaster walls, the thinness of his mattress, or the holes in his cardigan. Sofaer boasted of his international connections. He had visited London long ago and he had family in Iran and Israel. As we stood up to leave, he said, "Ask about me in Israel; they know me there." In a gesture of tenderness that was touching to observe, Samir handed him a packet of high-protein biscuits and kissed the old man's head. He would visit again in a few days, he said. Sofaer nodded, too weary to respond.

Emad Levy liked to think of himself as the engine behind the community, the person who drove things forward and who injected heart and purpose into an otherwise lifeless group. "I am the honorary rabbi," he told me, laughing. But he was deadly serious. The more time I spent in Baghdad, the more apparent it became that the real power in the community resided in Marcelle Daoud, a tiny, raven-haired matriarch, now seventy-nine, who had not stepped outside her front door in almost a year. I'd heard that Marcelle was a formidable character and was told that she would probably refuse to meet me. So I had gone to the trouble of acquiring a calling card she'd find hard to resist: a handwritten letter from her niece in London, into which were folded a handful of up-to-date family photographs. My ruse worked rather too well, and, to my dismay, Marcelle Daoud dissolved into quiet sobs before we'd so much as exchanged a word. She had not seen her niece Farah in more than twenty years and wanted nothing more than to join her in London.

Marcelle was more open and talkative than I'd expected. She told me about her life, her work as a teacher in the Menahem Daniel School, and her time as principal of one of the leading government schools. She was hospitable too, offering me orange soda and custard creams and asking me about my life in England. If anything, it was I who was guarded, not knowing quite how to convey the jarring essence of London living into the subdued environment of Marcelle's

old-fashioned and darkened living room. When we moved on to matters of faith and identity, Marcelle spoke about Judaism the same way
that Emad and Samir had done. She said: "I have always had a strong
faith in God. My roots are Jewish, and I can't cut my roots. My father
was a deeply religious man. He used to go to synagogue every day
and we always kept the Sabbath." Judaism, it appeared, was one of the
two pillars of her private faith. The other was mathematics.

When she retired from teaching in 1982, Marcelle wanted to get involved in community administration, so she began volunteering her
accounting skills at the Jewish Committee Office, where a skeleton
staff worked full time collecting rents owed on properties owned by
the community. Formerly these had been schools, synagogues, and
clubs, but such buildings had been destroyed one by one, and shops
and tenements were erected in their place. The result was that the
community acquired thousands of tenants, and because Saddam chose
not to interfere in community finances, allowing the Jews to retain
and reinvest the rental income, its wealth grew to be considerable.
How rich the community was, Marcelle wouldn't say, though she
knew better than anyone what its assets were worth. Indeed, she had
whispered to someone else, who later whispered to me, the astonishing figure of forty million dollars.

It is Marcelle who decides where, when, and how much to invest in
bonds and unit trusts, who creates endowment funds to educate the
children of the remaining Jews, and who determines what the
monthly stipend paid out to all community members of adult age
should be (the Jews called it their "salary," and at the time I visited it
was roughly equivalent to the take-home pay of a policeman before
the war). Similarly, if someone has a medical expense for hospital
treatment or surgery, they take the bill to Marcelle, and she pays the
hospital directly. She also undertakes to pay any educational establishment or training facility where Jews have enrolled for courses. When I
made the delicate observation that the community's outgoings were
proportionally, well, rather small compared to its income, Marcelle
narrowed her eyes and said, "We don't like to show that we have
money because everyone is always against the Jews."

It is a difficult trick to maintain the illusion of power when you've confined your sphere of operations to your living room, and Marcelle pulled it off with mixed results. On the one hand, I sensed the shrewish intelligence that had earned her the fear and respect of the other Jews: she evidently knew how to keep others in line as well as how to juggle sums. But perhaps because I'd seen (indeed caused) her veneer to crack, I had also glimpsed her underlying vulnerability. She may even have found some relief in being able to admit, albeit unwittingly, that Baghdad had somehow defeated her.

For all her intelligence and obvious capability, Marcelle was clearly exhausted, worn down by the sheer strain of living in this tumultuous city. Though she said she wanted to join Farah in London, she was scarcely able to make it sound believable: there simply wasn't the will there to match the intent. I began to think that the only agency capable of getting her to leave Iraq was supernatural. So it hardly surprised me that when Samir teased her, saying, "Who will lead our small ship if you go?" Marcelle had replied, "God."

"Imagine yourself to be a Robinson Crusoe and you will know how we are," said Jacob Shahrabani, inviting me to step into his shoes and contemplate being marooned in a sea of otherness, starved of the company of loved ones and with little hope of relief. This was how the last Jews of Baghdad viewed themselves, as quasitragic, quasiromantic figures, isolated, stranded, immobilized.

But how did they see me?

I was an emissary from the world beyond, a place where Iraqi Jews led unimaginably different and infinitely more settled lives. Through me Jacob, Emad, Marcelle, and the others could picture the kind of lives their brothers, mothers, or nieces were leading elsewhere, and perhaps even project their own futures onto that partially colored canvas. But my role had clear limitations. While I was able to serve as a cipher for escapist dreaming and as a conduit for trafficking memories, letters, heirlooms, and even hard cash between them and their relatives elsewhere, I was no savior. At no time was I more mindful of my fundamental inability to improve the lot of these Jews than when

Violet Tweg—resilient Violet Tweg, four feet ten inches tall in her slippered feet and threadbare woolly hat; mother, doctor, and octogenarian—turned to me and said: "If I want to leave, will you carry me?" I couldn't make such promises. I could only offer feeble reassurances. Emotionally invested as I was in the Baghdadi Jews, I was painfully conscious of my own shortcomings: I knew that their futures would have to be brokered by others.

And so we come to Rachel and Carole. I cannot count the times these names dropped into my conversations with the Baghdadi Jews. "If Rachel comes, will you go?" was a commonplace question, usually answered with a noncommittal shrug. While "Carole says that more Jews may come" was a phrase that fell from people's lips like a witchy incantation—something almost magical yet only half believed. It seemed that no discussion of the future was complete without mention of these two women. Rachel Zelon and Carole Basri represented the fork in the road that stretched out ahead of the last Jews of Baghdad. One path took the Jews to Israel; the other led precisely nowhere.

As an officer of the Hebrew Immigrant Aid Society in New York, Rachel Zelon has spent much of her career organizing airlifts to get Jews out of trouble spots to a safe haven in Israel. She has worked in Bosnia and Kenya, helped evacuate Jews from Argentina, and most recently her office has set up rescue programs in Uruguay and Chad. Rachel began working in Iraq during the sanction era, when she aided Iraqi Jews to escape to Jordan and from there negotiated their resettlement in England or Holland. If not for her efforts, my mother's long-lost cousin Aziza and her family would have never made new lives for themselves in London. In their eyes Rachel is practically a saint, and they've never been able to fathom why more of the Baghdadi Jews did not put their faith in her.

After the Iraq war, when evacuating Iraqi Jews became a wholesale proposition, at least from the perspective of a rescue-obsessed West, Rachel made several trips to Baghdad. She coaxed and cajoled and pleaded with the Jews to leave, promising them every convenience and safeguard. But only six elderly Jews, among whom Emad's father, Ezra, was, at seventy-five, the sprightliest, agreed to be flown to Israel in August 2003. The rest of the Jews prevaricated or simply strung her along, never intending to make the leap in the first place. Rachel found the apathy she encountered bewildering and frustrating by turn, while they found her urgency and haste unpersuasive. However much she tried to convince them that there was no future for them in Iraq, they were reluctant to turn their backs on what they knew.

To me Rachel complained about the condition in which the Jews were living; the squalor that old men like Tawfiq Sofaer, the synagogue caretaker, endured, the neglect, the ostensible yet nonsensical poverty of many of the Jews, the complete lack of expert care. She told me how one of the old women who had been flown to Israel had been living in miserable conditions in a community home for the aged. Regina Sion had a spine so crooked, said Rachel, she'd been bent at right angles, and she was almost blind with cataracts. Marcelle used to visit her occasionally, or else dispatch Mohammed from the synagogue to take her food, but according to Rachel the portions were meager and the poor woman was starving to death. Once Regina had been hospitalized in Israel it was discovered that she had diabetes and tumors on her back. "No one had been taking care of her," railed Rachel.

The truth, of course, was more complex. As Rachel herself would probably concede, the Jews believed that they were taking care of their own as best they could in trying circumstances. It was proving difficult for them to shed habits of caution and stealth that had shaped and comforted them over the decades. And they remained terrified of appearing to have wealth, resolute in their mistrust of outsiders. These were not people who could bite the bullet, seize opportunities, or embrace radical change.

When Rachel realized she wasn't going to get the response she'd hoped for, she had urged Marcelle to raise the Jews' salary from fifty dollars a month to five hundred dollars, on the grounds that no one monitored how they spent their money anymore. But Marcelle had been reluctant to comply. Rachel had also encouraged Marcelle to increase the food rations. But while she remained determined to improve conditions on the ground for the Jews, Rachel could not comprehend why they kept making excuses to stay. Violet Tweg's daughter, who I'll call Amal, was clearly desperate to get out of Iraq. Still in her mid-thirties, still single, and a qualified dentist with good spoken English, she could see her future gurgling down the sinkhole. But she refused to leave her mother behind, not trusting her older bother to care for her properly. Even Emad, who had so much energy to bring to a new life, loitered indefinitely, claiming that he needed to wind up his affairs before he could join his father, and protesting that it was impossible to sell the family home when the legal apparatus governing such transactions had disintegrated.

Though it was clear to me that the community was in conflict over disbanding, half convinced that individuals who chose to abandon Iraq were committing a crime against the past, it wasn't at all obvious that there was anything to be gained by staying. Carole thought otherwise.

Carole Basri is slight in build, with large, intense eyes, long blonded tresses and an urgent, almost hyperventilated way of talking. When she speaks, people listen. An adjunct law professor at the University of Pennsylvania and a longtime campaigner for the rights of displaced Arab Jews, she was offered the plum job of joining the small team of legal eagles appointed in July 2003 to advise CPA chief Paul Bremer on how best to transition Iraq to a smoothly functioning, modern economy. As part of the Iraqi Reconstruction Development Council, Carole worked on anticorruption legislation and helped draft the inspector-general statutes, whistleblower statutes, and Foreign Investment Act, all of which became integral to the constitution inherited by Iyad Allawi's interim government. Like her colleagues in the vanguard of Iraqi reconstruction, she did much to spread the CPA's almost recklessly optimistic vision for the country.

To the last Jews of Baghdad, Carole represented authority: her words carried weight, her promises the glitter of almost certain realization. It helped that Carole was herself an Iraqi Jew—one, moreover, who could boast pedigree lineage: her great-grandfather was the chief rabbi unseated by Sassoon Khedouri, and her uncle was the celebrated poet and former Iraqi civil servant Meir Basri.

According to Jacob, Carole Basri had been urging the Jews to remain in Baghdad by reminding them of how much there was to lose: "You represent twenty-seven hundred years of Babylonian Jewish history," she told them. Later she told me: "It is very important to keep the community intact, largely for communal reasons; you've got safer torahs, you have an identity, you have a history." Jacob, for one, was more of a pragmatist than either Rachel or Carole gave him credit for. Though his heritage was something he took pride in, he was not about to sacrifice his happiness to its preservation. The main reason he wanted to stay in Baghdad, he told me, was to finish his Ph.D.

But what about the medium and long term? Did Jacob and Samir really imagine themselves living in Baghdad when every other Jew had either died or emigrated? And how did they propose to meet Jewish women to settle down with? After all, there's little point in representing twenty-seven hundred years of a proud and vibrant history if that history ends with you.

Jacob and Samir had thought a good deal about this prickly issue, taking heart when Carole offered to help them contact the Jewish community in Tehran—a community of ancient standing that currently numbers roughly twenty-five thousand people. Perhaps, with a little romantic luck, Samir and Jacob could start the process of repopulating the community in Baghdad. I didn't want to pour cold water on the plan. But it was no easy thing to picture Samir or Jacob in front of a potential life partner, trying to sell her a vision of a glowing future in war-torn Baghdad. The task had a steep uphill aspect to it, not unlike inviting someone to share your prison sentence with you. Still, with Carole's encouragement, Samir had made provisional plans to visit Iran.

Though our paths failed to cross in Baghdad, I had met Carole once before when, fresh off the plane from Iraq, she visited London at the end of 2003 to address a gathering of Iraqi Jewish exiles at the Spanish and Portuguese Synagogue on Lordadale Road, Maida Vale. It was a highly charged evening. The assembled group of listeners, each invested to their core in the fate of Iraq, was eager for every bit of news she could yank into the light from what had essentially become a blackout zone, and they had hung greedily on her measured words. The picture she painted of life in Baghdad at the time was less grim than most had imagined. Sure, the city was groaning under water shortages and electricity blackouts, she told us. Its phones didn't work. Its streets were unsafe. But people were doing just fine: they were free, after all, and they were more than happy to tolerate some inconvenience in order to remain free.

After her talk she screened a video that she had made to commemorate the life of her grandfather Frank Iny, the businessman and philanthropist responsible for building the eponymous school on Emad's street. Then she showed us slides from her own recent visits to Baghdad. Many of these offered vistas of the Old City that had remained virtually unchanged in the half century since the Jews left *en masse,* and they were greeted with audible delight by an audience now openly homesick with recognition. But the slide that remained fixed in my own mind was a shot of her hotel room. Well appointed in the western style, lushly carpeted, with soft cream furnishings, it was a far cry from the basic and barely hygienic accommodation I would later end up with. Though I did not know it then, it underscored the top-down perspective that Carole had of Baghdad—a perspective one could get only if one flew in military planes, resided in relative luxury in the fiercely defended Green Zone, and availed oneself of armored escorts at every opportunity.

In the course of making regular visits to Baghdad on CPA business, Carole had taken the opportunity to befriend the last Jews. As a result she had become as intimately concerned with their future and survival as Rachel was. She'd even organized a community election in order to meet new ordinances issued by the Ministry of Religion and the *waqf,* which required individual communities to obtain official recognition in order to collect rents. And she'd drawn up a new budget for Marcelle. Unlike Rachel, Carole urged the Jews to stay put. Once the nation's present travails had passed, she argued, the position of Jews in Iraqi society would almost certainly improve. Eventually, Carole hoped, Iraqi Jews would once again enjoy prominence and respect in a rebuilt Iraq that was both confident enough and secure enough to embrace democracy, the free market, and Western-style multiculturalism.

Carole was not alone among Iraqi Jews in such thinking. Naim Dangoor, patron and proprietor of *The Scribe*—a quarterly journal devoted to the history of Babylonian Jewry—and a London-based philanthropist of considerable standing, shared the same vision. To this end, he raised almost twenty million dollars to put at the disposal of Iraqi Jews willing to move back to Baghdad and rebuild the Jewish community. At ninety Dangoor was too old to return himself, but he joked about reviving his business interests in Iraq, where he was once the bottler of Coca-Cola.

At the same time Iraqi Jews who had pinned their hopes on Ahmed Chalabi's Iraqi National Congress were similarly enthused and did much to talk up the prospect of return. In the immediate postwar period, Chalabi, a secular Shiite, political moderate, and cousin of Iyad Allawi, enjoyed considerable U.S. patronage, and he had made encouraging public remarks about Iraq's chances of making peace with Israel. Chalabi has since fallen from grace, but such were the delusions fostered by Iraqi Jews in Britain and America during the false dawn of 2003 that legions of them began to think about going back, if not for good, then at least to visit—in some cases clutching the title deeds belonging to homes and businesses that had been stolen from them. As Carole later told me: "If the security situation improves, there'll be more commerce, people will start going in and out and visiting religious sites. I don't see the rebirth of a vibrant community; I see Baghdad as an outpost."

If there was little substance to support such pipe dreams, there was certainly a whirl of symbolic activity that pointed in hopeful directions, much of it generated by the American-appointed Iraqi Governing Council. Members of the IGC had been handpicked to represent as broad a swath of Iraqi society as possible. They had responded favorably to the campaign led by Carole Basri and others who argued for the restoration and rehabilitation of Iraq's ancient Jewish shines. And prior to Ali al-Sistani's public dismissal of Jewish rights, IGC members were said to have been contemplating various ways in which Iraqi Jews electing to return from abroad and help rebuild the country might be repatriated.

Given its diverse ethnic makeup, the IGC was big on inclusiveness. Another of its failed gestures toward building a more tolerant Iraq involved unveiling a revolutionary new design for the Iraqi flag, purged of the partisan colors of Arab nationalism. It was to have two blue stripes representing Iraq's two rivers, a yellow stripe representing the ethnic Kurd minority, and a blue crescent of Islam. The flag was roundly rejected by the majority of Iraqis. If not an early sign of the convulsive changes that the country would soon undergo, it was a powerful signal that Iraq was not yet ready to embrace multiculturalism. Some journalists even complained that the proposed flag seemed similar to the Israeli flag, and this was before anti-Semitism had sunk its teeth into the nation.

Carole's appeal to the last Jews of Baghdad belonged to an unreal moment when a window of opportunity had been forced open and the champions of peaceful progress, racial tolerance, and a radical free-market economy had rushed in on a gust of breezy enthusiasm. When the window promptly slammed shut behind them, the generals, the administrators, the image makers, contractors, lawyers, and consultants, experts one and all, were left openmouthed and incredulous, unwilling to believe that a country as clearly in need of modernization as Iraq could reject what they had to offer, never mind that the terms of the offer were largely favorable to them.

In the months following Iraq's subsequent descent into renewed violence, Rachel managed to whisk four more Jews off to Israel, leaving just eighteen behind in Baghdad. The airlift took place only days before Iyad Allawi's interim government assumed the reins of government. Its timing was critical because thereafter Iraqi Jews no longer qualified as refugees of war: under a restored government they became Iraqi citizens once more, and from then forward any move on the part of HIAS or the Jewish Agency to petition ministers to allow further airlifts became politically sensitive.

Since that summer, Tawfiq Sofaer has died, and one family of five that appeared to maintain its Jewish identity solely in order to benefit from community largesse (its children's university places were funded out of Arab rents) has severed almost all its ties with the last Jews.

That leaves twelve. Unless the community's numbers are augmented by Jews emigrating from Iran or returning from exile elsewhere, in another generation—or, at the most, in two—there will be no more Jews left in Iraq.

Violet Tweg's daughter Amal made a solo bid for freedom in 2005. She hired a driver to take her to the Jordanian border and somehow managed to get herself across it without any kind of exit visa and with an invalid passport. She camped in Amman for more than a week and took her case to the British Embassy in that city on a daily basis. She had friends in Britain, she told embassy officials. She was a qualified dentist. She could speak the language. There was nothing for her in Iraq. But her pleas fell on deaf ears, and Amal was forced to hire another driver to take her back to Baghdad.

As the daughter and granddaughter of Iraqi Jews who did manage to leave, I find myself returning over and over to the matter of Amal's plight. What might have transpired if Regina had also been forced to turn back? It could have happened. Indeed, it very nearly did. And if it had happened, would Regina have been able to muster the energy for a fresh attempt at escaping? Would my family, now including me, have paid Kurdish smugglers to take us over the mountainous border with Iran? Or would we have stayed in Baghdad, hoping against the odds that things would eventually improve? What if we had struggled on through the long years of Saddam Hussein's rule? Through the war with Iran, the American bombs, and the UN sanctions? What if we found ourselves cut off from the outside world, our confidence sapped, our hopes turned to ashes? What if my life had been Amal's?

The thread of counterfactual logic that puts me in Amal's place leaves me unmoved by any temptation to mourn aloud the prolonged demise of a once-great community of ancient standing, since in almost every way my life is better than Amal's. By the same token, I cannot bring myself to make the case that the last Jews should remain in Iraq, proud standard bearers of a 2,700-year-old heritage, since added to the everyday facts of their difficult lives that heritage is just one more burden.

The truth is that the once-great community of Babylonian Jewry was abruptly wiped out in Iraq long ago, between the years 1950 and 1951. The Jews who stayed on after that qualify only as a remnant. They were never more than part of a whole, trying to function as a whole, and never more obviously so than when their numbers began drastically diminishing and they lost their rabbis, their schools, their synagogues, their center.

Now there are twelve souls left, and twelve souls can scarcely be expected to kick-start a new community, much less revive a formerly great one. It is simply too much to expect from a handful of struggling people trying to make their way in an embattled nation. The irony is that in a world where such things have for the most part ceased to matter, each of these twelve people has had to confront the same question their forebears faced in 1950 and 1951: are they Jews first and then Iraqis, or Iraqis first and then Jews?

For now they have elected to be Iraqi.

As for me, I'm all the more grateful in light of their stoicism that in the Diaspora this choice is not one I need to make.

EPILOGUE

There was an unexpected reunion for Regina in 1979 when Nessim moved to London in the wake of Ayatollah Khomeini's Islamic revolution in Iran. Under the shah, in Tehran, life had treated him well. He had prospered, and his children had thrived among a community of Jews who enjoyed greater civic freedoms than their Iraqui counterparts had ever had. *"Wallah,* there was no prejudice," he would tell Regina, clearly thinking that in some ways it was a shame it was all over.

But in other ways London represented a new start. Nessim set himself up in Kensington. He dabbled leisurely in a little business, and doted on his sons, who'd relocated with him and whose yet-to-be-born children would grow up speaking English as a first language, just as I did. Once in London, and with Nessim more or less retired, he used to spend long hours with Regina in Hounslow drinking Turkish coffee and talking about old times in Baghdad. From 1979 the family was less divided than it had been before.

Solomon was still in Israel with his wife and daughter, all of them switching back and forth between Arabic and Hebrew as they moved between family and friends who'd left Iraq with them and the newer company of European settlers, some of whom had been there for generations. Solomon never went in for the kibbutz life. He settled in the fast-growing coastal town of Tel Aviv, where he managed to parlay his banking experience into a career as an insurance broker.

Solomon was one of the lucky ones. The majority of Iraqi Jews arriving destitute in Israel found themselves entirely dependent on an overburdened state that hadn't the resources to absorb so many people on terms that favored such things as individual choice and personal aspiration: the Iraqi Jews therefore had little or no say in what they or their children would become. The Sehayeks, by contrast, had gotten a lot of their money out of Iraq illegally in the months prior to the *taskeet,* and within weeks of being dumped into stinking and overcrowded transition camps along with everyone else were able to elbow their way into something that resembled a normal life. By 1979 Solomon, his younger sister, Marcelle, and Josephine, who had moved from Calcutta to Israel after Regina left for London, had almost thirty years of pioneering behind them, and not one of them had once picked up a pitchfork, or hoe.

Ezra passed away in 1963, having reached the milestone of ninety. In celebration of his arriving at what the Baghdadi Jews call "the year of two ages" because it bridges two ordinary life spans, Solomon had given gifts of clothing and food to the poor. Ezra was delighted with this act of charity, undertaken in his honor. "What will you do when I turn one hundred?" he'd teased his son. Salha, meanwhile, lived on until 1978, when she turned ninety-three, though with Ezra gone she never felt quite at home in the world. She'd become pickier and snappier and grown bent as an old doornail. Yet she remained a fighter to the end. Once, when she fell and broke her leg, she managed to haul herself to the telephone and call for help. She was in her eighties at the time and living alone in a small apartment in Ramat Gan, a Tel Aviv suburb that the Ashkenazi Jews dubbed "Little Baghdad."

Although Salha had spent almost three decades living in Israel, she never learned to speak Hebrew. She acquired enough of the language to recite her daily prayers, but otherwise she made do with Arabic. While I like to think that at some level she was fighting the good fight, trying, through this small rearguard action, to keep a vital piece of the old world alive, it's more likely that she simply considered herself past adapting. In fact, it's easy to picture her protesting to Ezra that she was too old to learn how to live a new life in a new country with a new language and new ways. "What good will Hebrew do me?" she would have balked. While she was proud of her loyalty to Israel, which she trumpeted loudly down the years, Salha belonged to a generation for whom Baghdad would always remain home.

The manner and extent to which Baghdadi Jews were assimilated into Israel's essentially European mainstream culture poses many thorny questions, highly charged both politically and emotionally. For as long as Iraq's Jews remained in Iraq, the matter of their dual allegiance was purely theoretical. Once they'd landed in Israel however, they were expected to reinvent themselves as Israelis. In practice that meant embracing the language and culture, adopting new, "enlightened" values, and becoming acclimated to living off the land.

All of this would have been fine had the 124,638 Iraqi Jews who fled Iraq between 1948 and 1953 not arrived in Israel mostly as the kind of "penniless displaced persons" that Foreign Minister Moshe Sharett had vowed the country would not "in any circumstances" take in. If Iraqi Jews had been allowed to bring their assets with them, the story of their assimilation might have been a happy one: they could have purchased land, built homes, started businesses, and opened schools. They could have bought their way into a burgeoning society by building on the life they already knew. Instead they found themselves as "guests of the State." And if they were going to settle down and build new lives for themselves it was going to be on the state's terms.

As a matter of urgency the Israeli state needed cheap labor. It needed farmhands, construction workers, and factory workers, not merchants, artisans, bankers, and civil servants, and it was equally desperate to recruit young blood into the military to make up for lives lost in the Arab-Israeli War. Once the Iraqi Jews arrived on Israeli soil, their needs, both as individuals and as a community, were subsumed by those of the state.

This was profoundly shocking to Iraqi Jews nurturing dreams of salvation. The differing expectations of the immigrants and the state were painfully apparent from the moment the Iraqis arrived in Lydda Airport dressed in their finest clothing—their suits, synagogue hats, and silver watches—and expecting nothing less than a glorious homecoming. How many times had emissaries such as Enzo Sereni promised them a welcome beyond their dreams? Instead they were sprayed with DDT, bundled into the back of transport trucks, and shipped out to transition camps furnished with regulation khaki tents, surrounded by barbed wire fences, and guarded day and night by Polish commandants who apparently thought they were running concentration camps.

The Sehayeks spent only a month in the Nes Ziona camp south of Tel Aviv, huddling together on upturned vegetable crates inside a drafty tent. As they sipped watery tea out of dirty tin cups, Salha mourned aloud for the precious china she'd been forced to leave behind in Iraq. Ezra meanwhile quickly grew depressed. He said virtually nothing when he had to trudge across the muddy camp to line up for kerosene to light the oil lamps, and he spent long hours sitting hunched and unshaven inside the tent, wild thoughts of despair running through his head. The food was terrible. Every day there were powdered egg rations served on plates that smelled of disinfectant, and stale bread that had gone moldy. There was no work in the camp, and everyone was bored. Fights regularly broke out over the silliest things, such as hoarding rations or gaining privileges with the camp guards. Only Solomon kept the family going by reminding them that soon they'd be moving on, that there were better things in Israel than dirty tents, ringworm, and rotten fruit.

As I said, the Sehayeks were lucky. Some families spent up to seven years in the camps, or ma'abarot, growing increasingly angry and disillusioned with Israel. Other families had their children stolen from them.

The Baghdad-born Israeli novelist Eli Amir has written with wry humor and engaging frankness of his boyhood experiences of being "re-educated" in Israel: plucked out of the miserable ma'abarot, torn from the bosom of his family, and transported by cattle truck to an out-of-the-way kibbutz, there to imbibe the European philosophy of the state's founding fathers. Amir would have his "Asiatic" preconceptions knocked out of him. At the kibbutz he recalled that Fawzias became Ilanas and Abd el-Azizes became Avners and that blond-headed youth leaders taught them Yiddish slogans and gave them lessons in "how to behave, what to sing, how to dance, what to read and how to be different from what we were."

Amir's novelized account of his confusing coming-of-age pertinently captures the Iraqi Jews' sense of pain and betrayal when they discovered that the values of the Jewish state were European through and through. Although Israel was made up of myriad Jewish subcultures living cheek by jowl, the dominant national culture was Ashkenazi. Unless the Iraqi Jews signed up to it unquestioningly, they would remain second-class citizens. The Iraqi Jews were dismayed. "In Iraq we were Jews, but here, in Israel, we are Arabs," they complained. Just as comfusingly, they were regarded as primitives: their religiosity was seen as backward, their culture impoverished. As one Iraqi Jewish writer plaintively protested: "The God of Israel is Yiddish."

When the American anti-Zionist rabbi Elmer Berger visited Israel in 1955 he reported that "Arab Jews are discriminated against in Israel; they are given the lowest work, such as bricklayers, labour drainage works and so on, even though they are well educated, whilst the European Jews are treated as if they were the masters and the Arab Jews their slaves or servants."

As a further indictment of Israel's two-tier society, the Palestinian historian Abbas Shiblak notes that Iraqi Jews, along with Jews from Morocco, Aden, the Yemen, and Kurdistan, were settled in strategically exposed development towns and border settlements and in economically disadvantaged rural collectives, or *moshavim*. They were given smaller plots of land than those allotted to their European counterparts, and fewer educational opportunities. Since economically underprivileged parents produce culturally deprived children, it is hardly surprising that within a couple of decades of moving to Israel the urbane community of Iraqi Jews, who in Baghdad had valued nothing so much as education, had produced a generation of delinquents.

If being sacrificed for the sake of Iraq's national cause was the Iraqi Jews' first tragedy, then this cultural demise surely qualifies as their second.

Many Jewish apologists, and not a few Iraqi Jews among them, will protest that Israel was never guilty of racism, or even neocolonialism.

The problems that Iraqi and other Arab Jews encountered in the Holy Land were the result of logistical, practical, and material difficulties, the birth pangs of a new nation. A war had just been fought, the national coffers were close to empty, and hundreds of thousands of newly arrived immigrants urgently needed work and shelter. This much is all true. And the immigration numbers are certainly staggering. In the years following the founding of the Israeli state more than eight-hundred thousand Jews from Arab lands were forced, like the Palestinian Arabs, to pack their bags and leave their homes, and of these refugees more than six-hundred thousand ended up in Israel. However, the question of their absorption posed not just logistical but ideological issues. At the very highest levels of Israeli society, it was felt that the arrival of so many Arab Jews constituted a threat to the essential character of the nation.

Addressing the Knesset in 1960, Prime Minister David Ben-Gurion explained that Jews in Muslim countries "have lived in a society that was backward, corrupt, uneducated and lacking in independence and self-respect." The older immigrants from these countries would never change fundamentally, he said, but the younger ones had to be imbued with the "superior moral and intellectual qualities" of those who created the State of Israel. "If, heaven forbid, we do not succeed . . . there is a danger that the coming generation may transform Israel into a Levantine state." Defense Minister Moshe Dayan agreed, claiming "it will take two or three generations before we can bring them up to our European standards."

Before long, such pompous declamations were being parroted by the Israeli intelligentsia. Raphael Patai, an Israeli professor of cultural anthropology who went on to teach at a number of American universities, said: "The Oriental Jews are in need of a complete re-education . . . their entire being and thinking must be re-shaped in the European image." And the Romanian-born Zionist and essayist Maurice Samuel wrote that many of the Eastern immigrants "had no feeling whatsoever for the Jewish state, and knew nothing of the spirit that had built the country for them." Now the Iraqi Jews were ingrates as well as primitives!

In light of such comments one cannot help but feel cynical in reviewing Israel's motives for absorbing so many Mizrahi Jews. The country had been ravaged by war, its economy was in tatters, and its infrastructure desperately needed rebuilding. Manpower was needed to run its fledgling industries, farmers to reclaim fields abandoned by Arabs, and soldiers to defend its borders. When Israel's leaders looked toward the Jewish refugees from Arab lands, what they saw, according to one Iraqi Jewish writer, was a "human windfall."

Political historian Elie Kedourie has gone further, calling Israel's deal with the Iraqi government to sweep up the entirety of its indigenous Jews, a "monstrous" complicity, born of a desire to make Israel a fait accompli by concentrating as many Jews within its fragile borders as possible. For this gain Israel would help Iraq achieve its national unity.

Even before the Iraqi Jews had left the *ma'abarot,* there sprang up among them a militant group of politicized youth who would fight back against the discrimination and cultural oppression. They called themselves the Black Panthers, and they produced reams of radical literature denouncing the Israeli imperialists. How, they asked, could a community that used to produce "splendid sons" in Iraq produce only "handicapped" sons in Israel? How could a community that "ruled over most of the resources of Iraq" be turned into "a ruled group, discriminated against and oppressed in every aspect"?

The Black Panthers never succeeded in winning over the majority of their compatriots. But one of their songs has weathered the years. It was sung by Iraqi Jews in Israel long after they'd left the camps, and then, with increasing irony, at weddings and festive occasions. It goes as follows:

> *What did you do Ben-Gurion?*
> *You smuggled in all of us!*
> *Because of the past, we waived our citizenship*
> *And came to Israel.*
> *Would that we had come riding on a donkey and we*
> *Hadn't arrived here yet!*
> *Woe, what a black hour it was.*
> *To hell with the plane that brought us here!*

ACKNOWLEDGMENTS

This is a true story. It is largely based on my grandmother's life and the varied experiences of my extended family, but I hope that it also reflects the experiences of thousands of other Iraqi Jews who gave up their citizenship and were cast into exile in 1950 and 1951, or who left Iraq as refugees in the years following. Most of these Jews have succeeded in building new lives for themselves in the West. Their children speak not Arabic but English, Hebrew, or French. Their grandchildren know even less about their heritage: often it is not for lack of trying, but there's so little left that's tangible. This book has tried to capture some of that heritage before it slips out of cultural memory and into the obscurity of the forgotten past.

Without the unstinting support of my family, I could never have embarked on this project, since it required so much of their time, talking and remembering and reminiscing. My mother, Marcelle, and my aunt Bertha, in particular, spent long hours with me, delving into their past and generously sharing their memories. Sometimes my questions took them to places they would rather not have revisited, even in their heads, but they always remained brave and unbiased in their recollections. Likewise, my great-uncle Solomon and my great-aunt Khatoun were invaluable guides to the family's past. Other members of the Sehayek, Levy, and Nissan clans, too numerous to mention individually, brought the past to life by digging up photographs, anecdotes, family trees, letters, and memoirs. I would like to offer them all my deepest thanks and appreciation: I enjoyed their stories immensely.

Thanks are also due to Elli Timan, who let me read his father-in-law's unpublished memoirs, to Maurice Bekhor for sharing with me his recollections of life in Baghdad in the 1920s, and to Richard Moshe for introducing me to, among others, the renowned Iraqi Jewish poet Meir Basri, whose death at the end of 2005 occasioned great sadness in the Iraqi Jewish community. Basri was almost one hundred when he died and one of the very last representatives of my grandmother's generation: I am grateful to have had the chance to talk to him about his life and times in Baghdad. I was also lucky enough to meet Violet Battat and Abraham Shohet, both of whom have also since died. If ever there was a reminder of the urgent timeliness of this project, these sad losses to the community were it.

Now that the Iraqi Jewish community is dispersed across the globe, in Israel, America, England, and elsewhere, it relies on the written word as a mode of communication and commemoration. Among those who have made sterling efforts to transmit and preserve the Iraqi Jews' rich and fascinating history are Naim Dangoor, Eileen Khalastchy, and David Dangoor, the team behind *The Scribe, Journal of Babylonian Jewry*. I'd like to thank them for allowing me into their offices to read books and browse through photographs. Similar thanks go to the scholars at the Babylonian Heritage Center at Or-Yehuda, in Israel who produce the journal *Nehadrea;* and to Lyn Julius, who writes an online newsletter about Jews from Arab Lands. Lyn was hugely supportive and enthusiastic.

I would also like to thank Sylvia Haim, Sami Zubeida, and Lilian Joury for lending me their time and academic expertise and Hanan al-Shaykh and Linda Mnuchin for valuable introductions to Iraqi expats in London and Tel Aviv. Maurice Shohet, Jack Silas, and Valerie Monchi lent me rare books I was unable to obtain easily elsewhere. Alice Hecht and Carole Basri gave me useful perspectives on postwar Baghdad. Lydia Collins lent me her genealogical expertise and shared her research into the Levy family tree. And Ingrid Simler and John Bernstein gave me space in which to write when deadlines loomed.

Naturally, I am deeply indebted to a host of people who advised and materially helped me get into Baghdad. They include Patrick Cockburn, Tim Judah, Rachel Zelon, Rabbi Mitchell Ackerson, Phil Coburn, Ian Twigg, and Rania Kadri. Aziza Darwish and her lovely family furnished me with introductions to the "last Jews"; my guardian angel Mahmoud Shaker got me out of Baghdad safely; and, of course, my time in Baghdad would not have been complete without meeting the Jews who welcomed me so warmly, but especially Emad Levy, Khalida Mouallem, and Samir and Jacob Shahrabani.

Thanks must also go to my Arabic teachers at the University of Westminster, Hania Dvorak-Salter and 'Ali al-Malaki, for persevering with me; to the wonderful staff at the British Library, where I wrote much of the book; the archivists at the *Alliance Israélite Universelle* in Paris; the librarians at the *Jewish Chronicle* offices in London; and to Simon Rabson, archivist at P&O Shipping.

I have been most fortunate to work with consummate professionals at Free Press, especially Liz Stein and Maris Kreizman, and my agent, Henry Dunow, is an absolute star.

Finally I would like offer Greg Klerkx praise for his patience with a project that for almost three years has dominated both the discussion space and the office space in our house. His suggestions and comments on successive drafts of this book continually spurred me on and encouraged me when the weight of writing the book felt too heavy to bear. I am grateful to him beyond words.

NOTES

Chapter 2 Baghdad

16   "[Jews] have literally monopolized the local trade," H. D. Shohet, "Account of the Jewish Community at Baghdad," prepared for the British Consulate General in 1910, reprinted in Elie Kedourie, *Arab Political Memoirs and Other Studies* (London: Frank Cass, 1974), p. 268.

17   "breathless impatience," ibid., p. 271.

22   "The Chief Rabbi is simply a mouth-piece . . ." ibid., p. 268.

22   "It is these persons who discuss measures together in cases of emergency," ibid.

Chapter 3 Jews and Pomegranates

34   "It was soon rumoured that a door had fallen from heaven," Morris Cohen, "Superstitions Among the Jews in Baghdad," *The Scribe* 46 (Jan. 1991), p. 4.

Chapter 4 Very Nice to Meet You

46   "battered tins of potato meal, bully beef or sacks of flour," C. Hughes, quoted by Dorina L. Neave in *Remembering Kut* (London: Arthur Barker Ltd., 1937), p. 63.

46   "I am faced with the sorrowful necessity of abandoning Baghdad," Khalil Pasha, quoted in Richard Coke, *Baghdad, City of Peace* (London: Thornton Butterworth, 1927), p. 292.

48   "Our armies do not come into your cities and lands as conquerors or enemies," General Maude's proclamation, ibid., p. 294.

48   "I am commanded to invite you, through your nobles and elders," ibid., p. 296.

56   "a make-believe kingdom, built on false pretenses," Elie
Kedourie, "The Kingdom of Iraq: A Retrospect," in *The Chatham House Version and Other Middle Eastern Studies* (1970. Reprint, Chicago: van R. Dee, 2004), p. 278.

Chapter 6 Independence

75   "until such time as they could stand on their own,"
League of Nations, Article 22, April 28, 1919. The full sentence reads: "Certain communities formerly belonging to the Turkish Empire have reached a stage of development where their existence as independent nations can be provisionally recognized subject to the rendering of administrative advice and assistance by a Mandatory until such time . . . " in Edwin Black, *Banking on Baghdad: Inside Iraq's 7,000-Year History of War, Profit, and Conflict* (New York: John Wiley & Sons, Inc., 2004).

75   "All the time he takes our money he will have to take our directions," Winston Churchill to Sir Percy Cox, November 29, 1921. Quoted in Peter Sluglett, *Britain in Iraq: 1914–1932* (St. Anthony's College, Oxford: Middle East Centre and London: Itheca Press, 1976), p. 72.

81   Ruth Montefiore received notification in 1992 that the moneys had been "distributed." See *The Scribe* 57 (Mar. 1993), p. 7.

Chapter 7 Arabs Before Muslims

90   "We are Arabs before being Muslims," Quoted in Sylvia Haim, ed., *Arab Nationalism: An Anthology* (Berkeley and Los Angeles: University of California Press, 1962), p. 35.

91   "the soul and life of the nation" and "its memory and its consciousness," Sati' al-Husri, quoted in Reeva Simon, *Iraq Between the Two World Wars: The Creation and Implementation of a Nationalist Ideology* (New York: Columbia University Press, 1986), p. 32.

94   "Sixty years ago, Prussia used to dream," Sami Shawkat, "On the Profession of Death," in Haim, *Arab Nationalism*, p. 99.

95   "national home," a "paradise," "Give us good government and we will make this country flourish," in Arnold Wilson, *Loyalties: Mesopotamia, 1914–1917* (Oxford: Oxford University Press, 1930). The Jews added, "Here shall be liberty and with it opportunity! In Palestine there may be liberty, but there will be no opportunity," pp. 305–6.

97   "re-establish[ing] the ancient glory of Israel" and "virulent

antipathy of the high class . . . indifferent to national redemption" and "Mesopotamian Jews will not stay behind forever deaf and dumb admirers in front of the activities displayed abroad," Solomon Shina, "Letter to the World Zionist Organization," July 30, 1924, reprinted in Norman A. Stillman, *The Jews of Arab Lands in Modern Times* (Philadelphia and New York: Jewish Publication Society, 1991), pp. 337–39.

98   "It is the feeling of every Arab . . . that it [Zionism] is a violation of his legitimate rights, which it is his duty to denounce and fight to the best of his ability," "any sympathy with the Zionist Movement is nothing short of a betrayal of the Arab cause," "unless he gives proof of an unimpeachable loyalty to his country and avoids with care any action that may be misconstrued." Menahem Daniel, letter to the Zionist Organization, quoted in Nissim Rejwan, *The Jews of Iraq: 3000 Years of History and Culture* (London: Weidenfeld Nicolson, 1985), pp. 207–9.

101   "Ghazi shook London and made it cry," in Simon, *Iraq Between the Two World Wars,* p. 121.

101   "full and complete protection of life and liberty," from "Declaration on the Subject of Minorities," 1932. Quoted in Simha Horesh, "The Jews of Iraq between 1920 and 1970," in *The Scribe* 21 (1987), p. 6.

103   Chief Rabbi Sassoon Khedouri's "Declaration" was originally published in the right-wing nationalist paper *al-Istiqlal* in October 1936. It is reprinted as "A Public Declaration by the Head of Iraqi Jewry Disassociating Himself and his Community from Zionism at the Time of the Arab General Strike in Palestine," in Stillman, *The Jews of Arab Lands,* p. 389. A Baghdadi schoolmaster called Ezra Haddad expressed similar sentiments in an article published in *al-Bilad,* under the heading "We were Arabs before we became Jews." Quoted in Rejwan, *The Jews of Iraq,* p. 219.

Chapter 8 Writing on the Wall

110   "dressed out in uniforms": The full quote is, "Here, as elsewhere, thoughtful parents have been saddened and wearied by the sight of their schoolboys marching on all occasions, dressed out in uniforms, provided with battle-cries, excited with sham enthusiasms, their hearts and minds twisted from the gentler ways of learning to which their age belonged." Freya Stark, *East is West* (London: Arrow Books, 1991), p. 209.

112　　"a Jewish youth in the Arab countries expects nothing from Zionism except colonialism and domination," Ya'qub Balboul, quoted in Rejwan, *The Jews of Iraq*, p. 219.

112　　"Reconstructions of historical geography, if accepted as political theory," Yusef Elkabir, quoted in Abbas Shiblak, *The Lure of Zion: The Case of the Iraqi Jews*, (London: Al Saqi Books, 1986).

119　　"fifth column" and "internal enemy," in Simon, *Iraq Between the Two World Wars*, p. 153.

120　　"crackling like thorns under a pot." The phrase is Freya Stark's. See *East is West*, p. 160.

Chapter 9 Brothers

129　　Nessim's view that "They chose to look the other way" echoes those of—among others—Freya Stark and Somerset De Chair, a British intelligence agent who accompanied British relief force across the desert in May 1941. De Chair said that a British intervention during the *farhud* would have been "lowering to the dignity of our ally, the Regent, if he were seen to be supported on arrival by British bayonets." See *The Golden Carpet* (London: Faber & Faber, 1943), p. 118.

131　　"being forced to make great existential decisions," Stillman, *The Jews of Arab Lands*, p. 139.

133　　"the lack of enthusiasm among the Baghdadi Jews for Palestine" and "the Jewish talent for adapting and forgetting," in Ruth Bondy, *The Emissary: A Life of Enzo Sereni*, trans. Shlomo Katz (London: Robson Books 1977), p. 203.

134　　Elie Kedourie made his observations in an essay entitled "Minorities," printed in *Chatham House*, p. 311.

135　　"The Jewish people have no fatherland of their own . . . ," Leo Pinsker, *Auto-Emancipation: A Call to His People by a Russian Jew* (London: Rita Searle, 1947), p. 10. And on p. 12: "Fear of the Jewish ghost has been handed down and strengthened for generations and centuries."

136　　"'vague and concealed,' rebelliousness," Bondy, p. 201.

Chapter 10 Three Evils

145　　"Jews have no cause other than their surrounding societies," General Secretary Zilcha, quoted in Shiblak, *The Lure of Zion*, p. 61.

147　　"to poison the atmosphere" and "perfect peace and harmony" for "thousands of years," Muhammed Fadhil al-Jamali, quoted in Rejwan, The Jews of Iraq, pp. 235–6.

148 "useless, aimed at deceiving the Arabs," Shiblak, The Lure of Zion, p. 62.

150 "the Iraqi people in their fight for freedom," ibid., p. 56.

151 "the rescue of Palestine," quoted in Rejwan, The Jews of Iraq, p. 237.

152 "death to the Jews," Ibid.

152 "the three evils: the Communists, the Zionists and the Jews." The same paper described Israel as a "Communist plot against the Arabs," quoted in Shiblak, The Lure of Zion, pp 65–66.

154 "a Zionist smell about it," Colonel Abdullah Nafsani, quoted in The Scribe 41 (June 1990), p. 2.

156 "liberate the people from the economic slavery and domination imposed by the Jewish minority," Shiblak, The Lure of Zion, p. 66.

161 "retour à soi." Albert Memmi coined the phrase in his autobiographical novel The Pillar of Salt. See Stillman, The Jews of Arab Lands, p. 137.

Chapter 11 A Fair Exchange

164 "stormy debate and much opposition," Ramallah Radio, quoted in Joseph Schechtman, "The Repatriation of Iraqi Jewry," Jewish Social Studies 15 (1952), p. 158.

168 "sorting out" of ethnically mixed populations in the Middle East would lead "to the greater stability and contentment of all involved," quoted in Kedourie, Chatham House, p. 311.

168 "an arrangement whereby Iraqi Jews moved into Israel [and] received compensation for their property from the Israeli government," and "Iraq would be relieved of a minority whose position is always liable to add to the difficulties of maintaining public," Henry Mack, quoted in Shiblak, The Lure of Zion, p. 83.

169 "could not in any circumstances agree to receive the Iraqi Jews as penniless displaced persons," Moshe Sharett, quoted in ibid, p. 87.

171 "O Children of Zion . . . You are the backbone of your people and its main support. Do not let the torch be extinguished in the

darkness of exile. . . . Israel is calling to you—Get out of Babylon!" Reprinted in Stillman, *The Jews of Arab Lands*, p. 527.

171 "the price of houses and also rents, which until recently were excessively high, particularly in Baghdad, have dropped by about 80 per cent," in "Iraqi Jews Denounced," article in *Jewish Chronicle*, Mar. 31, 1950.

171 "alleged that Jewish furniture, which is being sold daily by auction, is contaminated with a special poison sent to Iraqi Jews in small parcels." From notice in *Jewish Chronicle*, Apr. 21, 1950.

Chapter 12 Last Train to Basra

177 "in many cases, officials have destroyed the meagre personal belongings of the passengers." *Jewish Chronicle*, Sept. 22, 1950.

177 "one family of three . . . were ordered by three officials to unpack their luggage . . ." *Jewish Chronicle*, Sept. 29, 1950.

179 "every Jew has the right to come to this country." Law of Return 5710–1950, July 5, 1950. Israeli Ministry of Foreign Affairs, www.mfa.gov.il/mfa.

187 "I declare willingly and voluntarily that I have decided to leave Iraq permanently . . ." Joseph Schechtman, "The Repatriation of Iraqi Jewry," *Jewish Social Studies*, p. 160.

189 "clearly a racist law, conforming to the spirit and letter of the Nazi Nuremberg laws". Public announcement by the U.S. State Department, quoted in Schechtman. "The Repatriation of Iraqi Jews." The British also condemned the law, but then in January 1952, when the question arose regarding property in the United Kingdom owned by Iraqi Jews residing in Israel, the government refused to release Jewish assets. See Itamar Levin, *Locked Doors: The Seizure of Jewish Property in Arab Countries*, trans. Rachel Neiman (Westport, Conn., and London: Praeger, 2001), p. 56.

189 "the position of the Jews in Iraq is deteriorating rapidly. Shops, restaurants, and other establishments belonging to Jews . . . " in *Jewish Chronicle*, 30 March, 1951.

190 "forty 'liquidation committees' have been set up and these have seized hundreds of business premises, cars, and large quantities of merchandise", in *Jewish Chronicle*, 30 March, 1951.

190 "Reign of Terror," headline in *Jewish Chronicle*, Apr. 6, 1951.

Chapter 13 The Anniversary

201   "cruel Zionism": the phrase comes from David Hirst, *The Gun and The Olive Branch: The Roots of Violence in the Middle East* (London: Faber and Faber, 1977). p. 160.

202   "State's Messianic pretensions towards all Jews"; "the Jews here are Arabs. They speak Arabic," Elmer Berger, *Who Knows Better Must Say So* (New York: The American Council for Judaism, 1955). See pp. 4, 12.

203   "lusty and bustling," ibid., p. 29.

203   "We did not lose our heads," p. 38, and "Why didn't someone come to see us instead of negotiating with Israel," ibid., p. 34.

212   "'lackey' national sovereignty". The phrase is Norman Daniel's. See "Contemporary Perceptions of the Revolution in Iraq on 14 July 1958," in Robert A. Fernea and William Roger Lewis, eds., *The Iraqi Revolution of 1958: The Old Social Classes Revisited* (London and New York: I.B. Tauris & Co., Ltd., 1991).

212   "national unity through revolutionary rebirth," Simha Horesh, "The Jews of Iraq Between 1920 and 1970," in *The Scribe* 26 (Apr. 1988), p. 2.

Chapter 14 The Last Jews of Baghdad

222   "the atmosphere was electric," in Itamar Levin, *Locked Doors*, p. 71.

222   "Families were left without anything, everything dwindled down until they reached their last crust of bread," ibid., p. 74.

222   "We couldn't travel more than 10 kilometres without informing the police, we couldn't be in groups, and each police officer defined the size of a group his own way," Edwin Shukur in Samantha Ellis, "Out of Arabia: The Past and Future of London's Iraqi Jews," *Jewish Quarterly* 50, no. 2 (Issue 190), p. 6.

223   "white revolution" and "we could hear the tanks" in the streets, Carmen Hakham, ibid.

0223   "come and enjoy the feast," from "The Martyrdom of Fouad Gabbay," in *The Scribe,* 47 (Mar. 1991), p. 4.

223   "just swaying in the wind," Ellis, "Out of Arabia" p. 6.

224   "a slow death or extinction," Levin, *Locked Doors,* p. 82.

Epilogue

250   "how to behave, what to sing, how to dance, what to read and how to be different from what we were," Eli Amir, *Scapegoat*, trans. Dalia Bilu (London: Weidenfeld Nicolson, 1987), p. 72.

251   "In Iraq we were Jews, but here, in Israel, we are Arabs," and "The God of Israel is Yiddish," Shimon Balas, *Ha-Ma'vara* [*The Transition Camp*] (Tel Aviv: Am Oved, 1964), p. 16. Quoted in Max Sawdayee, *The Baghdad Connection: The Impact of Western European Education on the Jewish Millet of Baghdad: 1860–1950* (Ph.D. dissertation 1977; revised, 1991). p. 145.

251   "Arab Jews are discriminated against in Israel; they are given the lowest work such as bricklayers," Berger, *Who Knows Better*, p. 78.

152   "have lived in a society that was backward, corrupt, uneducated and lacking in independence and self-respect" and "superior moral and intellectual qualities" and "If, heaven forbid, we do not succeed . . . there is a danger that the coming generation may transform Israel into a Levantine state." Ben-Gurion quoted in Kedourie, *Chatham House*, p. 448.

0252   "it will take two or three generations before we can bring them up to our European standards." Moshe Dayan in the May 4[h] *New York Times Magazine*, 1980. Quoted in Sawdayee, *The Baghdad Connection*. The quote reads; "The so-called Oriental Jews make up half the population now . . . while many of our top elite, the youth of European parents are leaving the country. Most of the newcomers have a minimal education . . . . It will take two or three generations . . . ."

252   "the Oriental Jews are in need of a complete re-education . . . their entire being and thinking must be re-shaped in the European image," Raphael Patai, quoted in ibid., p. 149.

252   "had no feeling whatsoever for the Jewish state, and knew nothing of the spirit that had built the country for them," Maurice Samuel, *Level Sunlight* (New York: Knopf, 1953). See pp. 64–86. Samuel goes on to say, "The tide of Eastern immigration to Israel should have been controlled as far as it could be, and not whipped up artificially."

253   "human windfall," Sawdayee, *The Baghdad Connection*, p. 136. See also Nissim Rejwan, "Israel: The Two Kinds of Jews," in *Israel: The Arabs and the Middle East*, ed. Irving Howe and Carl Gershman (New York: Bantam Books, 1972).

253   "monstous complicities," Elie Kedourie, *Chatham House Version*, p. 312.

253   "splendid sons" and "handicapped" sons "ruled over most of the resources of Iraq," and "a ruled group, discriminated against and oppressed in every aspect," David Hirst, *The Gun and the Olive Branch*, p. 160.

253   "What did you do Ben-Gurion? You smuggled in all of us!" from *Black Panther Magazine* 9 (1972). Quoted in ibid., p. 164.

BIBLIOGRAPHY

Almog, Shmuel, ed. *Zionism and the Arabs*. Jerusalem: Historical Society of Israel and the Zalman Shazar Center, 1983.

Amir, Eli. *Scapegoat*. Translated by Dalia Bilu. London: Weidenfeld Nicolson, London, 1987.

Anderson, Jon Lee. *The Fall of Baghdad*. New York: Penguin Press, 2004.

———."The United States' de-Baathification Program Fuelled the Insurgency. Is It Too Late for Bush to Change Course?" *The New Yorker,* Nov. 15, 2004.

Basri, Carole. "The Jewish Refugees from Arab Countries: An Examination of Legal Rights—A Case Study of the Human Rights Violations of Iraqi Jews." *Fordham International Law Journal* 26, no. 3 (March 2003).

———."The Jews of Iraq: A Forgotten Case of Ethnic Cleansing." *Institute of the World Jewish Congress, Policy Forum* 26 (2003).

Basri, Meir. "Review of Operation Babylon by Shlomo Hillel," *The Scribe* 27 (June 1988).

———."Killings and Rescue in Baghdad 1972–73, *The Scribe* 52 (January 1992).

Baum, Phil. *The Jews of Iraq*. New York: Commission on International Affairs, American Jewish Congress, 1969.

Batatu, Hanna. *The Old Social Classes and the Revolutionary Movements of Iraq: A Study of Iraq's Old Landed and Commercial Classes and of its Communists, Ba'thists, and Free Officers*. Princeton, N.J: Princeton University Press, 1978.

Bekhor, Gourji. *Fascinating Life and Sensational Death: The Conditions in Iraq Before and After the Six-Day War*. Tel-Aviv: Peli, 1990.

Bell, Gertrude. *Amurath to Amurath*. London: William Heinemann, 1911.

————. The Letters of Gertrude Bell. Edited by Lady Bell in two volumes. London: Pelican Books, 1927.

————. Review of the Civil Administration of Mesopotamia. House of Commons, Session 1920, vol. 51, cmd. 1061.

Berger, Elmer. Who Knows Better Must Say So. New York: American Council for Judaism, 1955.

Black, Edwin. Banking on Baghdad: Inside Iraq's 7,000-Year History of War, Profit and Conflict. New York: John Wiley & Sons, 2004.

Blanc, Haim. "Communal Dialects in Baghdad." Cambridge, Mass.: Harvard Middle East Monograph Series 10, 1964.

Bondy, Ruth. The Emissary: A Life of Enzo Sereni. Translated from the Hebrew by Shlomo Katz, with an afterword by Golda Meir. London: Robson Publishing, 1978.

Callwell, C. E. The Life of Sir Stanley Maude. London: Constable and Co., Ltd., 1920.

Candler, Edmund. Long Road to Baghdad. 2 vols. London: Cassel & Co., 1919.

Chouraqui, André. Cent ans d'histoire: L'Alliance Israélite Universelle et la renaissance juive contemporaine. Paris: Presses Universitaires de France, 1965.

Christie, Agatha. They Came to Baghdad. 1951. Reprint, London: Harper-Collins, 2001.

Cockburn, Patrick. "Special Report on Iraq." Independent on Sunday, May 15, 2005.

Cohen, Hayyim J. The Jews of the Middle East 1860–1972. New York: John Wiley and Sons, and Jerusalem: Israel Universities Press, 1973.

————. "The Anti-Jewish Farhud in Baghdad, 1941." Middle Eastern Studies 3 (1966–67).

————. "A Note on Social Change Among Iraqi Jews, 1917–1951." The Jewish Journal of Sociology 8 (Dec. 1966).

Cohen, Morris. "Superstition Among the Jews of Baghdad." Anglo-Jewish Association Review 25 (1895–96). Reprinted in abridged form in The Scribe 46 (Jan. 1991).

Coke, Richard. Baghdad: City of Peace, 1927. London: Thornton Butterworth, 1927.

Daniel, Norman, "Contemporary Perceptions of the Revolution in Iraq on 14 July 1958." In The Iraqi Revolution of 1958: The Old Social Classes Revis-

ited, edited by Robert A. Fernea and Wm. Roger Lewis. London and New York: I. B. Tauris & Co. Ltd., 1991.

Danielson, Virginia. *The Voice of Egypt: Umm Kulthum, Arabic Song, and Egyptian Society in the Twentieth Century*. Chicago and London: University of Chicago Press, 1997.

De Chair, Somerset. *The Golden Carpet*. London: Faber & Faber, 1943.

Deshen, Shlomo. "Baghdad Jewry in Late Ottoman Times: The Emergence of Social Classes and of Secularization." In *Jews Among Muslims: Communities in the Precolonial Middle East*, edited by Shlomo Deshen and Walter P. Zenner. London: Macmillan Press, 1986.

Egan, Eleanor Franklin. *The War in the Cradle of the World*. London: Hodder & Stoughton, 1918.

Elliot, Matthew. *"Independent Iraq": The Monarchy and British Influence, 1941–1958*. London: Tauris Academic Studies, 1996.

Ellis, Samantha. "Out of Arabia: The Past and Future of London's Iraqi Jews," *Jewish Quarterly* 50, no. 2, (Summer 2003).

"Fifty Years On." Anniversary edition of *The Scribe: remembering the Rashid Ali coup* 48 (May 1991).

Gat, Moshe. *The Jewish Exodus from Iraq, 1948–1951*. London: Frank Cass, 1997.

Golany, Gideon. *Babylonian Jewish Neighbourhood and Home Design*. Mellen Studies in Architecture. Lampeter, N.J.: Edwin Mellen Press, 1999.

Gourgey, Percy. "The Jews of Iraq in 1990." *The Scribe*, No 43 (Aug. 1990).

Haddad, Heskel M. *Jews of Arab and Islamic Countries: History, Problems, Solutions*. New York: Shengold, 1984.

Haim, Sylvia, G., ed. *Arab Nationalism: An Anthology*. Berkeley and Los Angeles: University of California Press, 1962.

———. "The Situation of the Arab Woman in the Mirror of Literature". *Middle Eastern Studies*. 17 (Oct. 1978): pp. 510–30.

———. "Love in an Arab Climate." *Encounter* 50 (1978): pp. 86–92.

———. "Aspects of Jewish Life in Baghdad under the Monarchy." *Middle Eastern Studies*, 12, no. 2 (May 1976).

Halpern, Orly. "The Iraqi Jews' Dilemma." *Jerusalem Post*, June 20, 2005.

Hamdi, Walid. *Rashid Ali Al-Gailani and the Nationalist Movement in Iraq, 1939– 1941: A Political and Military Study of the British Campaigns in Iraq and the National Revolution of May 1941*. London: Darf, 1987.

Hecht, Alice. *By the Waters of Babylon*. Paper circulated by the author.

Heller, Joseph. "The Anglo-American Commission of Inquiry on Palestine 1945–46: The Zionist Reaction Reconsidered." In *Zionism and Arabism in Palestine and Israel,* edited by Elie Kedourie and Sylvia G. Haim. London: Frank Cass, 1982.

Hillel, Shlomo. *Operation Babylon.* Translated by Ina Friedman. London: Collins, 1988.

Hirst, David, *The Gun and the Olive Branch: The Roots of Violence in the Middle East.* London: Faber and Faber, 1977.

Hirszowicz, Lukasz. *The Third Reich and the Arab East.* London: Routledge & Kegan Paul, 1966, and Toronto: University of Toronto Press, 1966.

Horesh, Simha. "The Jews of Baghdad between 1920 and 1970." *The Scribe* 21 (Jan. 1987); 22 (Apr. 1987); 23 (Oct. 1987); 26 (Apr. 1988).

Husry, Khuldun. "The Assyrian Affair of 1933." *International Journal of Middle Eastern Studies* 5, nos. 2 and 3 (Apr. and June 1974).

Hyman, Mavis. *Jews of the Raj.* Bristol, U.K.: Longman Press, 1995.

"Iraq." Annual report on internal conditions. *American Jewish Yearbook,* 52 (1951); 53 (1952); 54 (1953); 55 (1954); 56 (1955).

"Jewish Doctors in Iraq in Modern Times." Includes note on Agha Elazar Levy, in *The Scribe* 57 (Mar. 1993).

"The Jews of Iraq—The Sequel." Extract from a *New Yorker* article by Milton Viorst. Reprinted in *The Scribe* 29 (Oct. 1988).

Kattan, Naim. *Farewell, Babylon.* Translated from the French by Sheila Fischman. Toronto: McClelland and Stewart, 1976.

Kazzaz, David. *Mother of the Pound: Memoirs on the Life and History of the Jews of Iraq.* New York: Sepher-Hermon Press, 1999.

Kedourie, Elie. *The Chatham House Version and Other Middle Eastern Studies, 1970.* New edition with an Introduction by David Pryce-Jones. Chicago: Ivan R. Dee, 2004.

———. *Arab Political Memoirs and Other Studies.* London: Frank Cass;1974.

———. *England and the Middle East, the Destruction of the Ottoman Empire, 1914–1921, 1956.* London: Mansell, 1987.

———. "The Break Between Arabs and Jews in Iraq." In *Jews Among Arabs: Contacts and Boundaries,* edited by Mark Cohen and Abraham L. Udovitch. Princeton, N.J.: Princeton University Press, 1986.

———. and Sylvia Haim. *Zionism and Arabism in Palestine and Israel.* London: Frank Cass, 1982.

Khalastchy, Eileen. "Customs and Life in Baghdad." *The Scribe* 65 (Mar. 1996) and 67 (Apr. 1997).

Khadduri, Majid. *Independent Iraq, 1932–1958: A Study in Iraqi Politics.* London and New York: Oxford University Press, 1960.

———. *Independent Iraq: A Study in Iraqi Politics since 1932.* Oxford: Oxford University Press, 1951.

———. *Republican Iraq: A Study in Iraqi Politics Since the Revolution of 1958.* London and New York: Oxford University Press, 1969.

Khazoum, Eliahu. "An Arab View of the Jews of Iraq." *Middle East Review* 9, no. 2 (1976–7).

Klein, Naomi. "Getting the Purple Finger." Feb. 10, 2005, www.nologo.org.

———. "Baghdad Year Zero: Pillaging Iraq in Pursuit of a Neo-Con Utopia." *Harper's Magazine,* Sep. 2004. See also www.nologo.org.

Laskier, Michael M. "Aspects of the Activities of the *Alliance Israélite Universelle* in the Jewish Communities of the Middle East and North Africa: 1860–1918." *Modern Judaism* 3: 2 (May 1986).

Lesch, Ann Mosely. *Arab Politics in Palestine, 1917–1939: The Frustration of a Nationalist Movement.* Ithaca, N.Y.: Cornell University Press, 1979.

Levin, Itamar. *Locked Doors: The Seizure of Jewish Property in Arab Countries.* Translated by Rachel Neiman. Westport, Conn., and London: Praeger, 2001.

———. "Confiscated Wealth, the Fate of Jewish Property in Arab Lands." Institute of the World Jewish Congress, *Policy Forum 22 (2000).*

Lewis, Bernard. *The Jews of Islam.* Princeton, N.J.: Princeton University Press, 1984.

Longrigg, Steven Hemsley. *Iraq, 1900–1950: A Political, Social and Economic History.* London and New York: Oxford University Press, 1953.

Luks, H. P. "Iraqi Jews During World War II." *Wiener Library Bulletin* 30 (1977).

Makiya, Kanan [aka Samir al-Khalil]. *Republic of Fear: The Politics of Modern Iraq.* Berkeley and Los Angeles: University of California Press, 1989.

Mardor, Munya. *Strictly Illegal.* Translated from the Hebrew by H. A. G. Shmuckley. London: Robert Hale, 1964.

Marr, Phebe. *The Modern History of Iraq.* Boulder, Colo.: Westview Press, and London: Longman, 1985.

Mattar, Philip. *The Mufti of Jerusalem: Al-Hajj Amin al-Husayni and the Palestinian National Movement*. New York: Columbia University Press, 1988.

Melamed, Ora, ed. *Annals of Iraqi Jewry: A Collection of Articles and Reviews*. Translated by Edward Levin. Jerusalem: Eliner Library, 1995.

Michael, Sami. *Victoria*. Translated from the Hebrew by Dalia Bilu. London: Macmillan, 1995.

Pinsker, Leo. *Auto-Emancipation: A Call to His People by a Russian Jew*, London: Rita Searle, 1947.

Rabbie, Victoria. "Iraqi Jews in Iran." *The Scribe* 59 (Sep. 1993).

Rejwan, Nissim. *The Jews of Iraq: 3000 Years of History and Culture*. London: Weidenfeld Nicolson, 1985.

———. *Elie Kedourie and His Work: An Interim Appraisal*. Jerusalem: Leonard Davis Institute, 1997.

———. *Israel in Search of an Identity: Reading the Formative Years*. Gainesville: University Press of Florida, 1999.

———. *The Last Jews of Baghdad. Remembering a Lost Homeland*. With a Foreword by Joel Beinin. Austin: University of Texas Press, 2004.

———. "Life Among the Muslims: A Memoir." *Present Tense* 9: 1 (Autumn 1981).

———. "Israel: The Two Kinds of Jews." In *Israel, the Arabs and the Middle East*, edited by Irving Howe and Carl Gershman. New York: Bantam Books, 1972.

Resner, Lawrence. *Eternal Stranger: The Plight of the Modern Jews from Baghdad to Casablanca*. New York: Garden City Press, 1951.

Rubin, Barry. *The Arab States and the Palestine Conflict*. New York: Syracuse University Press, 1981.

Samuel, Maurice. *Level Skylight*. New York: Knopf, 1953.

Sassoon, David. *A History of the Jews in Baghdad*. Welwyn Garden City, Herts., U. K.: Alcuin Press, 1949.

———. "The History of the Jews in Basra." *Jewish Quarterly Review* 17 (July 1926–Apr. 1927): pp. 407–480.

Sassoon, Shaoul Hakham. "My Terrible Time in Saddam's Prison: An Account of the Author's Imprisonment in 1967. Privately published.

Sawdayee, Max. *The Baghdad Connection: The Impact of Western European Education on the Jewish Millet of Baghdad: 1860–1950*. Ph.D diss. 1977; revised, 1991.

Schechtman, Joseph B. *On Wings of Eagles: The Plight, Exodus, and Homecoming of Oriental Jewry.* New York and London: Thomas Yoseloff, 1961.

———. *The Mufti and the Fuehrer: The Rise and Fall of Haj Amin el-Husseini.* New York and London: Thomas Yoseloff, 1965.

———. "The Repatriation of Iraqi Jewry." *Jewish Social Studies,* 15 (1952).

———. "The Repatriation of Yemenite Jewry." *Jewish Social Studies* 16 (1953).

Shiblak, Abbas. *The Lure of Zion; The Case of the Iraqi Jews.* London: Al Saqi Books, 1986.

Shulewitz, Malka Hillel, ed. *The Forgotten Millions: The Modern Jewish Exodus from Arab Lands.* London: Cassell, 1999.

Silverfarb, Daniel. *Britain's Informal Empire in the Middle East: A Case Study of Iraq, 1929–1941.* London and New York: Oxford University Press, 1986.

Simon, Reeva. *Iraq Between the Two World Wars: The Creation and Implementation of a Nationalist Ideology.* New York: Columbia University Press, 1986.

———. "Arab Nationalism and Jewish Education in Iraq." In *Studies in History and Culture of the Jews in Babylonia,* edited by Yitzhak Avishur and Zvi Yehuda. Or-Yehuda Israel: Babylonian Jewry Heritage Center, 2002.

Sinderson, Harry. *Ten Thousand and One Nights: Memories of Iraq's Sharifian Dynasty.* London: Hodder & Stoughton, 1973.

Sluglett, Peter. *Britain in Iraq 1914–1932.* Oxford: Middle East Centre, St. Anthony's College: London: Itcheca Press, 1976.

Smooha, Sammy. *Israel: Pluralism and Conflict.* London: Routledge & Kegan Paul, 1978.

Snir, Reuven. "The Arabic Literature of Babylonian Jewry." *The Scribe* 62 (Sept.1994).

Stark, Freya. *Dust in the Lion's Paw: Autobiography, 1939–1946, 1961.* London: Century Publishing, 1985.

———. *Baghdad Sketches, 1937.* London: John Murray, 1946.

———.*East is West. 1945.* London: Reprint, Arrow Books, 1991.

Stillman, Norman. *The Jews of Arab Lands in Modern Times.* Philadephia and New York: Jewish Publication Society, 1991.

"The Martyrdom of Fouad Gabbay." *The Scribe* 47 (Mar. 1991).

"The Torat Area." *Nehadrea, Journal of the Babylonian Jewry Heritage Center* 10 (Nov. 1997).

"The Jews of Iraq—The Sequel." Extract from a *New Yorker* article by Milton Viorst. Reprinted in *The Scribe* 29 (Oct. 1988).

Tibi, Bassam. *Arab Nationalism: A Critical Enquiry.* Edited and translated by Marion Farouk Sluglett and Peter Sluglett. London: Macmillan, 1981.

Tripp, Charles. *A History of Iraq.* 2nd Ed. Cambridge: Cambridge University Press, 2002.

Tweena, Abraham. "The Diary of Abraham Tweena." *The Scribe* 12: 11 (May–June 1973):

Uriel, Dan. *Iraq Under Qassem: A Political History, 1958–1963.* New York: Praeger, 1969.

Wallach, Janet. *Queen of the Desert: The Extraordinary Life of Gertrude Bell, Adventurer, Adviser to Kings, Ally of Lawrence of Arabia.* London: Weidenfeld Nicolson, and New York: Doubleday, 1996.

Wasserstein, Bernard. *The British in Palestine: The Mandatory Government and the Arab-Jewish Conflict 1917–1929.* London: Royal Historical Society, 1978.

Wilson, Arnold T. *Loyalties, Mesopotamia, 1914–1917.* Oxford: Oxford University Press, 1930.

Woolfson, Marion. *Prophets in Babylon: Jews in the Arab World.* London: Faber & Faber, 1980.

Yahia, Mona. *When the Grey Beetles Took Over Baghdad.* London: Peter Halban, 2000.

Yehuda, Zvi. *Jewish Schools in Baghdad, 1832–1974: A Picture Album,* Or-Yehuda: Babylonian Jewry Heritage Center, 1996.

———."Daily Life in the Community in Baghdad at the End of the 19th Century." *Nehardea* 9 (Dec. 1996).

Yosef, Meir. "Al-Tawrat, A Baghdad Neighbourhood." *Nehardea* 10 (1997).

Zangana, Haifa. "Chewing on Meaningless Words, the Battle over the Constitution Is Regarded by Most Iraqi Women, Confined to Their Homes, as Meaningless," in *The Guardian,* Aug. 17, 2005.

Zubaida, Sami. "To Be an Iraqi and a Jew." Published in French in *Monde Arabe Maghred/Machrek,* 163, 1999.

———. "Entertainers in Baghdad, 1900–1950." In *Outside In: On the Margins of the Modern Middle East,* edited by Eugene Rogen, London: I.B. Taurius, 2002.

———. "The Rise and Fall of Civil Society in Iraq." In *La Societé Irakienne;*

communautes, pouvoirs et violences, edited by Hocham Dawod and Hamit Bozarslan. Paris: Karthala, 2003.

———."Community, Class and Minorities in Iraqi Politics." In *The Iraqi Revolution of 1958: The Old Social Classes Revisited,* Edited by Robert A. Fernea and William Roger Lewis. London and New York: I.B. Tauris & Co., Ltd., 1991.

INDEX

ABOUT THE AUTHOR

MARINA BENJAMIN is the author of *Rocket Dreams* (short-listed for the Eugene Emme Award) and *Living at the End of the World*. She has worked as arts editor for Britains' *The New Statesman* and the *London Evening Standard,* and has had columns in the *Daily Express* and *Scotland on Sunday.* Currently she holds the Royal Literary Fund Fellowship at the London School of Economics.

Last Days in Babylon

the exile of Iraq's Jews, the story of my family

৵৽৽

MARINA BENJAMIN

Reading Group Guide

A Conversation with Marina Benjamin

ABOUT THIS GUIDE

The following reading group guide and author interview are intended to help you find interesting and rewarding approaches to your reading of *Last Days in Babylon*. We hope this enhances your enjoyment and appreciation of the book. For a complete listing of reading group guides from Simon and Schuster, visit BookClubReader.com.

READING GROUP GUIDE

DISCUSSION QUESTIONS

1. "I, too, had come to the Old City in search of the past, my family's past, colored by fond memories I'd been spoon-fed down the years." How would you compare Benjamin's expectations for Baghdad with the reality of what she encounters on her first visit there in 2004? Why are Benjamin's walks through Rashid Street and the Shorja, the open-air souk in the Jewish Quarter, especially frustrating? What prompts her to write that her grandmother, Regina, would find herself a stranger in Iraq, were she to visit today?

2. At one point, Baghdad's citizens included Jews, Sunnis, Shias, Kurds, Turkomans, Assyrians, Armenians, and Yazidis. How has nearly a century of Arab-Zionist conflict impacted the city's ethnic diversity? What religious, social, and political phenomena help explain the presence of a vibrant Jewish population in Iraq in the early twentieth century?

3. "[M]y grandmother never lost sight of the fact that her married life had begun as it was meant to continue—with a test." In what respects was Regina's betrothal to Elazar typical of the era? How would you characterize their marriage, and what role—if any— did their age difference seem to play in terms of their obligations and expectations?

4. How did Iraq's gain of independence in 1932 serve to formalize the indirect rule of the country by the British? In what ways did the emerging forces of Arab nationalism and Zionism that coalesced around this time come to threaten the stability and security of the Jewish minority population in Baghdad?

5. "The *farhud* [of June, 1941] was pivotal to the consciousness of this generation, for which it functioned as a kind of awakening." Why did the *farhud* serve to polarize brothers Nessim and Solomon Sehayek in terms of their political philosophies? How did this act of violence against Jews by Iraqis underscore the complex nature of political and religious affiliation in the Middle East?

6. What effect did the shifting international allegiances during World War II have on the Jews in Iraq? To what extent were Jews perceived by Iraqis as affiliated with the British?

   How did the rioting and widespread mayhem during the *farhud* affect the relationship between the Jews and the British in Iraq?

7. In what respects did the Iraqi policy of denaturalization and the Israeli government's Law of Return alter the political landscape for Jews in Iraq the 1950s? How did Regina and her family's flight from Basra to Bombay reflect the challenges faced by ordinary people to keep their families intact during times of political upheaval? To what extent did her experiences on board the *Dumra* seem typical of the time?

8. According to Benjamin, some 124,000 Iraqi Jews fled Iraq between 1948 and 1953. How did their treatment in Israel differ from the treatment of European Jews fleeing persecution? How significant was their inability to emigrate with their assets to the success of their assimilation? To what extent was their assumption into the Israeli state a convenient solution to the nascent country's need for cheap labor?

9. "This was how the last Jews of Baghdad viewed themselves, as quasi-tragic, quasi-romantic figures, isolated, stranded, immobilized." How do many of the Jews that Benjamin encounters living in Baghdad in 2004 feel about their decision to stay in Iraq? How would you characterize their plight? What keeps them in Baghdad?

10. How does the author's use of personal anecdotes and experiences from her family's history enhance your appreciation of the story of Iraqi Jews? What aspects of the narrative of *Last Days in Babylon* did you find especially surprising or illuminating, and why?

ENHANCE YOUR BOOK CLUB

1. Marina Benjamin smuggles vast quantities of kosher meat to the Iraqi Jews she meets in Baghdad, as a kind of "calling card" that will give her access to their secretive community. If you lived in isolation, with limited access to abundant sources of fresh food, what kinds of meals would you crave? Bring a recipe or a favorite dish to your next book club gathering—one that embodies the kind of food that you would get you to open your door to a stranger. Share your food (and your cravings) with your fellow book club members.

2. Benjamin writes that her grandmother, Regina, would hardly recognize some of Baghdad's most revered and historic neighborhoods in the aftermath of the many conflicts that have devastated the city in the last few decades. How has your childhood home and neighborhood changed over the course of your life? If you were to return now, how much would you discover has changed? How many of the neighbors and friends you knew as a child would you encounter? If time allows, revisit your old community and observe the changes. Or, connect with friends who are part of your past and reminisce about the way of life you enjoyed back then.

3. In *Last Days in Babylon*, author Marina Benjamin confesses that a photograph of her grandmother offers her a "silent rebuke" for not having been interested in her grandmother's life until after her death. What photographs of family members trigger powerful memories for you? Gather some of your most beloved photographs and bring them to your next book group to share with your friends. What emotions do these photographs elicit from you, and why? Do any of your photographs offer a "silent rebuke"?

A CONVERSATION WITH
MARINA BENJAMIN

1. **What role did having a child play in your decision to explore your family's past in Iraq?**

   It encouraged me re-examine my own identity anew, in light of knowing that at some point in my daughter's future she would want to know where she came from. I thought I'd better have the answer when that time came.

   As the project progressed, I increasingly came to see the book as a gift to her—the story of her lineage between two covers.

2. **How did your immediate family feel about your willingness to put yourself in harm's way in order to research your book?**

   They were understandably anxious, of course. But I shall be eternally grateful to my husband, because he never once said 'don't go': he simply said that he wanted to be assured that my plans to travel to Iraq were as watertight as they could be; that I had back-up plans B, C, and D covered, if plan A proved impossible to implement; and that I had contacts, guides, interpreters and transport sorted beforehand.

   My mother, who is one of the most cautious and in some ways fearful people I know, was in contrast buoyant and excited at the prospect of my going to Baghdad. I think there was a lot of projection on her part; a feeling that I was actually going to do something that she had longed to do for years, but which, in her heart of hearts, she knew she never would. Though she would never express it this way herself, it was a vicarious thrill that she derived from my visit.

3. **Why did you decide to explore the lives of Iraqi Jews through the lens of your grandmother's experiences?**

   There was never any doubt that my grandmother would be the

central character in this book. I wished to acknowledge and pay tribute to her life, to honor her, as it were, for great deeds gone unrecognized. I also wanted to get close to her once again, to somehow close the gap on her actual absence by remembering what I knew of and reconstructing what I didn't know about her life. There was definitely a personal and emotional element to my choice.

That said, part of my reason for choosing to hang the story on my grandmother's experiences was writerly. It was a narrative contrivance. I felt that her life was the perfect vehicle for carrying a highly-textured tale about what life in Baghdad was like pre-Saddam—and I felt I had license to borrow from her life story in a way I could never do with a living relative. More importantly, I felt that the dramatic account of her exile provided the book with a natural climax.

4. **What surprised you most about your encounters with Jews living in Iraq today?**

How open they were . . . I have always been quite skeptical about the idea—common among many Jewish people—that there's somehow a deep implicit bond between coreligionists; that whenever one Jew meets another Jew, there's a natural understanding and warmth in place, kind of a priori, and that this forms the foundations for good communication. And yet in Baghdad I experienced exactly that. In the book I speculate that this immediate bond arose out of a common identification of being Other. Until my visit to Iraq, I had never been in a country where Jews were openly vilified, where subterfuge was considered necessary, and where persecution was potentially round the corner. That vivid sense of being different—and being overtly identified as such—created an enormous empathy.

I was also surprised by how strongly the last Jews of Iraq felt themselves to be Jews. There are so very few of them left. Their community structure, such as it is, is in tatters, and the pressures to assimilate and convert have, over the decades, been persistent and nagging. The fact that people somehow managed through all this to hold on to and cherish their Jewish identities was something I admired hugely.

5. **In your estimation, how has the situation changed for Jews in Iraq since you visited?**

It has without a doubt worsened. Since I met the last Jews one of their tiny number has been kidnapped. His brother coughed up a large sum in ransom, but the victim was never returned. The chances are that the kidnappers killed him, perhaps even before they were paid.

I think that I visited Baghdad at the end of what I call in the book "the false dawn"—a time when there was still a small residual sense of optimism that as a result of the invasion and the deposing of Saddam, things might actually improve. Since then of course, the situation has only worsened. And I can only imagine the sense of despair that must pervade the Iraqi people as a whole.

6. **Why do you think the history of Jews living in Iraq is unknown to so many of your readers?**

I believe that the history of all Jewish people outside of Europe has been dwarfed into near invisibility by an almost exclusive focus—by Jewish and other critics and historians—on the holocaust. It is almost as if there's an unconscious need for a one-narrative-fits-all approach to minority cultures. As if it's simply too bothersome for people to acknowledge that there are multiple Jewish experiences of the 20th century and that the holocaust is only one among many.

In some ways, though, the focus on the holocaust is understandable; never before have so many people been systematically killed, never before has ethnic cleaning been conducted with such mechanical efficiency. But if Jews from other parts of the Diaspora, from China, or India, or the Middle East want their experiences and histories to be given voice, too, then they have to write them. I can only speak for Babylonian Jews, of course, but until recently there has not really been a culture of writing for a wide public audience.

7. **To what extent do you trace the partition of Palestine as the trigger for the tension between Arabs and Jews in the Middle East?**

I think that without Partition, there's a very good chance that there would still be a Jewish community in Iraq. Although I make it quite clear in the book that it was the parallel rise of two forces—Zionism and Arab nationalism—and the inevitable conflicts between them that account for the Jews' expulsion.

8. **If your grandmother were to read your book, what would surprise her about your account of the experiences of Iraqi Jews?**

I don't think anything I say about the community as a whole would surprise her. However, I've no doubt that she would be deeply embarrassed by the fact that I confide many details about her private life—not least the horrors of her wedding night! Iraqi Jews are culturally conservative and they absolutely do not believe in airing personal matters in public.

9. **You describe your visit to the Jewish cemetery in Baghdad and the special closeness to your grandfather that you felt there. Why do you think that plot of land (now in Sadr City) hasn't seen more desecration in the wake of the U.S. invasion?**

It's simply a case of people not knowing that it exists. It's like a secret garden.

10. **Would you go back to Iraq today? Do you plan to visit there with your children?**

I would love to go back at some point in the future, but I've grown increasingly pessimistic about the country's prospects for peace since I visited in 2004.

11. **What do you miss most about your grandmother?**

I miss her presence at family gatherings. I miss that sense of completeness that her presence conferred, the sense that everyone was present and counted and that everything therefore was alright with the world. I often wish that she could have read my book: unwanted revelations aside (!) I think she would have been proud of me for writing it.

12. What is next for you?

I'm not one of those writers who writes the same book over and over. I'll be moving on to something very different . . . ...watch this space . . ..